中国文化精粹

汉英释本

A Chinese-English Interpretation of the Essences of Chinese Culture

殷凌云　编译

ZHEJIANG UNIVERSITY PRESS
浙江大学出版社
·杭州·

图书在版编目（CIP）数据

中国文化精粹汉英释本 / 殷凌云编译. — 杭州：浙江大学出版社，2022.11
ISBN 978-7-308-22923-4

Ⅰ. ①中… Ⅱ. ①殷… Ⅲ. ①中华文化—汉、英
Ⅳ. ①K203

中国版本图书馆CIP数据核字（2022）第149075号

感谢范景中、吴敢、王超三位老师授权使用其研究成果。

中国文化精粹汉英释本
殷凌云　编译

责任编辑　徐凯凯
责任校对　蔡　帆
封面设计　杭州林智广告有限公司
出版发行　浙江大学出版社
（杭州市天目山路148号　　邮政编码　310007）
（网址：http://www.zjupress.com）
排　　版　杭州林智广告有限公司
印　　刷　广东虎彩云印刷有限公司绍兴分公司
开　　本　710mm×1000mm 1/16
印　　张　21.75
字　　数　512千
版 印 次　2022年11月第1版　2022年11月第1次印刷
书　　号　ISBN 978-7-308-22923-4
定　　价　88.00元

序言

中国文化博大精深，其精粹也非这样一本小书可以涵盖的。编纂本书的诱因是一次对大学生中国文化知识的问卷调查，调查结果出乎意料，许多大学生对中国文化知识所知寥寥，更不要说用英语表达和阐释。这一结果引发了我的思考，了解中国文化、学习如何用英语等外语介绍、诠释中国文化，这是一件重要的事。这促生了本书的形成。

在知识爆炸的今日，坚守自己民族的文化，增强文化底蕴，是民族兴旺的根本。文化具有多维性，从语言到艺术、生活，民族文化的精粹永远在历史的长河中闪耀。对比其他有关中国文化及艺术方面的读物，本书将长期被人弱化的、独具中国文化特色的内容收入其中，譬如中国图书艺术、版画艺术、织绣和饰品等；因为文化源自生活，而最终又从各个维度体现于生活中。

本书没有按照常见的中国文化读物的惯常思路排列篇章结构，而是自成一家，采用汉英对照形式，旨在帮助读者了解一些中国文化知识并熟悉英语的阐释方式。以汉语语言为开篇，每一部分包括选读材料、注释、词汇等，采用汉英双语形式。其中有幸得到像范景中、吴敢、王超等大家赐稿，为本书增添了更丰厚的精神内涵。在此深表谢意。

首先，语言是最实用、最有趣、最高深、最富有变幻的文化形式。天生万物，人类为万灵之首，无言却无以为继，语言是人类区别于其他生物的首要标志，是人类智慧的体现。斯蒂芬•卢卡斯在《发表演讲》中阐述了语言的作用:“通过语言，我们分享经验，阐明价值观，交流思想，传播知识，传承文化。的确，语言对于思考本身是至关重要的。与普遍的信仰相反，语言并非简单地反映现实，而且通过发掘事件的意义，帮助我们形成对现实的感悟。”[1] 语言是人类文明之血脉，语言是人类思想之化身，语言是人类智慧最重要的标志之一，文字的形成使人类的内在思想有了外在抒发的媒介，使人类历史有了确切的书面记载。人自一出生就需要学习、理解自己的母语。汉语是中华民族文明的源头，因而是中国文化的首要篇章。

语言的形成开启了文明的发展历程，先有口语进而形成文字。对于汉字的起源，说法多样，譬如仓颉造字说、结绳记事说、契刻记事说、河图洛书说等，无论是何种起源，文字的形成都是由人类生活的需要促生的。辜鸿铭在《中国人民的精神》一书中的“汉语”一文中破除了人们对汉语难学的误解，自豪地向西方读者昭示汉语不仅易学，而且优美简洁。

语言文字的形成催生了文字的物理形态——图书。图书作为艺术形式，一直处于边缘化状态，在语言形成文字到印刷术的发明这一文明进化的过程中，图书是最高级的文明象征，装帧、字体、页面设计等属于外在的视觉艺术范畴，文字内容则属于精神美学，外在和内在达到完美和谐就成为一种艺术。因此，许多藏家都狂热痴迷图书收藏和鉴赏。在“图书”部分，本书节选了范景中的文章《书籍之为艺术》，展现了图书作为文化艺术的载体所发生的故事。“书法”部分主要以吴敢的授课话语录再现书法艺术的理论与实践的融合；在“绘画”部分，本书编译了王超关于版画的论述，证明中国版画艺术的源远流长。

书法是文字的书写形式，可分为汉字书法、英文书法、蒙古文书法、阿拉伯文书法等，本书中的书法指汉字书法，这是中国文化艺术中所特有的一门传统艺术形式，是一种展现汉字美感的艺术表现形式，它不同于任何其他文字的书写方式。

1　斯蒂芬·卢卡斯是威斯康星大学麦迪逊分校传播艺术系教授，教授公共演讲、修辞批评和美国公共演讲。他获得了加州大学圣巴巴拉分校的学士学位，宾夕法尼亚州立大学的硕士和博士学位。他的著作《造反的征兆：1765—1776年费城的修辞与革命》获得美国传播学会1977年度金奖，并获普利策奖提名。1988年，他获得了威斯康星大学麦迪逊分校的校长杰出教学奖。这段话引自《发表演讲》，转引自罗立胜主编：《学术综合英语》，上海外语教育出版社，2015年，第15页。

汉字书法享誉世界，可用于字形设计、石刻题字、图案设计等诸多领域。从字面意义理解，书法指书写的法度。书法一词可以指具体的书写作品，也可以表示一种书写汉字的艺术类别。狭义而言，中国书法是指用毛笔书写汉字的方法和规律。书法技法包括执笔、运笔、点画、结体、布局、章法等。书法从广义讲是指语言符号的书写法则。换言之，书法是指按照文字特点及其涵义，以其书体笔法、结构和章法写字，使之成为富有美感的艺术作品。汉字书法主要分为五种书体：篆书（包含大篆、小篆）、隶书（包含古隶、今隶）、楷书（包含魏碑、正楷）、行书（包含行楷、行草）、草书（包含章草、小草、大草、标准草书）。汉字书法讲究美感：整体形态美、点画结构美、墨色组合美等。

尽管汉字形态原本呈现正方形，但是通过伸缩点画、扭动轴线，也可以形成不拘一格的动人形态，从而组合成优美的书法作品。点画结构美的构建方式主要有两种：一是指各种点画按一定的组合方式，直接组合成各种美的独体字或偏旁部首。二是指通过将各种部首按一定的方式组合成各种字形。汉字由部首组成，组字方式多样，有左右式、左中右式、上下式、上中下式、包围式、半包围式等，按照审美原则组字，点画结构合乎美感的字须合乎比例、结体均衡、富有韵律、节奏合度、笔画简洁等。

汉字书法作品的主要材质是毛笔、宣纸和墨。汉字的结体、墨色组合的艺术性主要是指其组合的秩序性。作为艺术形式的书法，墨色必须浓淡有致、虚实相间、均衡渐变。同时，必须注意点画墨色的平面结构，还要注意点画墨色的层次呼应，从而增强书法艺术的表现力。

谈到书法，人们经常会把书法与法书相混淆。法书不等同于书法。法书是对古代名家墨迹的尊称，包含着书法作品的楷模之意。自古以来，皇室、宫廷就喜欢收集历代法书作品，尤其唐宋明清宫廷内府集中了很多藏品，其情形见于宋徽宗时所撰《宣和书谱》、康熙朝所纂《佩文斋书画谱》和乾隆、嘉庆朝所编《石渠宝笈》等著录中。不论是尺牍、诗文，还是写经、抄本，无不意涉瑰奇，思逸神超。中国人运一支笔，始于一画，留下无数墨宝，把虚无的心印之美呈现为实在的文字之美。

国画，在西方称为中国画，可见其在世界艺术领域中的独特性，自成体系。首先，中国画具有地域性，发源、兴盛于中国。中国画的工具异于其他画类，中国画使用柔软的毛笔、单色的墨、柔软的宣纸和绢素以及矿物质制作的彩色颜料等。画类按主题可分为山水、人物、花鸟、虫鱼、界画等。画类按风格可分为普通绘画、文人画、禅画等，其中人物画从晚周至汉魏、六朝渐趋成熟。山水、花卉、鸟兽画等至隋唐之际始独立形成画科；在魏晋、南北朝、唐朝和明清等时期，它们先后受到佛教艺术和西方绘画艺术的影响。五代、两宋流派竞出，水墨画随之盛行，山水画蔚成大科。文人画在宋代已有发展，而至元代大兴，画风趋向写意；明清和近代续有发展，日益侧重达意。

山水画作为中国画的一种，主写山川自然景色，也描写人物、屋宇等次要主题，“在中国绘画的众多主题中，山水充分代表着中国艺术家的成就，不仅体现了他们对自然美景和奇观的欣赏，还体现了他们对宇宙运作方式的深刻理解以及对人类在世界上的地位的了解”[1]。中国人物画则有别于西方人物肖像画，独具特色，这在高居翰的著作中论述颇深。

从技法上中国画可分为工笔、写意、勾勒、设色、水墨等，设色又可分为金碧、青绿、没骨、泼彩、淡彩、浅绛等。总之，中国画主要运用线条和墨色的变化，以勾、皴、点、染，浓、淡、干、湿，阴、阳、向、背，虚、实、疏、密和留白等表现手法来描绘物象与经营位置。[2]

装裱工艺形态上中国画大致可分为壁画、屏障、卷轴、册页、扇面等形式。中国书法与中国画同源，两者在达意抒情上都和用笔、用墨有着紧密的联系，因此绘画与书法、篆刻相互影响，形成了中国画艺术显著的艺术特征。

随后有建筑、织绣、陶瓷、哲学、文学、饮食、中医、影视和饰品等部分，在展现中国文化精粹的同时，以英语介绍这些中国文化知识，以利于中国文化的对外传播。

书中部分插图为自摄照片，更加真实，也避免出现版权问题。

---

1 J. Turner, *The Dictionary of Art*, Volume 6, Grove, 1998, pp. 787–789.

2 尤汪洋主编：《中国画技法全书》，河南美术出版社，2002年，第122页。

Preface

Chinese culture is vast and profound, and its essence cannot be covered by such a small book. The motivation for our compiling this book was a questionnaire survey on Chinese cultural knowledge of college students. The results of the survey were unexpected, showing many college students knew little about Chinese cultural knowledge, let alone expressed and explained it in English, which triggered my thinking about it. It is important to understand Chinese culture and learn how to introduce and interpret Chinese culture in English and other foreign languages. This leads to the formation of this book.

In today's explosion of knowledge, sticking to the culture of one's own nation and restoring the cultural heritage is the foundation of national prosperity. With culture of multidemension, from language to art to life, the essence of national culture will always shine in the long river of history. Compared with other books about Chinese culture and art, this book incorporates the unique Chinese cultural characteristics that have been weakened for a long time, such as Chinese book art, print art, weaving and embroidery, and accessories.

This book does not arrange the chapter structure according to the usual thinking of common Chinese cultural readings. Instead, it is a self–contained book, using a Chinese–English format to help readers understand some Chinese cultural knowledge and familiarize themselves with English interpretation. It starts with Chinese language, with each part including a brief overview, anecdotes, optional reading materials, notes, and vocabulary, all in both Chinese and English. Fortunately, such famous scholars like Fan Jingzhong, Wu Gan, Wang Chao, etc. allow me to use their manuscripts, which adds a richer spiritual connotation to this book. I'm greatly thankful to them.

Language is the most practical, the most interesting, the most profound and the most changeable form of culture. With all things born in nature, human beings are the head of all souls. Without languages, there would be nothing sustainable. Language is the primary sign that distinguishes humans from other creatures, the obvious manifestation of human wisdom. Stephen Lucas expressed his ideas about the function of language in "Presenting a Speech" as the following: "Through language we share experiences, formulate values, exchange ideas, transmit knowledge, and sustain culture. Indeed, language is vital to thinking itself. Contrary to popular belief, language does not simply mirror reality but also helps to create our sense of reality by giving meaning to events."[1] Language is the bloodline of human civilization; language is the embodiment of human thoughts; and language is one of the most important signs of human wisdoms. The formation of words gives human internal thoughts an external expression medium, and therefore human history enjoys an accurate written record. People need to learn and understand their mother tongue since born. The Chinese language is the source of the Chinese civilization and therefore the most important chapter of Chinese culture.

The start of civilization began with the creation of language, and oral languages came into being ahead of written characters. There are various theories about the origin of Chinese characters, such as the one that Cangjie

---

1 Stephen Lucas, a professor, teaches public speaking, rhetorical criticism, and American public address in the Department of Communication Arts at the University of Wisconsin–Madison. He received his bachelor's degree from the University of California, Santa Barbara, and his master's and doctorate degrees from Penn State University. Lucas has been recognized for his work as both a scholar and a teacher. His book *Portents of Rebellion: Rhetoric and Revolution in Philadelphia, 1765–1776*, won the National Communication Associations Golden Anniversary Award in 1977 and was nominated for a Pulitzer Prize. In 1988, he received the Chancellor's Award for Excellence in Teaching at the University of Wisconsin–Madison. This is taken from "Presenting a Speech", in *Comprehensive Academic English for Graduates*, Luo Lisheng ed., Shanghai Foreign Language Education Press, p.15.

created Chinese characters, the one that a rope was tied to record a story, the one that a deed was carved to record a story, the one of *Hetu Luoshu*, etc. No matter what the origin is, the formation of Chinese characters is promoted by the needs of human life. Gu Hongming's article "The Chinese Language" in his book *The Spirit of the Chinese People* dispells the misconception that Chinese is difficult to learn, proudly showing to Western readers that Chinese is not only easy to learn, but also beautiful and concise.

The creation of language and characters gave birth to its physical form — books. However, books have always been marginalized as an art form. In the process of civilization evolution from the formation of words to the invention of printing, books are the most advanced symbol of civilization. Binding, fonts, page designing, etc. belong to the category of external visual arts; text content belongs to spiritual aesthetics, and the perfect harmony of external and internal forms becomes a kind of art; therefore, many collectors have been in great fever of book collections and appreciation. In the chapter of Chinese books, it mainly revolves around Fan Jingzhong's essay "Books as an Art", showing the story of books as a carrier of culture and art. Then there is a chapter of calligraphy, which mainly reproduces the fusion of theory and practice of calligraphy art based on Wu Gan's lecture between the teacher and students. In the painting part, Wang Chao's exposition on printmaking proves the long history of printmaking skills in China.

Calligraphy is the way that the text is written, which can be divided into the calligraphy of Chinese characters, English handwriting, Mongolian handwriting, Arab handwriting and so on. The chapter of calligraphy in this book refers to Chinese calligraphy, a traditional art form unique to Chinese culture and art, a kind of art form of expression of beauty in writing Chinese characters, different from any other ways of writing.

Chinese calligraphy enjoys a worldwide reputation, which can be used in font design, stone inscriptions, pattern design and many other aspects. In the literal sense, calligraphy refers to the practice of writing. The word "calligraphy" can refer to a specific work of writing; it can also represent an artistic category for writing Chinese characters. In a narrow sense, calligraphy refers to the methods and rules of writing Chinese characters with a brush. Calligraphy techniques include brush holding, stroke handling, stroke composition, layout, structure and so on. In a broad sense, calligraphy refers to the rules of writing language signs. In other words, calligraphy is to write according to the characteristics of characters and their meaning, with its style, structure and composition, so that it becomes an aesthetic work of art. Chinese calligraphy is mainly divided into five styles: seal character (Zhuan shu, including big seal character and small seal character), official/clerical script (Li shu, including ancient and modern scripts), regular script (Kai shu, including Wei bei style and regular block script), running script (Xing shu, including running regular script and running cursive script), and cursive script (Cao shu, including Zhang cao / cursive, small cursive, big cursive and standard cursive scripts). Chinese calligraphy stresses aesthetic feelings: the beauty of the overall form, the beauty of the dot stroke structure and the beauty of the combination of ink colors.

Although the original form of Chinese characters is square, it can also form an eclectic and touching form by stretching the dots and twisting the axis, so as to combine into beautiful calligraphy works. There are two main ways to construct the beauty of stroke structure. One is to directly combine various dots into various single characters and radicals of beauty in a certain combination way. The other is to combine various radicals into various glyphs in a certain way. Chinese characters are composed of radicals, and they are grouped in various ways, such as the left–right, the left–middle–right, the top–bottom, the top–middle and bottom, the surrounded, and the semi–surrounded. The characters are grouped according to aesthetic principles. The characters with aesthetically pleasing structure and composition should be in proportion, balanced and full of rhythm, rhythm fit, concise strokes, and so forth.

The main materials of Chinese calligraphy written with are brushes, rice paper and ink. The shape of the character and the artistry of the combination of ink mainly refer to the order of the stroke combination. As an art form of calligraphy, the ink color must be orderly, not chaotic, alternate with reality, be balanced and gradual. One must pay attention to the plane structure of the ink color of the strokes, but also to the level of the echo of ink color, so as to enhance the depth of the performance of calligraphy art.

Calligraphy is often mixed with fashu 法书 , when it comes to calligraphy. Fashu is not the same as it. Fashu is an honorific title of respect for the works by ancient masters, which contains the meaning of the model of calligraphy works. Since ancient times, the royal court has been interested in collecting the works of all dynasties. There are particularly many collections in the palaces of the Tang, Song, Ming and Qing dynasties, which can be found in the compilation of *Xuanhe Shupu* compiled by Emperor Huizong of the Northern Song Dynasty, the Compilation of *Peiwen Zhai Painting and Calligraphy* compiled during the reign by Emperor Kangxi of the Qing Dynasty, and the three compilations of *The Shiqu Baoji, Treasured Paintings and Calligraphies,* compiled during the period by Emperor Qianlong and Emperor Jiaqing in the Qing Dynasty. Whether they are letters and poetry or scriptures and transcripts, all are magnificent and super wonderful. When Chinese people move a brush, starting with a stroke or a line and leaving countless ink handwriting, the beauty of the nihilistic impression of the heart is presented as the beauty of the real characters.

Traditional Chinese Painting is known as Chinese Painting in the West, from which we can see this kind of painting art has great uniqueness with its own system in the world of art. First of all, Chinese Painting is regional, originated and thrived in China. The tools and materials used in Chinese Painting are different from those for other kinds of painting, with soft brushes, monochromatic ink, soft rice paper and silk, and color pigments made from minerals. Traditional Chinese Painting, from the theme, can be divided into landscape, figures, flowers and birds, insects and fish, boundary painting, etc. From its style, it can be divided into ordinary painting, literati painting, Zen painting, etc. Among them, figure painting gradually became mature from the late Zhou Dynasty to the Han and Wei dynasties and Six Dynasties. Landscape, flowers, birds and animals paintings started to become the independent formation of painting till Sui and Tang dynasties. In the Wei and Jin dynasties, the Southern and Northern Dynasties, the Tang Dynasty and the Ming and Qing dynasties, they were successively influenced by Buddhist art and western painting art. There were great competitions among different schools of the Five Dynasties and the Song Dynasty, when ink painting became popular and landscape painting a major subject. The literati painting developed since the Song Dynasty, and in the Yuan Dynasty the painting style tended to freehand brushwork, which in Ming and Qing dynasties and modern times continued to develop, increasingly focused on the expression of meanings.

Chinese Landscape Painting, as a kind of Chinese Painting, mainly describes the natural scenery of mountains and rivers, as well as minor subjects such as figures and buildings. "Among many themes in Chinese Painting, landscape paintings fully represent the achievements of Chinese artists, reflecting not only their appreciation of the beauty and wonders of nature, but also their deep understanding of the way the universe works and of human's place in the world."[1] Chinese Figure Paintings are different from western portrait paintings with unique characteristics, which is deeply discussed in James Cahill's book.

From the techniques, Chinese Painting can be divided into meticulous brushwork, freehand brushwork, outlining, coloring, ink–washed and other forms; colored paintings can be divided into golden, blue–and–green, boneless, colored, light colored, light purpled and other several. It mainly uses the changes of lines and ink, to describe the object image and composition through outlining, brushing, dotting, dyeing, thick, light, dry, wet, Yin, Yang, fasade, back, hollow,

1 J. Turner, *The Dictionary of Art*, Volume 6, Grove, 1998, pp. 787–789.

solid, thin, dense and empty and other expression techniques.[1]

From the mounting craft form, Chinese Painting can be roughly divided into fresco, screen, scroll, album, fan and other physical manifestations. Chinese calligraphy and Chinese Painting have the same origin, both of which are closely connected with the use of brush and line movement in expressing feelings and emotions. Therefore, painting and calligraphy as well as seal carving influence each other, forming the remarkable artistic characteristics of Chinese Painting art.

Following are architecture, weaving and embroidery, ceramics, philosophy, literature, food, traditional Chinese medicine, movies, and accessories with cultural stories about them. While demonstrating the essence of Chinese culture, it also introduces the knowledge of Chinese culture in English to facilitate the spread of Chinese culture to the outside world.

Some of the illustrations in the book are photographs taken by ourselves to avoid copyright issues, which are also more realistic.

---

1 You Wangyang ed., *Zhongguo Huihua Jifa Quanshu* (*The Complete Book of Chinese Painting Techniques*), Henan Art Publishing House, 2002, p.122.

目 录

语　言

The Chinese Language

文书误一字[1]

洪迈

文书一字之误，有绝系利害者，予亲经其三焉，至今思之，犹为汗下。乾道[2]二年冬，蒙恩召还，过三衢，郡守何德辅问奏对用几札，因出草稿示之，其一乞蠲减鄱阳岁贡诞节金千两事，言此贡不知起于何时，或云艺祖初下江南，郡库适有金，守臣取以献长春节[3]，遂为故事。误书“长春”为“万春”，乃金主褒节名也。德辅读之，指以相告，予悚然面发赤，亟改之。三年，以侍讲[4]讲毛诗，作发题，引孔子于论语中说诗处云：“不学诗，无以言。”误书

1　（宋）洪迈：《容斋随笔》卷四，北京燕山出版社，第777页。本书以引文中的故事说明语言文字的重要性。在此故事中，若误字未能发现，皇帝可能会因此而惩罚他，甚至会危及生命。

2　乾道：中国南宋年号，公元1165—1173年。

3　长春节：长春节就是在公元960年为庆贺北宋赵匡胤出生设立的节日。“长春”的意思是长寿。

4　侍讲：官名。（1）汉唐：一种附加在正式官职上的有声望的头衔，以表示被任命者有资格，有时被期望作为皇帝的伴侣和古典导师；这个头衔没有自己的品级，也没有俸禄。（2）宋清：翰林院正式成员。（3）宋：指定为皇太子和每个王府侍读。［美］贺凯：《中国古代官名辞典》，北京大学出版社，2008年，第422页。

“言”为“立”，已写进读正本，经筵吏[1]袁显忠曰：“恐是言字。”予愧谢之。淳熙十三年在翰苑[2]，作赐安南国历日诏云：“兹履夏正，载颁汉朔。”书“夏正”为“周正”，院吏以呈宰执[3]，周益公见而摘其误，吏还以告，盖语顺意同，一时不自觉也。

---

1 经筵吏（官）：职名。经筵是帝王为讲论经史而特设的御前讲席，是皇帝与首都各行政机关、翰林院、国子监等高级文官的聚会，以阅读和讨论古典和历史文献；直到明朝才定期每年春秋开始排定会议；参加者获特别但有声望的委任为讲官等。在元代，最负盛名的参与者被称为艺文官。经筵参与者通称经筵吏（官）。

2 翰苑：翰林院别称。

3 宰执：宰相与执政的简称。

A Wrong Character in the Document[1]

Hong Mai

Sometimes one mistaken character in the document can absolutely result in a deadly effect, which I have undergone three times, so that I am still sweating fearfully thinking about it so far. In the winter of the second year of the Gandao[2] Era, I was called back by the emperor. Passing by Sanqu, He Defu, Commandery Governor, asked me how many letters should be used to present to the emperor, and then I showed him the drafts, one of which was to beg to reduce the one–thousand–liang money for the Poyang New Year's tribute. It read that it was unknown when the tribute started, and it was said that when the ancestor of Yi came to the south of the Yangtze River, there happened to be gold in the county treasury, and the guards presented it for the Changchun (Long Spring) Festival[3], as the story went. The term "Changchun" was mistaken as "Wanchun", which is also the name of the Bao Festival for the Emperor of Jin Dynasty. When Defu saw it, he showed it to me, and I was so horrified as to change it immediately and urgently. In the third year, I taught *The Book of Poems* as the Expositor–

---

1 Hong Mai, Song Dynasty, *Rongzhai's Essays*, Four, Beijing Yanshan Publishing House, p.777. The story in the quotation is used to illustrate the importance of language. If none of the mistakes had been found in the text, then the emperor might have punished him, or even sentenced him to death as result of the carelessness.

2 Gandao Era: Year name of Southern Song Dynasty, 1165–1173 AD.

3 Changchun (Long Spring) Festival: "Long Spring Festival" was established in 960 AD to celebrate Zhao Kuangyin's birthday in the Northern Song Dynasty. Long Spring means longevity.

in–waiting[1]. I wrote about the topic, citing Confucius' remarks about poetry in the *Analects*: "If you don't study *The Book of Poetry*, you can't well at all." I made a mistake to write " 言 yan" as " 立 li", which has already been written into the formal. Yuan Xianzhong, Classics Colloquium[2], said: "I'm afraid it is the character 言 ." I am ashamed and thankful to him. In the thirteenth year of Chunxi Era in Hanlin Yuan, I wrote an edict for the Annan National Calendar: "I will hereby honor the formal Calendar of Xia Dynasty and present the annual Han's." I worte 夏正 as 周正 by mistake, and then the official Participant in the Classics Colloquium [3]there sent it to the prime minister Steward[4]. Zhouyi found out the mistake and told him about it, and he returned to let me know. It may be resulted from that it was so fluent to read with the same meaning that I didn't realize it at first.

---

1 shih chiang 侍讲: an official title, Expositor–in–waiting, an attendant skilled in explaining classical texts. (1)Han–Tang: a prestigious title added to a regular title to signify that the appointee was worthy, and sometimes expected, to serve as companion and classical tutor of the Emperor; the title had no rank of its own and carried no salary. (2) Song–Qing: regular members of the Hanlin Academy (Hanlin Yuan); (3) Song: one assigned to the household of the Heir Apparent and to each Princely Establishment (wang–fu) as shih–tu, reader–in–waiting. Charles O. Hucker, *A Dictionary of Official Titles in Imperial China*, Peking University Press, 2008, p.422.

2 Ching–yen kuan 经筵官/吏, an official title. Ching–yen 经筵: Classics Colloquium, a gathering of the Emperor with eminent civil officials of the general administrative agencies in the capital, of the Hanlin Academy (Han lin yuan), of the Directorate of Education (kuo–tzu chien) etc., for the reading and discussion of classical and historical texts; irregular until the Ming Dynasty, when sessions began to be scheduled every spring and autumn; participants were given ad hoc but prestigious designations as Lecturer (chiang–kuan) etc. In the Yuan Dynasty the most prestigious participant was called the Translator (I–wen kuan). ching–yen kuan refers to all the official Participant in the Classics Colloquium.

3 Hanyuan: Another name for the Hanlin Academy.

4 Steward: Prime Minister and Grand councillor ruling for short.

汉 语

辜鸿铭[1]

所有学过汉语的外国人都说汉语是一门很难学的语言。那么中文是一门难的语言吗？然而，在我们回答这个问题之前，让我们先了解一下汉语是何意思。众所周知，在中国有两种语言——我不是指方言——口语和书面语。现在，顺便说一句，有人知道为什么中国人坚持使用这两种不同的语言口语和书面语吗？我将在这里告诉你原因。

在中国，人们被恰当地分为两个截然不同的阶层，受过教育的和没有受过教育的。口语是未受过教育的人使用的语言，而书面语言是真正受过教育的人使用的语言。这样，这个国家就没有受过一半教育的人了。我说，这就是为何中国人坚持要有两种语言的原因。现在想想一个国家只有一半受过教育的人会有什么后果。看看今天的欧洲和美国。

在欧洲及美国，由于废弃了拉丁语，口语和书面语之间的明显区别消失了，出现了一个受过一半教育的阶层，他们被允许使用与真正受过教育的人相同的语言，他们谈论文明、自由、中立、军国主义和泛奴役主义，却根本不知道这些词到底是何意思。人们说普鲁士军国主义是对文明的威胁。然而，在我看来，当今世上那些受过一半教育的人，才真正是对文明的威胁。然而，这无关紧要。

1　辜鸿铭（1857—1928）是中国晚清时期的一位杰出学者，他精通九种语言：英语、法语、德语、拉丁语、希腊语、马来语等。他的主要作品包括《中国牛津运动的故事》（原名《清流传》），《中国人民的精神》（原名《春秋大义》），《论语》（译著），《中庸》（译著），等等。本文选自《中国人民的精神》一书中的《汉语》一文。《中国人民的精神》原载1914年的《中国评论》，1915年更名《春秋大义》在京出版，并很快被译成德文。本书着力阐述中国传统文化对西方文明的价值，在当时中国文化面临歧视、中华民族遭受欺凌的情况下，影响尤为特殊。本书也是一本极为宝贵的关于中国文化的英语读物。辜鸿铭在序言中说："本书的目的是试图阐释中华文明的精神和价值。"这本书是由前言、介绍和六篇选择的文章——"中国人的精神"、"中国女人"、"中文"、"约翰·史密斯在中国"、"一个伟大的汉学家中华物种"、"中国奖学金"（第一部分和第二部分）组成。

现在来看看这个问题：汉语是一门难学的语言吗？我的回答是，是又不是。让我们先看看口语。我说，汉语不仅不难，而且与我所知道的六种语言相比，是除马来语之外世界上最容易的语言。汉语口语很容易，因为它是一门极其简单的语言。它是一种无格、无时态、无规则和不规则动词的语言；事实上，无语法或任何规则。但有人对我说，汉语难就是因为它简单，即使它既没有规则或也没有语法。然而，这是不可能的。马来语和汉语一样，也是一种简单的语言，无语法或规则；然而学习它的欧洲人并不觉得很难。因此，就汉语本身而言，口语至少不是一门难学的语言。

然而，对于受过教育的欧洲人，尤其是那些来到中国的受过一半教育的欧洲人来说，即使是口语或口语汉语也是一门非常难的语言：为什么呢？因为汉语口语，正如我所说，是没有受过教育的人的语言；事实上是儿童语言。现在举例证明，我们都知道欧洲的孩子学习口语或汉语口语是多么容易，而博学的哲学家和汉学家坚持说汉语是如此难。汉语，口语，我再说一遍，是儿童语言。因此，我对想学汉语的外国朋友的第一个建议是："像童子一样，你不仅能进入天国，而且你也能学会汉语。"

现在我们来谈谈书面语言或书面语，书面汉语。在我深入论述之前，我想说的是，也有不同种类的书面中文。传教士把它们分为易文礼和难文礼两类。但在我看来，这不是令人满意的分类。我认为，正确的分类应该是，素衣裹身的中文、身着中国官方制服的中文以及完全身着宫廷礼服的中文。如果你喜欢用拉丁语，就叫它们：litera communis 或 litera officinalis（普通或商务汉语）；litera classica minor（古典腔调较少的汉语）和文学经典专业（高级文言文）。

现在很多外国人自称为中国学者或被称为中国学者。三十多年前，我在北卡《华北每日新闻》[1]上发表了一篇关于中国学术的文章，啊，我！我于是说："在中国的欧洲人中间，只要能用一些地方方言发表几段对话，或者汇集

1 《华北每日新闻》（北卡罗来纳州每日新闻字林西报），是一份英文报纸，是当时中国最具影响力的外国报纸。创刊为《北华捷报》周刊，创始人是英国拍卖师亨利·谢尔曼，中文名字奚安门。亨利·谢尔曼初在上海经营拍卖业，兼任一英商驻沪代表。清道光三十年（1850）六月二十六日，其在上海独资创办《北华捷报》，兼编辑；办报宗旨是唤起英国人"一股热情"，支持同中国"建立更加密切的政治联系，更加扩大对华贸易的主张"，"并看到这个巨大帝国拥有惊人的丰富资源"。《华北日报》于1864年6月1日创刊。它的发行量最高为7817份。

了一百句中国谚语，就可以说是中国学者了。”

“当然”，我说，“名义上无害，而且根据条约中的治外法权条款，在中国的英国人可以不受惩罚地自称孔子，如果他喜欢的话。”现在我想说的是，有多少外国人自称是中国学者，他们知道中国文学中蕴藏着一种文明的财富，我称之为古典文学，也就是穿着中国宫廷服装的文学吗？我之所以说它是文明的资产，是因为我相信，正如马修·阿诺德[1]在谈到荷马的诗歌时所说的那样，中国文学中的经典之作能够“使原始的自然之人变得精美：它们能够改变他”。

事实上，我相信，中国文学中的这首经典巨著，有一天也能改变那些以爱国者的身份在欧洲作战、但又具有野兽般的战斗本能的原始人类；把他们变成和平、温和、文明的人。文明的目标，正如拉斯金[2]所言，是使人类成为文明的人，他们将摒弃粗俗、暴力、野蛮和争斗。

莫急，且让我们言归正传。那么书面汉语是一种难学的语言吗？我的回答是，是又不是。我说，书面汉语，甚至我称之为完全宫廷腔调的汉语，古典汉语，并不难，因为，就像口语一样，极其简单。请允许我向你们展示一个随机抽取的样本，它是多么的简单，即使完全一副宫廷腔调，汉字也是如此。我取的样本是一首唐诗四行诗，它描述了中国人民为了保护自己的文明，抵御来自北方的野蛮的半开化的凶猛匈奴人所做的牺牲。

这首诗的中文版是：

誓扫匈奴不顾身，
五千貂锦丧胡尘，
可怜无定河边骨，
犹是春闺梦里人。[3]

1 马修·阿诺德（1822—1888）是英国诗人和文化评论家，担任学校督学。他的父亲是著名的拉格比学校校长托马斯·阿诺德，他的兄弟是文学教授汤姆·阿诺德和小说家、殖民行政长官威廉·德拉菲尔德·阿诺德。马修·阿诺德被认为是一位圣人作家，是一位对当代社会问题进行鞭策和指导的作家。

2 约翰·罗斯金（1819—1900）是英国维多利亚时代的主要艺术评论家，也是一位艺术赞助人、画家、杰出的社会思想家和慈善家。他的作品涉及地质、建筑、神话、鸟类学、文学、教育、植物学和政治经济学等多种学科。他的写作风格和文学形式都表现出多样性。他在所有的作品中，都强调自然、艺术和社会之间的联系。他还对岩石、植物、鸟类、风景、建筑结构和装饰进行了详细的素描和绘画。

3 唐代陈陶《陇西行四首（其二）》，参见《全唐诗》，http://www.qts.cn/#，2021年10月23日访问。

译成英文的意思是：

Swear sweep the Huns not care self,
Five thousand embroidery sable perish desert dust;
Alas! Wuting riverside bones,
Still are spring chambers dream inside men!

这首诗的自由体英文版本是这样的：

They vowed to sweep the heathen hordes
From off their native soil or die:
Five thousand tasselled knights, sable–clad,
All dead now on the desert lie.
Alas! The white bones that bleach cold
Far off along the Wuting stream,
Still come and go as living men
Home somewhere in the loved one's dream.

现在，如果你把它和我那拙劣的英文版本比较一下，你就会发现汉语原版语言多么文雅、风格多么鲜明、思想多么简单。语言、风格和思想是多么平淡、简洁，而思想又多么深刻，感情又多么深厚。

The Chinese Language

Ku Hung–Ming[1]

All foreigners who have tried to learn Chinese say that Chinese is a very difficult language. But is Chinese a difficult language? Before, however, we answer this question, let us understand what we mean by the Chinese language. There are, as everybody knows, two languages—I do not mean dialects—in China, the spoken and the written language. Now, by the way, does anybody know the reason why the Chinese insist upon having these two distinct, spoken and written languages? I will here give you the reason.

In China, as it was at one time in Europe when Latin was the learned or written language, the people are properly divided into two distinct classes, the educated and the uneducated. The colloquial or spoken language is the language for the use of the uneducated, and the written language is the language for the use of the really educated. In this way half educated people do not exist in this country. That is the reason, I say, why the Chinese insist upon having two

1 Ku Hung–Ming (1857–1928), an outstanding scholar in the late Qing Dynasty of China, proficient in 9 languages: English, French, German, Latin, Greek, Malay, etc. His main works include *The Story of a Chinese Oxford Movement, The Spirit of the Chinese People, The Discourses and Sayings of Confucius* (translation), *The Universal Order or Conduct of Life* (translation), etc. This passage is selected from the article "The Chinese Language" in the book *The Spirit of the Chinese People*, which in 1914 was originally published in the *China Review* in Beijing in 1915 under the name *Chunqiu Da Yi*, and soon translated into German. This book tries to explain the value of traditional Chinese culture to Western civilization, especially when Chinese culture was discriminated against and the Chinese nation was bullied. Besides, it is also an extremely valuable English book on Chinese culture. Ku states in the preface that "The object of this book is an attempt to interpret the spirit and show the value of the Chinese civilization". The book is composed of preface, introduction and six selected articles, namely "The Spirit of the Chinese People", "The Chinese Woman", "The Chinese Language", "John Smith in China", "A Great Sinologue", "Chinese Scholarship" (Part I and Part II).

languages. Now think of the consequences of having half educated people in a country. Look at Europe and America today.

In Europe and America since, from the disuse of Latin, the sharp distinction between the spoken and the written language has disappeared, there has arisen a class of half educated people who are allowed to use the same language as the really educated people, who talk of civilization, liberty, neutrality, militarism and panslavism without in the least understanding what these words really mean. People say that Prussian Militarism is a danger to civilization. But to me it seems, the half–educated man, the mob of half educated men in the world today, is the real danger to civilization. But that is neither here nor there.

Now to come to the question: is Chinese a difficult language? My answer is, yes and no. Let us first take the spoken language. The Chinese spoken language, I say, is not only not difficult, but as compared with the half dozen languages that I know, the easiest language in the world except Malay. Spoken Chinese is easy because it is an extremely simple language. It is a language without case, without tense, without regular and irregular verbs; in fact without grammar, or any rule whatever. But people have said to me that Chinese is difficult even because of its simplicity; even because it has no rule or grammar. That, however, cannot be true. Malay like Chinese, is also a simple language without grammar or rules; and yet Europeans who learn it, do not find it difficult. Thus in itself and for the Chinese, colloquial or spoken Chinese at least is not a difficult language.

But for educated Europeans and especially for half educated Europeans who come to China, even colloquial or spoken Chinese is a very difficult language: and why? Because spoken or colloquial Chinese is, as I said, the language of uneducated men, of thoroughly uneducated men; in fact the language of a child. Now as a proof of this, we all know how easily European children learn colloquial or spoken Chinese, while learned philogues and sinologues insist in saying that Chinese is so difficult. Chinese, colloquial Chinese, I say again is the language of a child. My first advice therefore to my foreign friends who want to learn Chinese is "Be ye like little children, you will then not only enter into the Kingdom of Heaven, but you will also be able to learn Chinese."

We now come to the written or book language, written Chinese. But here before I go further, let me say there are also different kinds of written Chinese. The Missionaries class these under two categories and call them easy *wen li* and difficult *wen li*. But that, in my opinion, is not a satisfactory classification. The proper classification, I think, should be, plain dress written Chinese; official uniform Chinese; and full court dress Chinese. If you like to use Latin, call them: *litera communis* or *litera officinalis* (common or business Chinese); *litera classica minor* (lesser classical Chinese); and *litera classica major* (higher classical Chinese).

Now many foreigners have called themselves or have been called Chinese scholars. Writing an article on Chinese scholarship, some thirty years ago for the *N. C. Daily News*,[1]—ah me! those old Shanghai days, *Tempora mutantur, nos et mutamur in illis*, I then said: "Among Europeans in China, the publication of a few dialogues in some provincial patois or the collection of a hundred Chinese proverbs at once entitles a man to call himself a Chinese scholar. "

"There is," I said, "of course no harm in a name, and with the extraterritoriality clause in the treaty, an Englishman in China may with impunity call himself Confucius, if so it pleases him." Now what I want to say here is this: how many foreigners who call themselves Chinese scholars, have any idea of what an asset of civilisation is stored up in that portion of Chinese literature which I have called the *Classica majora*, the literature in full court dress Chinese? I say an asset of

1 *The North China Daily News* (*N.C. Daily News*), was an English–language newspaper in Shanghai, China, called the most influential foreign newspaper of its time. The paper was founded as the weekly *North–China Herald*. Its founder was Henry Shearman, a British auctioneer, with his Chinese name Xi Anmen, who started his career in Shanghai as an auctioneer and a representative of British merchants in Shanghai. On June 26, 1850, in the thirtieth year of Daoguang of the Qing Dynasty, he founded *Beihua Jiebao*, a wholly owned newspaper in Shanghai. The purpose of the paper was to evoke "a wave of enthusiasm" in Britain in support of "claims for closer political ties and greater trade" with China, "and to see that this vast empire had an astonishing wealth of resources". A daily edition commenced publication on 1 June 1864 as the *North China Daily News*. Its circulation peaked at 7,817 copies.

civilisation, because I believe that this *Classica majora* in the Chinese literature is something which can, as Matthew Arnold[1] says of Homer's poetry, "refine the raw natural man: they can transmute him."

In fact, I believe this *Classica majora* in Chinese literature will be able to transform one day even the raw natural men who are now fighting in Europe as patriots, but with the fighting instincts of wild animals; transform them into peaceful, gentle and civil persons. Now the object of civilisation, as Ruskin[2] says, is to make mankind into civil persons who will do away with coarseness, violence, brutality and fighting.

But *revenons a nos moutons*. Is then written Chinese a difficult language? My answer again is, yes and no. I say, written Chinese, even what I have called the full court dress Chinese, the *Classica majora* Chinese, is not difficult, because, like the spoken or colloquial Chinese, it is extremely simple. Allow me to show you by an average specimen taken at random how extremely simple, written Chinese even when dressed in full court dress uniform, is. The specimen I take is a poem of four lines from the poetry of the Tang Dynasty describing what sacrifices the Chinese people had to make in order to protect their civilisation against the wild half–civilised fierce Huns from the North.

The words of the poem in Chinese are:

誓扫匈奴不顾身，
五千貂锦丧胡尘，

1 Matthew Arnold (1822–1888) was an English poet and cultural critic who worked as an inspector of schools. He was the son of Thomas Arnold, the famed headmaster of Rugby School, and brother to both Tom Arnold, literary professor, and William Delafield Arnold, novelist and colonial administrator. Matthew Arnold has been characterized as a sage writer, a type of writer who chastises and instructs the reader on contemporary social issues.

2 John Ruskin (1819–1900) was the leading English art critic of the Victorian era, also an art patron, draughtsman, a prominent social thinker and philanthropist. He wrote on subjects as varied as geology, architecture, myth, ornithology, literature, education, botany and political economy. His writing styles and literary forms were equally varied. In all of his writing, he emphasized the connections between nature, art and society. He also made detailed sketches and paintings of rocks, plants, birds, landscapes, and architectural structures and ornamentation.

可怜无定河边骨，

犹是春闺梦里人。[1]

which translated into English word for word mean:

Swear sweep the Huns not care self,

Five thousand embroidery sable perish desert dust;

Alas! Wuting riverside bones,

Still are Spring chambers dream inside men!

A free English version of the poem is something like this:

They vowed to sweep the heathen hordes

From off their native soil or die:

Five thousand tasselled knights, sable–clad,

All dead now on the desert lie.

Alas! the white bones that bleach cold

Far off along the Wuting stream,

Still come and go as living men

Home somewhere in the loved one's dream.

Now, if you will compare it with my poor clumsy English version, you will see how plain in words and style, how simple in ideas, the original Chinese is. How plain and simple in words, style and ideas: and yet how *deep* in thought, how *deep* in feeling it is.

1 Chen Tao, Tang Dynasty, *Longxi Xing·Four* (The second). See *Poetry of Tang Dynasty*, http://www.qts.cn/#.

Word bank

1. dialect n. 方言，土话
2. insist upon 坚持
3. colloquial adj. 用于日常交谈的；口语的；非正式的；非文学的
4. distinction n. 不同；差异；优秀；杰出
5. civilization n. 文明；文化；文明进程
6. liberty n. 自由；自由活动的权力；自由女神像
7. neutrality n. 中立；中性；中立立场
8. militarism n. 军国主义；穷兵黩武主义
9. panslavism n. 泛奴役主义
10. mob n. 人群；暴民；乱民；乌合之众 v. 成群围住；围攻；成群袭击；蜂拥进入
11. simplicity n. 简明；简易
12. philogue n. 哲学（家）
13. Sinologue n. 汉学家
14. Kingdom of Heaven 天国
15. Missionary n. 传教士
16. full court dress Chinese 完全身着宫廷礼服的中文
17. common or business Chinese 普通或商人腔调的汉语
18. lesser classical Chinese 古典腔调较少的中文
19. higher classical Chinese 高级文言文
20. scholarship n. 学术研究；学术成就；学问；奖学金
21. publication n. 出版；发表；出版物；发布；公布
22. provincial adj. 省的；京都大邑以外地方的；外地的；低俗的；思想褊狭的；偏执的；乡气的 n. 省内居民；外省人
23. patois n. 方言；土语；行话；圈内用语；黑话
24. proverb n. 谚语；格言
25. extraterritoriality n. 治外法权
26. treaty n. 条约；协定

27. impunity n. 不受惩罚；免罪；不受损伤

28. Confucius 孔子

29. asset n. 物品；人才；品质；优点；资产

30. homer n. 本垒打；信鸽；偏袒主队的裁判

31. Homer n. 人名：荷马；霍默

32. transmute v. 变形；变质；变化；将（贱金属）变成金银

33. patriot n. 爱国者；爱国主义者

34. coarseness n. 粗糙；劣等；粗；粗度

35. brutality n. 残忍；暴行；野蛮

36. random adj. 胡乱的；无一定之规的；任意的；任意选取的

37. sacrifice n. 献祭；供奉；牺牲；v. 献祭；以……为祭品；牺牲；献出；弃子

38. fierce adj. 凶猛的；好斗的；残酷的；猛烈的；强烈的；adv. 非常；极其

39. swear v. 发誓；保证；诅咒

40. sweep v. 扫；拂；掠过；扫射；搜寻；向上（或向后）梳头发 n. 扫；挥动；延伸；绵延；囊括所有奖项

41. embroidery n. 刺绣；绣花；刺绣法；绣制品；渲染

42. sable n. 紫貂；黑貂；黑色；貂羚；貂皮；紫貂皮；丧服 adj. 黑色的

43. perish v. 死亡；经受酷寒；毁灭；消亡

44. Chamber n. 房间；会议厅；议院

45. vow n. 誓言；誓约 v. 宣誓；立誓；发誓；立誓奉献

46. heathen n. 异教徒 adj. 异教的

47. horde n. 一群人；一伙人；小而松散的社会组织；游牧队伍

48. bleach v. 漂白；晒白；使变成淡色；用漂白剂给……清洗；消毒；使失去实质内容 n. 漂白剂；消毒剂

49. tassel n. 流苏；穗；承梁木；承梁石 v. 用流苏装饰；抽穗

50. knight n. 披甲戴盔的骑马武士；爵士；骑士；护花使者 v. 封……为爵士

51. clothe (clad, clad) v. 给（自己、别人）穿衣；为……提供衣物；覆盖；赋予

52. clumsy adj. 笨拙的；笨手笨脚的；手脚不灵活的；毫无技巧的；不圆滑的

图　书

The Chinese Books

书籍之厄[1]

书籍是人类智慧和思想的实物体现。古籍图书不仅可以传承思想、知识和文化，图书本身也是一种艺术形式，因为其刊印、装帧、收藏等皆为中国文化艺术的精髓，譬如中国古籍装帧版式可分为线装版、经折装、蝴蝶装等多种形态。但是，在人类历史长河中，图书饱经厄运，多灾多难，既有天灾又有人祸。因而古籍珍本难求。

《史记·秦始皇本纪》载：

丞相臣斯昧死言："古者天下散乱，莫之能一，是以诸侯并作，语皆道古以害今，饰虚言以乱实，人善其所私学，以非上之所建立。今皇帝并有天下，别黑白而定一尊。私学而相与非法教，人闻令下，则各以其学议之，入则心非，出则巷议，夸主以为名，异取以为高，率群下以造谤。如此弗禁，则主势降乎上，党与成乎下。禁之便。臣请史官非秦记皆烧之。非博士官所职，天下敢有藏《诗》《书》、百家语者，悉诣守、尉杂烧之。有敢偶语《诗》《书》者弃市。以古非今者族。吏见知不举者与同罪。令下三十日不烧，黥为城旦。所不去者，医药卜筮种

1　编写此文时参考了司马迁的《史记》和洪迈的《客斋随笔》等文献。

树之书。若欲有学法令，以吏为师。”制曰：“可。”[1]

结果，公元前213年秦始皇下令焚烧秦国史书以外的各国史书。[2]

《容斋随笔》有：

梁元帝在江陵，蓄古今图书十四万卷，将亡之夕尽焚之。隋嘉则殿有书三十七万卷，唐平王世充，得其旧书于东都，浮舟溯河，尽覆于砥柱。贞观、开元募借缮写，两都各聚书四部。禄山之乱，尺简不藏。代宗、文宗时，复行采，分藏于十二库。黄巢之乱，存者盖鲜。昭宗又于诸道求访，及徙洛阳，荡然无遗。今人汉、隋、唐《经籍》《艺文志》，未尝不茫然太息也。晁以道记本朝王文康初相周世宗，多有唐旧书，今其子孙不知何在。李文正所藏既富，而且辟学馆以延学士大夫，不待见主人，而下马直入读书。供牢饩以给其日力，与众共利之。今其家仅有败屋数楹，而书不知何在也！宋宣献家兼有毕文简、杨文庄二家之书，其富盖有王府不及者。元符中，一夕灾为灰爆。以道自谓家五世于兹，虽不敢与宋氏争多，而校雠是正，未肯自逊。政和甲午之冬，火亦告遗。唯刘壮舆家于庐山之阳，自其祖凝之以来，遗子孙者唯图书也，其书与七泽俱富矣。于是为作记。今刘氏之在庐山者不闻其人，则所谓藏书殆亦羽化。乃知自古到今，神物亦于斯文为靳也。宣和殿、太清楼、龙图阁御府所储，靖康荡析之余，尽归于燕，置之秘书省，乃有幸而得存者焉。[3]

可见书籍命运之多舛，古籍善本之珍贵。

1 （西汉）司马迁：《史记》，中华书局，2011年。

2 沈善洪：《中国语言文化背景汉英双解词典》，商务印书馆，2010年，第113页。

3 （宋）洪迈：《容斋随笔》，北京燕山出版社，2008年，第443—444页。

Dooms of Books

Books are the physical embodiments of human wisdom and thoughts. Not only can ancient books sustain the heritages of classic ideas, knowledge and culture, but also the books themselves are an art form, because their printing, binding, and collection are of the essence of Chinese culture and art. In the long river of human history, books have suffered from bad luck, plagued by natural disasters and man–made ones. Therefore, rare ancient books are hard to find.

In "Emperor Qin Shihuang's Biography" of *Historical Records* can it be found out that:

Li Si, Prime Minister, risked his death to say: in ancient times, the world was scattered and no one could unify it. As a result, the princes rose together. They all said that they used the ancient to harm the present. They played false words to disturb the true reality, under the name of citing the ancient. People only appreciated what they had learned and accused the systems established by the government. Today, the emperor has unified the world, and everything is determined by the emperor alone, to distinguish right from wrong, black and white. However, private schools criticized the law together. When people heard that there was an order to introduce, they would discuss it according to what they had learned. When entering the court, they would criticize in their hearts, and when they left the court, they would go to the streets to discuss, boasting about themselves in front of the monarch in order to gain fame and fortune. They pursued strange claims to exalt themselves and take the lead in creating slanders and rumors among the people. If this is not forbidden, the power of the monarch at the upper will decrease, and the power of cronyism will form at the lower. I thought it was better to ban it. I asked the historian minister to burn all the classics that were not from Qin State. Except those under the control of the Doctor's Office, whoever dares to have a collection of *Shijing–The Book of Poems, Shang Shu–Classic of History,* and Zhuzi baijia –works by various scholars of various schools, should send them to the local officials to burn together. Whoever dares to discuss *Shijing–The Book of Poems* and *Shang Shu–Classic of History* will be sentenced to death to show to the public. Whoever dares to critisize the current by taking advantage of the ancient should be executed to death with all the family members. If an official does not report it while knowing about it, he shall be punished with the same crime as the accomplice. Those who do not burn the books 30 days after the order has been promulgated should be sentenced to the punishments like tattooing on their faces and building the city walls. What is not prohibited are books on medicine, divination, and planting. If someone wants to learn the law, he should follow the officials as his teacher. Emperor Qin Shihuang issued an edict and said: "Yes." [1]

As a result, in 213 BC, Emperor Qin Shihuang ordered to burn all the history books from other princely states except those of the Qin State.[2]

In *Rongzhai Suibi* we can see:

Xiao Yi, Emperor Yuan of Liang State in the Southern Dynasties collected 140,000 volumes of ancient books and the ones at that time in Jiangling. On the eve of the fall of Jiangling City by the Wei army, Xiao Yi's collection of books were burned out. The Jiaze Hall of the Sui Dynasty had a collection of 370,000 volumes. After the Tang army defeated Wang Shichong, they obtained the old books of the Sui Dynasty in Luoyang, the eastern capital. However, on the way to ship these old books along the Yellow River to Chang'an (now Xi'an), all overturned into the river at Gorge Sanmenxia. During the period of Zhenguan and Kaiyuan, the government of the Tang Dynasty called on scholars

---

1 (Western Han Dynasty) Sima Qian, *Historical Records,* Zhonghua Book Company, 2011.

2 Shen Shanhong, *A Chinese–English Dictionary with Cultural Background Information*, the Commercial Press, 2010, p.113.

and people nationwide to donate books. As with those owners unwilling to donate them, the government would borrow their books. After the copying was completed, the books would be returned to the owners. As a result, a large number of precious books were obtained. According to the four parts of Classics, History, Zi (the works of philosophers) and Collections, they were collected in Chang'an and Luoyang. However, during the Anshi Rebellion, these books were all burned out. During the period of Tang Daizong and Tang Wenzong, the government searched for classics on a large scale and stored them in twelve storehouses for treasuries. But after the Peasants' War in the late Tang Dynasty headed by Huang Chao, there were few books left. Tang Zhaozong had the whole country searched for books again, achieving remarkable results. When he moved to Luoyang, these books were all destroyed and disappeared. Nowadays, when people read *Jingji Zhi* or *Yiwen Zhi* in *Hanshu, Suishu,* and *Tangshu*, they often feel very sad full of various emotions when facing the abundance of famous books with non–content. Chao Yidao said that Wang Wenkang of our dynasty used to be Zhou Shizong's prime minister in his early years, and he had in his family a large collection of old books from the Tang Dynasty, but it is unknown where his descendants are now living. Li Fang, Duke Wenzheng, had a large collection of books, so he opened his own library for the majority of scholar–officials to study. Those who read books could directly enter the library to read, without having to visit the owner. At the same time, the host also provided free meals for readers to save their time, and he hoped to take advantage of his library with everyone else together. But unfortunately, till to day, there are only a few ruined houses left, and many of his collections have disappeared, whereabouts of which are unknown! Duke Xuanxian of the Song Dynasty took over the collections of Bi Wenjian and Yang Wenzhuang, and his collection was even richer and larger than that in the palace. However, during the Yuanfu reign of Zhezong, these collections were also burned overnight. Chao Yidao claimed that five generations of his family had devoted themselves to collecting books. Although the number of books in the collection cannot be compared with that of the Song family, the collation was by no means inferior to others'. In the winter of the forth year (AD 1114) in Zhenghe Era under Emperor Huizong, a fire broke out in Chao's family, and the books suffered heavy losses. Only Liu Zhuangao in the southern foothills of Mount Lu had books left to his descendants since his ancestor Liu Ning, so that his family's collection of books was as large as the waters of the Seven Great Lakes such as Yunmeng Lake and Dongting Lake. Therefore, I deliberately wrote an article to commend his family's beautiful traditions. Today, I have never heard of anyone from the Liu family still living in Mount Lu. If this is the case, then the so–called book collection of the Liu family may have long since disappeared and vanished. It can be seen that, since ancient times, the devine things are really stingy with the literati. The collections of books preserved in the imperial library such as Xuanhe Hall, Taiqing Tower, Longtu Pavilion of the Song Dynasty had been washed away by the battle of Jingkang during the Qinzong period, and all the remaining books were transported to the capital of Yanjing (now Beijing), stored in the Secretary Bureau, rare books that were lucky enough to be preserved.[1]

How many dooms is the fate of books full of, seen from above; and how precious the rare ancient books are!

1 (Song) Hong Mai, "Rongzhai's Essays", Beijing Yanshan Publishing House, 2008, pp. 44–43–4.

《尚书》与伏生

伏生保护、诠释并传播了《尚书》。《尚书》又称《书》或《书经》，是中国第一部古典文集和最早的历史文献，《尚书》即上古历史文书和后人追忆的古代史实的汇编。[1]此书自尧、舜时期到夏、商、周，跨越两千余年，是三坟五典[2]的可考记录。《尚书》被列为儒家经典之一，相传由孔子整理、选编成百余篇。后经秦朝焚书，损失极大。首先，阐明仁君治民之道是《尚书》的第一要旨；其次，它阐明了贤臣辅佐君王之道。

伏生，名胜，字子贱，秦朝济南郡邹平人，伏生系孔门弟子轁子贱后裔。自幼嗜古好学，博览群书，对《尚书》研读尤精，为儒学博士。公元前215年，秦始皇下令禁止民间私藏经书，焚书坑儒，伏生冒被诛杀之罪，将《尚书》藏于墙壁之夹层内，《尚书》由此逃过焚烧之难。秦末兵起，伏生流亡异乡。刘邦平定天下，伏生返回故里，其所藏《尚书》已损失大半，仅剩29篇，他抄录、整理，教授于齐鲁之间，主要弟子有济南张生及欧阳生。汉文帝时，文帝求能治《尚书》者，天下无有；后闻伏生之名，乃下令召见；然伏生年逾九十，不能出行，汉文帝遣晁错亲赴邹平。伏生年事已高，言语不清，由女儿羲娥代言，传授《尚书》。人们将伏生所记《尚书》整理、记录下来，补叙出所失篇章，才使《尚书》得以完整流传，后世称此为《今文尚书》。

1　《不列颠百科全书》第15卷，中国大百科全书出版社，1999年，第329页。

2　“三坟”指伏羲、神农、黄帝的书；“五典”指少昊、颛顼、高辛、唐、虞的书。三坟五典相传为我国最早的古籍。在中华民族的记忆中，先夏时期中国有四部名著，它们分别被称为三坟、五典、八索、九丘。有说法认为“三坟”是指《黄帝内经》《伏羲卦经》和《神农本草经》。

明 杜堇 《伏生授经图》 绢本设色 纽约大都会艺术博物馆藏

(Ming) Du Jin, Fu Sheng Transmitting the "*Classic of History*", ink and colour on silk, collected by Metropolitan Museum, New York.

古代有许多艺术家都描绘过这一主题，譬如唐朝名家王维有《伏生授经图》[1]，以及明代著名画家杜堇的人物画作《伏生授经图》[2]。关于这一主题，德国学者劳悟达在她的新著《中国艺术中芭蕉的图像学·叶展叶舒》中有详述。[3]

---

1 王维（701—761），《伏生授经图》，手卷，绢本，墨笔设色，画幅尺寸纵25.4厘米，横44.7厘米，大阪市立美术馆藏。

2 杜堇，《伏生授经图》，立轴，绢本，墨笔设色，画幅尺寸纵147厘米，横104.5厘米，纽约大都会艺术博物馆藏。

3 ［德］劳悟达著，殷凌云、毕夏译：《中国艺术中芭蕉的图像学·叶展叶舒》，中国美术学院出版社，2022年。

A Classic of History and Fu Sheng

Fu Sheng protected, interpreted and disseminated *Shang Shu—Classic of History,* also known as "*Book*" or "*Shujing* (*Shu Ching*)", is China's first collection of classical essays and the earliest historical documents. It mainly records the ancient historical documents and the ancient historical facts recalled by later generations [1]from Yao and Shun to Xia, Shang and Zhou, spanning more than two thousand years. It is the testable record of "Three Tombs and Five Classics"[2]. *Classic of History* is listed as one of the Confucian classics. According to legend, *Classic of History* was compiled and selected by Confucius into one hundred chapters. After the books were burned in the Qin Dynasty, it suffered a great loss. The first gist of the book is to interpret and clarify how good benevolent rulers govern the people. The second is about the way of wise ministers assisting the rulers.

Fu Sheng, with his name Sheng and the courtesy name Zijian, was born in Zouping, Jinan County of the Qin Dynasty, a descendant of Shi Zijian, a disciple of Confucianism. Since his childhood, he was fond of learning ancient knowledge, read extensively all kinds of books, and was especially good at studying *Classic of History*. He was a scholar of Confucianism. In 215 BC, Emperor Qin Shihuang banned the private collection of scriptures and ordered to

---

1 *Encyclopaedia Britannica International Chinese Edition*, Encyclopaedia of China Publishing House, 1999, vol. 15, p.329.

2 *San Fen* (*Three Tombs*): refers to the books of Fuxi, Shennong, and Huangdi; *Wu Dian* (*the Five Classics*): refers to the books of Shaohao, Zhuan Xu, Gao Xin, Tang, and Yu. According to legend, it is the earliest ancient book in our country. In the memory of the Chinese nation, there were four masterpieces in China during the pre–Xia period, and they were called "Three Tombs", "Five Classics", "Eight Suo", and "Nine Hills". It is said that the *Three Tombs* refer to the *Huangdi Neijing, Fuxi Gua Jing and Shen Nong's Materia Medica.*

burn books and buried Confucianists. Fu Sheng risked being punishably killed and hid one of *Classic of History* in the mezzanine of the wall, thus protecing it from burning. At the end of the Qin Dynasty, rebellions rose and Fu Sheng fled to a foreign land. After Liu Bang pacified the world, Fu Sheng returned to his hometown, seeking *Classic of History* in his collection, with most lost and only 29 chapters remaining. He transcribed it, sorted it out, and taught it in Qi and Lu, with Zhang Sheng and Ouyang Sheng from Jinan as the main disciples. At the time of Emperor Wen of the Han Dynasty, there was no such a person who could study and interpret *Classic of History.* After hearing Fu Sheng, he ordered to summon him. However, Fu Sheng was over ninety, too old to travel to the capital personally. Emperor Wen of the Han Dynasty sent Chao Cuo to Zouping. Fu Sheng was at a high age and his speech was slurred, so that his daughter Xi'e acted as an endorsement and interpreted his speech. Finally, *Classic of History* collected in Fu Sheng's chest was recorded with the missing chapters complemented, making it be completely spread, later known as "*Jinwen Shangshu*".

In ancient times, many artists painted the images of this theme, such as the painting *Fu Sheng Shou Jing* [1]by Wang Wei, a famous artist of the Tang Dynasty, and a figure painting with the same name *Fu Sheng Transmitting the "Book of Documents"* [2], by Du Jin, a famous artist of the Ming Dynasty. About this theme, Uta Lauer, a German scholar, detailed in her new book *Leaves Unfurl: The Iconography of the Banana Plant in Chinese Art.*[3]

---

1 Wang Wei (701–761). *Fu Sheng expounding the Classic*, handing scroll, ink and colour on silk, 25.4 × 44.7 cm, Osaka City Museum of Fine Arts.

2 Du Jin, *Fu Sheng Transmitting the "Book of Documents"*, hanging scroll, ink and colour on silk, 147 × 104.5 cm, Metropolitan Museum, New York.

3 (Germany) Uta Lauer, *Leaves Unfurl: The Iconography of the Banana Plant in Chinese Art,* translated into Chinese by Yin Lingyun and Bi Xia, China Academy of Art Press, March, 2022.

《书籍之为艺术》节选

范景中[1]

据上所述，对于《汲黯传》的评价已成僵局，不论是赞赏还是否定，都有权威人士的支持。因此想找一条新的路径来解答《汲黯传》的两个问题，此处我们不妨再回味一次张伯英先生的批评：

所谓“此刻”者，不知何所指，若亦为《汲黯传》，何以不言临，而曰手钞；所谓得其笔意者，得何书之笔意。即此数语可以断其伪矣。

“此刻”在《汲黯传》的语境中，只能有两种解释，或为刻石，或为刻本。否定者正是从第一种解释点出发的，因为不论从实物看，还是从文献看，直到今天都未发现可供赵孟頫取用的《汲黯传》刻石。这使我们不得不思考一下第二种解释，即刻本（冯誉骥已接近此看法），也自然使我们想到赵孟頫的藏书。根据资料，首先就是前述的收有《汲黯传》的《汉书》。遗憾的是《汉书》已化蝶天上，不能用来与《汲黯传》墨迹比对。好在还存有前人的鉴赏记录，可以帮助我们退而求其次。《汉书》在王世贞的家中时，王氏曾这样描述说：

桑皮纸，白洁如玉，四旁宽广，字大者如钱，绝有欧柳笔法。细书丝发肤致，墨色精纯，溪潘流沖。盖自真宗（918—1022）朝刻之秘阁，特赐两府，而其人亦自宝惜，四百年而手若未触者。前有赵吴兴小像。[2]

1　范景中，中国美术学院教授，博士生导师，著名学者，著作颇丰。此文原载《新美术》2008年第3期，有幸得到作者允许在此节选引用。

2　转引自《钦定天禄琳琅书目》卷二《清人书目题跋丛刊》本，中华书局，1995年。

有赵孟頫小像，赵氏宝爱之极，才有此举，不言而喻。有欧柳笔法，正与《汲黯传》相合。“此刻”的问题与书体的问题一并而解。不过，潘文协帮助我校勘的结果，却是《汲黯传》的文字更近似于《史记》，而疏远于《汉书》，因此，底本当为《史记》无疑。

赵孟頫所藏的《史记》，文献只记录了一部，已见前述，我已断为钞本而非刻本。这样，“此刻”之刻本具体何指，又将落空。在这里，我们碰到了一个历史研究最最常见的问题，诚如贡布里希所说：历史就像瑞士奶酪，有很多孔隙，在很多情况下都是空缺，留下了大量无解的问题，因为我们缺乏证据，而史学家的技巧就在于找出那些有可能得到回答的问题，他的智慧就在于感觉到哪一条探索线路能找到结果，能够使他有所发现。[1]

也许我们现在就遇到了一个没有答案、没有结果的问题。不过，如果我们仅仅盯住细节，而忘记了让想象的羽翼飞翔起来，可能就会失去一次提出有趣而有创造性问题的机会。换言之，我们不应该仅仅局限于记载，我们还要复原那些原本应有而没有文献记录的历史情境，还要靠我们在考试的终结处大胆显示智慧（Sapere aude）。因此，我们不妨假设，他也同样拥有高质量的《史记》刻本，我想这绝非牵强附会，相反，他这样的地位和身份，如果没有一部佳美的宋刻本《史记》，倒是不可思议的，毕竟他本人就是天潢贵胄，是从宋王室里走出来的人。这样设想，我们不仅首先轻而易举解释了上述的“此刻”与字体问题，而且还紧接着立刻提出一个更重要的艺术史问题，即本文的正题：书籍何以成为艺术。一旦确立了这个问题，就会得出一个有趣的结论，《汲黯传》以刻本的书籍为范本，书写而成，这就是为什么赵氏的跋语不称临，而曰手钞的原因。

在进一步说明这个假设之前，我们先看一个旁证。

《过云楼书画记·文彦可米庵图卷》：“张青甫得米襄阳《宝章待访录》……凡四千余字，相传为胜国赵文敏公物，有赵氏子昂印。在我明为陆冢宰所有，

1 E.H. Gombrich, The Museum's Mission, the Enjoyment of Art, the Problem of Critics', *Art News*, January 1974, pp. 54–57；中译本见E.H.贡布里希著，杨思梁、范景中、严善淳译：《艺术与科学：贡布里希谈话录和回忆录》，浙江摄影出版社，1998年，第121页。

内兄青甫氏从陆氏后人踪迹二十年余，始倾资购归，遂自号米庵。”[1]张丑是晚明收藏大家，竟以《宝章待访录》这部书命名斋号，可见其宝重之意。这在赵孟頫的书斋中也影响着他对书籍的看法，让他以艺术的眼光来看书籍，即《宝章待访录》是书也是艺术，我想是自然而然的。特别是此书后有明人张奉（字伯承，工隶书）的一通跋语，正与此处的论题有关，他说：“海岳小楷，世所罕睹，此《宝章待访录》全出泰和（李邕）家法，时杂欧褚笔仗，定为盛年真迹无疑。”[2]张青甫连作三跋，说的也是欧柳笔法。宋版佳刻，就有此风貌。

与此处问题最直接最重要的是赵孟頫在他的另一部藏书《六臣注文选》上写的跋语，此书没有他的小像，或不如《汉书》那样珍秘，但他的跋语却完全是崭新的眼光。

霜月如雪，夜读阮嗣宗咏怀诗，九咽皆作清冷。而是书玉楮[3]银钩[4]，若与灯月相映，助我清吟之兴不浅。[5]

萧萧数语，却是藏书史上的大事，在他之前，我们似乎还找不到这样的言论。宋人写书跋多者陆游算是一位，把他的《放翁题跋》翻阅一遍，就能体会到赵氏看待书籍的眼光是多么新颖，“玉楮”是书籍的材质，而“银钩”完全是用书法品评的术语作议论，这让赵孟頫成了把书籍当作艺术品欣赏的有文字可征的第一人。[6]

这通跋语光绪刻本作至正二年（1342）必是至大二年（1309）之误刻，至正二年赵氏已去世二十年，因此是刻本出了问题，倘是作伪，也不至于糊涂到

1　（清）顾文彬著：《过云楼书画记》，卷五，《续修四库全书》影印光绪刊本，第1085册，上海古籍出版社，1994—2002年，第238页。

2　见（清）卞永誉著：《式古堂书画汇考》，书法卷之四，《中国书画全书》本，上海书画出版社，1994年，第6册，第118页。

3　楮（chǔ）为构树之古名，树皮是制造桑皮纸和宣纸的原料。古时亦作纸的代称。亦如：楮知白、楮先生、楮生均为纸的别名。—编者注。

4　银钩意为：（1）一种银质的妇女饰物；（2）比喻遒媚刚劲的书法；（3）比喻弯月。在此处指书法。—编者注。

5　光绪十年（1884）长沙王氏刻本，卷三，第24页。

6　李清照《金石录后序》云：“每获一书，即同共勘校，整集签题。得书画彝鼎，亦摩玩舒卷，指摘疵病，夜尽一烛为率。故能纸札精致，字画完整，冠诸收书家。”（《四部丛刊》续编本）可称开书籍欣赏先声者，但似还在工艺欣赏的层次，赵孟頫可谓是进入艺术欣赏了。

如此地步。此书有王世贞、董其昌、王稺登、周天球、张凤翼、汪应娄、王醇、曹子念及乾隆馆臣过目的跋文，当是可信的赵氏藏书。

《天禄琳琅》的编者评曰："孟頫此跋作小楷书，曲尽二王之妙，其爱是书也，至足以助吟兴，则宋本之佳者在元时已不可多得矣。"[1]

为了说明书籍在赵孟頫眼中的景象，再引一条资料。陈继儒《读书十六观》引赵孟頫书跋云：

> 聚书藏书，良非易事。善观书者，澄神端虑，静几焚香，勿捲脑，勿折角，勿以爪侵字，勿以唾揭幅，勿以作枕，勿以夹刺，随损随修，随开随掩。后之得吾书者，并奉赠此法。[2]

关于这通书跋在藏书史上的影响，有兴趣者可参看我的《藏书铭印记》，此处我想把它和与赵孟頫相差八岁的汤垕（1262—1332）对鉴赏绘画的要求作一比较：

> 霾天秽地，灯下酒边，不可看画；拙工之印，凡手之题，坚为规避；不映摹、不改装以失旧观，更不乱订真伪，令人气短。[3]

这些话殊可相通互文，合在一起并论。只有对艺术品才须如此小心，如此挑剔。

说到此，我们可以简短的下一结论说，由于赵孟頫具备两个条件，而改变了书籍的命运。一是他的鉴赏眼光，一是他的书法家实践，他不仅欣赏书籍，而且还以书籍为样板，书写了我们至今还能见到的《汲黯传》，为他的书风又增添了一种样式。当然，最重要的条件还是赵孟頫是个大文人，书籍能像绘画一样助吟兴，也只能由他这样身份的人来宣布，也只能产生在像他这样身份的书斋中。帕赫特在研究文艺复兴时期书籍装帧艺术时说过一番话，其理

1　转引自《钦定天禄琳琅书目》卷三，版本同前。

2　（明）陈继儒著：《读书十六观》，道光刊本。

3　参见（元）陶宗仪辑：《说郛》，卷十三，民国十六年上海商务印书馆铅印本。

也正与此类似。他说：

No art has a better claim to be called "humanistic" than the book–decoration of the early Renaissance. For this art is closely linked with the professional activities of the humanists themselves, in fact the studio of the humanist scholars is its very birthplace.[1]

《汲黯传》写于赵孟頫67岁的晚年。恰好在赵孟頫去世的前十年这段时间之内，他的小楷取得了巨大的进展，他64岁书写的《七观帖》，早于《汲黯传》前三年即延祐四年（1317），杨大瓢和翁覃溪都认为代表了他的小楷高峰。张伯英那样的大鉴赏家看的是明人翻本，也赞叹道："松雪小楷传世固多，唯此（指《七观贴》）有《黄庭》《洛神》之遗，无平时侧媚习气，允为合作。"[2]其实，翻本已大失风神。而袁桷在《清容居士集》记赵孟頫在去世前的书法则可进一步印证他何以会作欧褚笔意的小楷。袁桷说："承旨公作小楷，著纸如飞，每谓欧褚而下不足论。此经（指《灵宝经》），距下世才两月，痛当作恸！"[3]"欧褚而下不足论"，正是胸中存有欧褚。恰好我们也有赵氏对欧阳询的评价。辽宁博物馆藏有《梦奠帖》，后有赵孟頫的题跋说："欧阳信本书，清劲秀健，古今一人。米老云：'庄若对越，俊若跳掷'，犹似未知其神奇也。向在都下，见《劝学》一帖，是集贤官库物，后有开元题识具全，笔意与此一同，但官帖是硬黄纸为异耳。至元廿九年闰月望日，为右之（郭无锡）兄书。吴兴赵孟頫。"这段话，出于1292年的赵孟頫之手，前此一年（1291），他书写了大名鼎鼎的《过秦论》。前此三年（1289），他写了《书姜白石兰亭序考》（台北故宫博物院藏），而姜白石正有一手典型的出自欧体的小楷，赵孟頫也见过那件《兰亭考》的原迹。他早年致力小楷，颇受姜白石的影响也是公论。

《抚州永安禅院僧堂记》书于赵孟頫逝世的前一年，款识云："至治元年正月廿四日，千江上人过余溪上，茗谈中话及无尽居士所作《永安禅院僧堂记》，

1 Fritz Saxl (1890–1948), *A Volume of Memorial Essays from his Friends in England*, ed., D. J. Gordon, London, 1957.

2 张伯英著：《张伯英碑帖论稿》，河北教育出版社，2006年，第312页。

3 《四部丛刊》初编本，卷四十六，第16—17页。

词意卓绝，深有抑扬宗旨、勉励后学之语。因上人求余书，故书此以归之。”[1] 观此跋语，知必精心所写。惜未见墨迹。乾隆年间曾藏沈虹屏春雨楼，《石渠宝笈》卷三亦记一册，不知是否即此卷。《春雨楼书画目》记曰：“此文敏晚年笔，即得十三行真迹后书也。书法奕奕有神，一洗平生甜熟之习，晋唐后小楷当以此为冠。”[2] 又有跋云：

> 文敏所传小楷，石本多矣。此真迹瘦硬通神，飘举欲仙，使不亲此，不知赵公真面目也。惜纸墨昏暗，安得能手响拓精钩，砻片石以传，一洗向来俗刻赵书种种甜熟之陋耶？姑宝藏以待。[3]

况且《大瓢偶笔》也引用过查异渠的话，说“湖州钱氏有赵承旨‘苏白堂’墨迹匾，又有‘介祉’匾，甚瘦劲有骨，与流传碑刻不同”。[4] 这些都足以说明仅从书体上难以否定《汲黯传》。如果我们把大德元年（1297）之后算作他书风的中期，延祐元年（1314）之后算作晚期[5]，那么，我们说，他晚期有向早期回归的倾向，或许也不失为一种有意味的眼光。我们注意到《汲黯传》“轨方峻劲”或“结体方劲”，不再以侧媚取胜，这可换用心理分析的方式来看，即：赵孟頫也许想抛弃那种“眼睛的筵席”（a feast for eye），毕竟那种风格倾向于甜蜜、甜美、甜腻（syrupy，saccharined，cloying），太诱惑我们的低级感官，太诉诸即时的快感，而最高价值的艺术则是庄严的，它要求用自我（ego）把本我（id）的冲动引向升华的方向，即心理分析所谓的 ego control（自我控制）。这样，赵孟頫又回到了早年学过的方劲的风格。[6]

当然，这只是猜测，赵孟頫即使确有此意，也无力阻挡他的侧媚之风在元代的漫弥。《汲黯传》是取径刻本，也许他万万想不到的是，刻本也取径他

---

1 参见《石渠宝笈》卷三，上海古籍出版社影印文渊阁《四库全书》本，1987年。

2 雪映庐抄本，无页次。

3 （清）沈虹屏著：《春雨楼集》，卷十三，乾隆刻本，第4—5页。

4 （清）杨宾著：《大瓢偶笔》，《中国书画全书》本，第8册，上海书画出版社，1994年。

5 傅申著：《书史与书迹》，台湾历史博物馆，1996年，第184页。

6 傅山著名的《训子帖》极诋赵孟頫字之软美，薄其为人，恶其书浅俗，力倡“宁拙毋巧，宁丑毋媚，宁支离毋轻滑，宁直率毋安排”，赞扬劲瘦挺拗的书风，认为这样才可以“回临池既倒之狂澜”，带有强烈的政治意味。赵孟頫在晚年向早期的书法风格回归（regress），是否也有一丝忏悔之意，心理分析在此或有用武之地。

的书法，而且竟一下子不可收场，几乎改变了元代刻书的面貌，一直影响到明代中期方休。此聊举一例。俞琰（1258—1327），字玉吾，赵孟頫题其居曰："石硐书隐。"学者因称之曰石硐先生。陆心源《皕宋楼藏书志》元刊元印本《周易集说》条记载："《上经》后跋曰：'嗣男仲温命儿桢缮写。谨锓梓于读易楼。'""彖传"后的跋语略同，惟改"命儿桢"为"命儿桢、植"。[1]"玉吾无子，以仲温为嗣。桢、植为玉吾孙，皆有书名。濡染家学，手书上板，故能精美如此。"这是自岳珂手书《玉楮诗稿》一百零七板以来难得的史料。[2]俞桢（1331—1401）善小楷，《书史会要续编》有传，他的书法很受赵氏影响，元代的刻书字体多用赵体，正是通过俞桢这类人的所为，把赵孟頫的书风推为刻书史上最重要的字体，为书籍成为艺术加重了砝码。

谈到俞桢，我们已在谈论赵孟頫的影响。此处不得不再谈一谈受他影响最大的俞和（1307—1382），俞和字子中，号紫芝生，原籍严州桐庐，其父俞章定居钱塘，遂为钱塘人。陈善（1514—1598）《杭州府志》说他"冲淡安怡，隐居不仕，能诗，善书翰，早年得见赵文敏用笔之法，临晋唐诸帖甚夥。行草逼真文敏，好事者得其书，每以赵款识，仓卒莫能辨。"他能得赵氏的真传，故对他又有不同的传闻。丰道生（嘉靖二年进士）《书诀》以为是赵孟頫的儿子，顾复《平生壮观》说是赵文敏甥，不管如何，他的书法可以乱真孟頫之书迹，众口一词。

1986年，张光宾先生在台湾《历史博物馆馆刊》第二卷第4期发表大作《俞和书乐毅论与赵孟頫书汉汲黯传》（第51—60页），提出了一个全新的看法：《汲黯传》是俞和戏拟赵孟頫的作品。张先生的主要依据是他们的书法风格差异，他说：

> 赵书与俞和最基本的差异，在于赵书无论点、横、直、撇、捺，起笔多逆入回锋而后运行，收笔顿折必向内敛；故其点画骨肉停匀，圆劲腴润。秀丽而醇雅，雍容而华美，有俊爽之气，且纸笔精良，笔性刚柔适度。尤其学养气度，恢宏博

1　光绪八年十万卷楼刊本，卷二，第16—17页。

2　岳珂《玉楮诗稿》跋云：集既成，遣人誊录，写法甚恶，俗不可观，遂自日录数纸。未知有宋本，或未刊板。岳元声万历刻本每卷首题"十六世孙元声等藏墨"，或依岳珂手录传写付梓者，板数相符，但字句间犹有晋豕，不知何故。

大，表现在字里行间，毫无寒伧、崄刻之象。

俞书，点画运转，直往直来，起笔切入，殊乏变化，收笔顿折、时显圭角。善于临仿，模拟形似，而气度神采，难求大家风范。所用纸笔亦非精良，习用强毫，锋芒毕露。无论临仿或自运，虽然出自松雪遗绪，风仪差易颇大。本非直接欧阳，而峻崄刻露，殊少含蓄。遂略呈率更外貌。

这里说的是两种风格的对比，其实并没有回答《汲黯传》的两个问题：书风问题和“此刻”问题。尤其没有解释俞和既是作伪，为何写了这样一通莫名其妙的跋语。因此他的结论似过于简单了。但他的结论有一个优点，它为徐一夔（1318—约 1400）撰写的俞和墓碣铭中描述的游戏翰墨的风情提供了一个传世的实例：

（俞和）篆楷行草，各臻于妙。一纸出，戏用文敏公私印识之，人莫能辨其真赝。至其临摹晋唐人法书，尤称妙绝。高堂广厦，风日清美，宾友会集，酒数行后，濡笔伸纸，一挥数十行。波戈趯磔，转换神速，真有惊蛇入草，飞鸟出林之态。已乃停笔按纸，诧众客曰：“颠长史[1]不我过也。”人争购之，以为珍玩。[2]

值得注意的是，一些当代书法鉴定家多有赞成张先生论定者，大陆学者王连起先生在《俞和及其行书兰亭记》中也断《汲黯传》为俞和所书，“因为它没有赵书的虚和委婉而有俞和的方峻刚利”。理由与张光宾先生相似。只是张氏认为《汲黯传》不及俞书《乐毅论》[3]朴厚典雅，尚非晚年之作，而王先生则认为：“《汲黯传》较《乐毅论》更趋精工老到，所作时间，或更晚一些。”[4]。对比一下这两位专家的见解，书法鉴定之难，可知也。

在此领域花费心血最大的傅申先生也是张先生看法的赞赏者，他说张先生“推理极为正确。盖俞氏虽学赵氏，然仍具个人特色。赵氏用笔实中有虚，

1　“颠长史”即张旭，唐朝著名书法家，擅长狂草，有“草圣”之称。

2　（明）徐一夔著：《始丰稿》，卷十三，光绪间钱塘丁氏嘉惠堂刻《武林往哲遗箸》本。

3　普林斯顿大学美术馆藏，至正二十年即1360年，俞和54岁时所书。

4　见《书法丛刊》，总第28期，文物出版社，1991年。

以韵胜而近晋人；俞和笔笔皆实，以法胜故近唐人”[1]。

傅、张二位先生的看法，确有警人之处。写到这里，不禁扪心自问，真有点儿想放弃这个论题，因为自己实在没有能力进行这种以书风论真伪的辨析，此处至少有两个妨碍的因素我无法逾越，首先是我看的真迹太少，眼力孱弱，根本没有参论的资格。但徘徊来，彷徨去，总觉得有些看法万一能成野人芹献，也是好事。我似乎感到，傅先生的意见也大可用来证明《汲黯传》为真，题跋中所谓的“有唐人之遗风”，不正要求“笔笔皆实，以法胜”吗？为了尽快逃避这个论题，我只想转引另一位赵孟頫研究专家黄惇先生的意见。他在慎重考虑了王连起先生的鉴定后说：“拙见以为仅凭书风方峻刚利即文徵明所言轨方峻劲便断《汉汲黯传》为俞和书，似证据稍欠，况以俞和小楷《乐毅论》与《汉汲黯传》相比，不仅欠于精工老到，且于神韵亦不可同日而语也。故从旧说。”[2] 这里的旧说，不仅包括文徵明、董其昌、安岐那样的古代大家，也包括徐邦达那样的现代大家。我们可能还记得前面引用过的徐邦达鉴定《汲黯传》的话，他和安都注意到了俞和伪造赵氏书法之事，但在赞美《汲黯传》上却是异口同声。也许正是他们对俞和造伪的看法启发了我们现代学者把《汲黯传》与俞和联系了起来。这样，第一流的鉴定家对《汲黯传》已分成两派，真伪如何，已成僵局，我们还是回到赵孟頫的藏书。

也许大家还记得，前述的赵氏藏书，除了《汉书》之外，还有一部《文选》。引人入胜的是，《文选》也像《汉书》一样，在明代受到了王世贞的赞美，只是王氏已无力收藏了。但是，我们不会忘记他的评价，他说：“余所见宋本《文选》亡虑数种，此本缮刻极精，纸用澄心堂，墨用奚氏。”王穉登还把此书与《汉书》作了比较，说它纸墨锓摹并出良工之手，与王氏所藏《汉书》绝相类。这些话也引逗我们猜测，赵孟頫所藏的《史记》刻本也当与此绝相类。

大概在万历五年（1577），此书由徐文敏处归汪仲嘉（1544—1613，名道会）易手之前，张凤翼曾留案头匝月，校对他将要出版的《文选纂注》。约21年后又归汤宾尹（1568—？，万历二十三年进士，宣城人，攻击东林党人的宣昆党之首），王醇曾往看，也记下了他的观感和羡慕：

1 傅申著：《书史与书迹》，台湾历史博物馆，1996年，第193页。
2 见《中国书法全集》（赵孟頫卷），荣宝斋出版社，2002年，下册，第475—476页。

予知仲嘉有宋版《文选》，心摇摇十余年矣。及造其庐，未遑索看。后逢嘉宾（汤氏）于讬山小有园，出陶隐居及唐宋墨迹示之，皆人间所未见者，业已夺人精魄，且许以此书出观，以瞑色不能，归去。役我魂梦越数日，始得一觏。纸墨之光射目，字楷而有致。竟日披览，得未曾有。时松风弄弦，远山横黛，是生平第一乐事。[1]

王醇与钱谦益有点儿交往，武功极棒，诗也写得好，在钱氏的《列朝诗集小传》丁集下中有记录。他明亡后当了和尚，著作遭禁罕传，只知杭大藏有抄本《宝蕊栖诗》一册，有兴趣者可往观。以上跋语，大都写于万历年间，与我在第一节的引文合在一起，可以想见其时其人对待书籍的态度，如果说赵孟頫把《汉书》和《文选》看作艺术品还是特立独拔的个人行为，那么到了明代万历年间已是文人圈子的集体行为了。我们已几次提到过张丑，他不厌其烦地记录法书名画，在他的《法书名画见闻表》中就是把宋板《文选》和文同的《晚霭横看》《此君图》等与王诜《梦游瀛山图》、黄山谷的《诸上座帖》等一起并置的（见“目睹部分”）。尤令人不敢置信的，《见闻表》还列有赵氏抄写的《左传》正文全部及《李太白集》（“的闻”部分）。

如果我们再往前上溯一些，看看华夏的真赏斋收藏，更是惊人，丰道生《真赏斋赋》的序言述其收藏，先是钟王法书，继而右丞等唐宋绘画，再标举碑帖，最后列述藏书，胪陈最夥。序说：

暨乎刘氏《史通》《玉台新咏》（上有“建业文房之印”），则南唐之初梓也。聂崇义《三礼图》、俞言等《五经图说》，乃北宋之精帙也。荀悦《前汉纪》、袁宏《后汉纪》（绍兴间刻本，汝阴王铚序），嘉史久遗；许嵩《建康录》、陆游《南唐书》，载纪攸罕。宋批《周礼》，五采如新；古注《九经》，南雍多阙（俞石硐藏，王守溪跋）。苏子容《仪像法要》，亟称于诸子；张彦远《名画记》，鉴收于子昂。相台岳氏《左传》、建安黄善夫《史记》《六臣注文选》，郭知达《集注杜工部诗》（共九家，曾噩校），曾南丰序次《李翰林集》（三十卷），《五百家注韩柳文》（在朱子前，斋中诸书，《文选》《韩柳》尤精），《刘宾客集》（共四十卷，内《外集》十

1 转引自《钦定天禄琳琅书目》卷三，版本同前。

卷),《白氏长庆集》(七十一卷)、《欧阳家藏集》(删繁补缺八十卷,最为真完)。《三苏全集》《王临川集》(世所传只一百卷,唯此本一百六十卷),《管子》《韩非》《三国志》(大字本,淳熙乙巳刊于潼州转运司公帑),《鲍参军集》(十卷),《花间集》(纸墨精好),《云溪友议》(十二卷,范摅著),《诗话总龟》(一百卷,阮阅编),《经鉏堂杂志》(八卷,雪川倪思著),《金石略》(郑樵著,笪氏藏),《宝晋山林拾遗》(八卷,孙光宪刻),《东观余论》(楼攻媿等跋,宋刻初拓,纸墨独精,卷帙甚备,世所罕见),《唐名画录》(朱景玄刻),《五代名画补》(刘道醇纂),《宋名画评》,《兰亭考》(十二卷,桑世昌集),皆传自宋元,远有端绪。

述此完毕,接着又言:"牙签锦笈以为藏,天球河图而比重,是以太史李文正公八分题扁曰:'真赏斋'。真则心目俱洞,赏则神境双融。翰林文正公为图为铭,昭其趣也。昔张彦远弱年鸠集,昼夜精勤,或嗤其为无益之事,则安能悦有涯之生。贷衣减粝,笃好成癖,以千乘为轻,以一瓢为适。米元章每得一书,既穷其趣,辄以良日,手自背洗,客拱而后示,屡濯而后展,谛视之际,迅雷不闻。与夫褚中令鉴定,若视黑白;黄长睿辨证,不漏毫发。揆兹雅抱,千载同符。斯东沙子所以淹留岁时,两忘忧乐,眇万物而无累,超四海而特行者乎。"[1]

连用鉴赏家的典故,造出一派艺术气氛浓郁的境界。这些文字写于嘉靖二十八年(1549),让我们再往前推半个世纪,即弘治十年(1497),尔时祝允明(1460—1527)为友人钱同爱(1475—1549,字孔同,号野亭)的《文选》写了一通跋语:

自士以经术梯名,昭明之《选》与酱瓿翻久矣。然或有以著者,必事乎此者也。吴中数年来以文竞,兹编始贵。余向蓄三五种,亦皆旧刻。钱秀才高本尤佳,秀才既力文甚竞,助以佳本,尤当增翰藻,不可涯尔。丁巳祝允明笔,门人张灵时侍笔砚。[2]

---

1 (明)丰坊著:《真赏斋赋》,光绪二十四年缪荃孙刻《藕香零拾》本。
2 见《汪氏珊瑚网法书题跋》,卷十六,《适园丛书》本,第1—2页。

迨至崇祯年间，此书似归汪砢玉所有，他在编《珊瑚网》时也为此书写了一通跋语，口气已是这样：

予家尚有宋板隶篆五经、左、国、诸子、史、汉、通鉴、文集种种，净拭棐几展玩，觉古香可爱。后苕溪镌五色朱批各书，错陈左右，牙签锦函，灿灿相映，奚百城之足云。[1]

五色朱批各书，若阅读，是陋书，前人已多有批评，若赏鉴，确实阅目，这已经进入了书籍成为艺术品、从实用中脱拔而出的年代；谢肇淛在《五杂组》中发的牢骚："吴兴凌氏诸刻，急于成书射利，又悭于倩人编摩其间，亥豕相望，何怪其然？至于《水浒》《西厢》《琵琶》及《墨苑》等书，反覃精聚神，穷极要眇，以天巧人士徒为传奇耳目之玩，亦可惜也！"[2] 以凌氏刻本与板画书相提并论，又从反面印证了那样一个时代。关于此问题，我写有专文讨论，此不赘述。但想补说一下汪砢玉生活的环境。他的父亲名汪继美，有书斋名东雅堂，李日华拜访过他，记下了亲见的景象："堂前松石梅兰，列置楚楚，已入书室中，手探一卷展视，乃元人翰墨也……已登墨华阁，列大理石屏四座，石榻一张，几上宋板书数十函，杂帖数十种，铜瓷花觚罍洗之属。汪君所自娱弄，以绝意于外交者也。"[3]

这里似乎越谈越远，我应该赶紧再回到赵孟頫的藏书和《汲黯传》，正是在这个起点上，我提出了一个假设，根据这个假设，不仅判断《汲黯传》为真迹，而且还提出了本节最中心的问题；书籍之成为艺术。我认为这一假说有一点漏洞，因为"此刻"到底是哪一部书，不能具体落实，但是，我也认为这不是大缺陷。它不妨碍我的更重要的论断，总的说来，我的假说比判断《汲黯传》单纯为真为假，要具有更多的优点。在我看来，一个假说要比另一个好，可由下面三点来作比较：

1 见《汪氏珊瑚网法书题跋》，卷十六，《适园丛书》本，第2页。

2 《新世纪万有文库》本，卷十三，第275页。

3 见李日华著：《味水轩日记》，卷六，万历四十二年十二月十八日条，《嘉业堂丛书》本，第72页。

一、简洁性：一个假说，或一个理论，越简洁明了，就越容易被人理解，更重要的是越容易被反驳。

二、包容性：包容量越大的假说，即所能解释的内容越多的假说越有优势。

三、创造性：能否提出新的有意思有创见的问题，这一点似乎非常重要。而对于人文学者来说，他的主要任务，毕竟是使过去的静态记录和文献获得勃勃的生机。

鉴于上述，我们不仅解决了《汲黯传》的两个看似难解的问题，没有轻易地把它推出大师杰作的行列，让它仍然熠熠放光，而且还以新的眼光解释了赵孟頫在《文选》上的一通题跋以及他的藏书训令，不仅如此，更重要的是，书籍的历史从此完全可以用一种新的观点来看待了。这种重新看待书籍历史的线索大致是：

首先，赵孟頫以独到的鉴赏眼光观看书籍，正与那时已完全成熟的书画鉴定眼光相同，他们是宋人高雅趣味的自然延伸，这种趣味王国维先生早在1928年发表于《国学论丛》（第一卷3号）上的《宋代之金石学》中就已阐明了。

接着就是上引《真赏斋赋序》所构造的那种时代气氛，其时在明代中期，一股复古的热潮大为流行，这包括文学、绘画、青铜、陶瓷，当然书籍是最重要的一项。现藏台北故宫博物院杜堇（约1465—1509）的《玩古图》上所绘器物不但有青铜、瓷器、玉器、书画卷轴，而且还有书籍，款识则曰："玩古乃常，博之志大；尚象别名，礼乐所在。日无礼乐，人反愧然；作之正之，吾有待焉。"可作为这种风气开始的标志。在这场风气中，宋板书不仅变成了古董，它的翻刻本还形成了一种新的字体——仿宋体。

行笔至此，我们不妨向西方眺望一下，看看约略同期的西方人是如何看待书籍的。菲拉雷特（Antonio Averlino Filarete）（约1400—1469）在《建筑专论》（*Trattato d' architettura*）中描绘了一幅皮耶罗·梅迪奇（Piero Medici，1414—1469）的硬笔肖像，说他："看着那屋里的书，好像它们是一堆金子。……让我们且不谈他的读书活动。有时，他的消遣可能就是让眼睛扫过这些书，以此来消磨时光，为眼睛提供娱乐。”

这段珍贵的材料曾为贡布里希所援引，尽管那些书都还是手写本。但在欧洲，早在 12 世纪，装饰手写本的圣经就成了艺匠的重要工作，特别是每章的首写字母，有时要用各种颜色，极尽其华丽，[1] 这样的一件华丽手写本，本身就是艺术品，欣赏价值要远远大于实用功能，它们往往数月乃至数年才能完成，价格更是不菲，15 世纪的最重要爱书者贝利公（Duke of Berry）的名贵藏书大抵如此。[2] 佛罗伦萨作家韦斯帕夏诺·达·比斯蒂奇（Vespasiano da Bisticci）《名人传》（*Live of Illustrious Men*）有这样一段话，谈到乌比诺公爵图书馆：“他的图书馆里只收藏手写本，如果有一本印刷的书，他会觉得丢脸。”[3] 其时印刷书在欧洲刚出现不久。不论如何，这些故事都给了我们机会，去揣想一次人类的普遍心理。贡布里希评论说：

> 我们并非常常能进入久远时代人的快乐，哪怕在想象中进入。不过，菲拉雷特关于皮耶罗的藏书的叙述仍然可以转译成视术语。许多明确地注明专为皮耶罗操写的或者专为他作插图的书现在仍然藏在佛罗伦萨的洛伦佐图书馆（Laurenziana），有西塞罗、普鲁塔克、约瑟夫斯（Josephus）、普林尼和亚里士多德的著作的插图。这些书为那些找出它们来的人“提供娱乐眼睛”的材料。[4]

我们再来回看一部宋板书《草窗韵语》护叶上的明人跋语，那可看作尔时人以书籍愉悦眼睛的自述：“万历庚寅端阳，余有齐鲁之行，过夏镇谒明復先生仙署，有此宋版佳刻，世所罕见，当为法帖中求也，漫纪喜尔。新都罗文瑞。”[5]

以书籍为法帖，这是赵孟頫的“玉楮银钩”的遥遥嗣响，完全是艺术的眼光。此时，即万历期间，成为独立艺术品的新型书籍终于出现，现在收藏在

1　Cf. Christopher de Hamel, *The Book: A History of the Bible*, London, 2001, pp. 83–84.

2　Cf. L. Febvre and H. Martin, *The Coming of the Book*, London, 1993, p. 27.

3　E.H. Gombrich, The Museum's Mission, the Enjoyment of Art, the Problem of Critics', *Art News*, January 1974, pp. 54–57；中译本见E.H.贡布里希著，杨思梁、范景中、严善淳译：《艺术与科学：贡布里希谈话录和回忆录》，浙江摄影出版社，1998年，第63页。

4　（英）贡布里希著，李本正、范景中编选：《文艺复兴：西方艺术的伟大时代》，中国美术学院出版社，2000年，第164页。

5　参见民国乌程蒋氏密韵楼景宋刊本。

法国国家图书馆的《湖山胜概》最堪代表，它把诗、书、画结合起来，以四彩套印出版，大约刊于万历三四十年间（1602—1612），[1]是杭州雕版印刷的杰作。《文字会宝》亦刊于此时，则是以各家墨迹上板的书法作品选。到了崇祯十三年秋天闵遇五刊刻《会真图》（1640），已达到了中国版画艺术的高峰，杜堇所谓的由玩古而博大，那时也形成气候，以图像构成百科知识、宇宙景观的书籍也应时出版，我们所熟知的《三才图绘》（1609）是最著名者。

有了这样的史观，我们可以重新评价许宗鲁（1490—1559）的刻书，他是书法家，所刻《国语》（嘉靖四年）、《吕氏春秋》（嘉靖七年），俱系古体字，而且还在明代中后期发生了影响，尽管后来查他山批评说："此不明六书之故，若能解释得出《说文》，断不敢用也。"但若放在复古风气中，或有别解。丰道生所制伪书，体势诘曲，傅山所作书法，多奇字，也可以从中寻绎一二。

到了清代，人们看待书籍的眼光，特别是乾嘉学者的眼光已与明人大不相同，但影响却不可能消失。金冬心玩弄古版书，最终写出了一笔新体书法，更是与赵孟頫合拍，都受了雕版书的启发。

书籍能成为一种艺术，而且反过来影响他种艺术，这一过程就像贡布里希所说，绝非一夜完成，绝非招之即来，它是经过了漫长的特殊的历史，这个特殊的历史或者一如赫伊津哈（Johan Huizinga）所言：某物之所以成为艺术，并非起因于人们对美的渴望，而是因其过剩的发展，当它在王宫贵族的宝库里堆积为宝藏，不再应用于实际生活，而是成为奢侈和珍奇之物受到观贯时，就发展出了它的艺术品格。

以上的勾勒只是略图。但已足以说明，我们对于书籍和书法的关系，书籍和绘画的关系，特别书是书籍自身的命运，虽有研究，却实在太浅，尚是一段有待开发的历史。

当然，古人没有艺术或美术的观念，对于他们来讲，只是古物或古董而已，但是古人描述书籍的语言是那么精美，例如隋江总（519—594）《皇太子太学讲碑》"紫台秘典，绿帙奇文，羽陵蠹迹，嵩山落简，外史所掌，广内所司，靡不饰以铅椠，雕以缃素"[2]，早就埋下了美的种子，以至从赵孟頫开始的

1　参见我的文章《套印本和刻本及其〈会真图〉》，《新美术》，2005年第4期，第77—82页。
2　见《江令君集》，卷一，光绪五年信述堂重刊《汉魏六朝百三家集》本，第18页。

鉴赏眼光在二十世纪的开端终于表达成了现代术语，这就是我在篇首所引述的那段话，现在我们又回到了起点。

返回头再看，张光宾先生的伪品论断，我觉得它虽能满足一个好假说的第一点，但与其他两点几乎无关。所以在没有确凿证据的情况下，我遵守旧说，不愿让这件宝物降格。本来我们的宝物就不多，因此要慎用奥卡姆剃刀，勿减实体。这是我们不介入单纯以眼力来鉴定作品讨论的第二个因素。

在结束之前，我想再谈一段与赵孟頫藏书有关的掌故，故事发生在1600年前后，记录在臧懋循（1550—1620，万历八年进士）《负苞堂文选》“题六臣文选跋”中，地点就发生在南京和杭州：

往予游白下，偕客过开之[1]署中，于时，梧阴满席，凉飔徐引，展几上《文选》，讽诵数篇以为适，盖开之平日所秘珍宋板书也。客有举杨用修（杨慎，1488－1559）云：“‘古书不独无谬处，并有古香，’不知香从何生？”予曰：“尔不觉新书纸墨臭味乎？”开之为绝倒。迨庚子（1600）秋访开之于湖上，方校刻李注《文选》，甚工，因索观前书。开之手取示予曰：“独此无恙。比虽贫，犹幸不为王元美《汉书》也。”予曾见元美《汉书》，有赵文敏跋。愧同吴兴人，不能作文敏书，以为此《文选》重。聊题数语识岁月云。[2]

这部文选不是赵孟頫所藏的那部，就在冯开之中进士的万历五年（1577），赵氏所藏的《文选》进了汪仲嘉的书斋，说来凑巧，汪仲嘉就是卖地给冯开之，让他在孤山建起著名的快雪堂的。此书经汪仲嘉转汤宾尹，最后也像《汉书》那样，入了内府，乾隆帝题曰：

此书（《文选》）董其昌所称与《汉书》《杜诗》鼎足海内者也。在元赵孟頫、在明王世贞、董其昌、王穉登、周天球、张凤翼、汪应娄、王醇、曹子念、并东南之秀，俱有题识。又有国初李楷跋。纸润如玉，南唐澄心堂法也。字迹精妙，北宋

1　冯梦桢（1546—1605），国子监祭酒，被劾归，于孤山买汪仲嘉地筑快雪堂。

2　（明）臧懋循：《负苞堂文选》，卷三，《续修四库全书》影印天启元年臧尔炳刊本，第1361册，上海古籍出版社，1994—2002年，第91页。

人笔意。《汉书》见在大内，与为连璧，不知《杜诗》落何处矣。天禄琳琅中若此者亦不多得。[1]

董其昌所艳称的宋板三宝，我们一宝都见不到了，今日大谈书籍艺术，不免让人惆怅，不由得想起钱谦益的几句感慨：水天闲话，久落人间，花月新闻，已成故事。

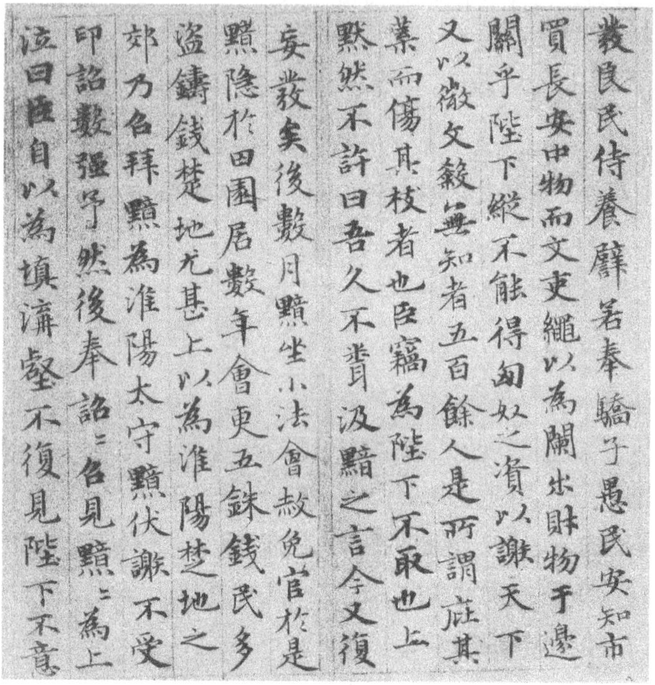
養良民侍養譬若奉驕子愚民安知市
買長安中物而文吏繩以為闌出財物于邊
關乎陛下縱不能得匈奴之資以謝天下
又以微文殺無知者五百餘人是所謂庇其
葉而傷其枝者也臣竊為陛下不取也上
默然不許曰吾久不聞汲黯之言今又復
妄發矣後數月黯坐小法會赦免官於是
黯隱於田園居數年會更五銖錢民多
盜鑄錢楚地尤甚上以為淮陽楚地之
郊乃召拜黯為淮陽太守黯伏謝不受
印詔數強予然後奉詔詔召見黯黯為上
泣曰臣自以為填溝壑不復見陛下不意

赵孟頫　小楷《汲黯传》卷首　日本东京永青文库藏

The front of *Ji An's Biography* in small regular script by Zhao Mengfu, a collection of Eisei Library in Tokyo, Japan

1　转引自《钦定天禄琳琅书目》卷三，版本同前。

Excerpts from Books as an Art

Fan Jingzhong[1]

According to the above, the evaluation of "*Ji An's Biography*" has reached a deadlock. Whether it is praised or negated, there is the support of authority figures. Therefore, I want to find a new way to answer the two questions of *Ji An's Biography*. Here we might as well recall Mr. Zhang Boying's criticism about it again:

> We do not know what the so–called "this engraved version" means. If it is also the *Ji An's Biography*, why not say copying, but say the hand writing; the so–called "getting the brushstrokes" is to say getting what brushstrokes. Through these it can be judged as fake.

"This engraved version" in the context of *Ji An's Biography* can only have be two interpretations, either as a carved stone or as a carved block copy. The negator started from the first point of interpretation, because from the actual object or from the literature, until today, no engraved stone of *Ji An's Biography* for Zhao Mengfu to use has been found, which makes us have to think about the second explanation, the carved block copy (Feng Yuji is close to this view), and naturally reminds us of Zhao Mengfu's collection of books. According to the data, the first is the aforementioned *Hanshu* containing the *Ji An's Biography*.

---

1 Fan Jingzhong is a famous professor of China Academy of Art, doctoral supervisor, and famous scholar, with many books and essays on art published. This article was originally published in the third issue of *New Art* in 2008, and it was fortunate to have the author's permission to quote this excerpt.

It is a pity that *Hanshu* has disappeared, and cannot be used to compare with the ink marks of *Ji An's Biography*. Fortunately, there are still records of the appreciation of our predecessors, which can help us to retreat to take them as a second reference. When *Hanshu* was collected in Wang Shizhen's home, Wang once described it like this:

> On mulberry paper, white and clean as jade, are big characters with the same size as a copper coin, surrounded by broad margins, absolutely in Ou's and Liu's brushwork. The brushstrokes are as slim as hair beautiful and flowing with the ink color pure. It is perhaps from the Secret Pavilion of Zhenzong (918–1022) of the Song Dynasty, especially given to the two families. The owners also cherished them themselves so much that they were clean as if they had not been touched by their hands after 400 years. There is a small portrait of Zhao Wuxing in front. [1]

It is self–evident that there is a small portrait of Zhao Mengfu in front because Zhao extremely loved it, which is in harmony with *Ji An's Biography*. The problem of "this engraved version" is solved together with the problem of the script. However, the result from which Pan Wenxie helps me to collate is that the text of *Ji An's Biography* is more similar to *Shiji* (*Records of the History*), and alienated from *Hanshu*. Therefore, the original copy is undoubtedly *Shiji* (*Records of the History*).

The *Shiji* (*Records of the History*) in Zhao Mengfu's collection is only recorded in one text. As mentioned above, I have asserted as a handwritten one instead of a carved block copy. In this case, it will be in vain again to find out what exactly the "this engraved version" does refer to. Here, we have encountered one of the most common problems in historical research, as Gombrich said: History is like Swiss cheese, with many pores, and in many cases

---

1 Quoted from "The Bibliography Inscription and Postscript Series of Qing Dynasty", Volume 2 of *Qinding tianlu linlang shumu (The Imperial Tianlu Linlang Bibliography)*, Zhonghua Book Company, 1995.

has vacancies, leaving a large number of unsolvable problems. Because we lack evidence, and the historian's skill is to find out the questions that are likely to be answered, and his wisdom is to feel through which line of exploration he can get results and discover something. [1]

Now, maybe we have encountered a problem without an answer or a result. However, if we only focus on the details forgetting to let our imaginary wings fly, we may lose an opportunity to ask interesting and creative questions. In other words, we should not limit ourselves to the records, but also to restore the historical context of those documents that were supposed to be undocumented and it is up to us to boldy show the wisdom of *Sapereaude* at the end of the examination. Therefore, we might as well assume that he also owned *Shiji* (*Records of the History*) of high quality. I think this is by no means far–fetched. On the contrary, it would be incredible he didn't own a beautiful copy of *Shiji* (*Records of the History*) engraved in the Song Dynasty in the right of his status and identity. After all, he himself is a nobleman, a person who was out of royal family of the Song Dynasty. With this assumption, not only did we easily explain this engraved version and script issues above mentioned, but also immediately raised a more important issue about art history, that is, the theme of this article: how books become an art. Once this question is established, an interesting conclusion will be drawn that *Ji An's Biography* is written using a block–printed book as a template. This is why it is not called copying in Zhao's epilogue, but handwriting.

Before further explaining this hypothesis, let's look at a circumstantial evidence.

In *Guoyunlou Calligraphy and Paintings·Wenyan Ke Mi'an Painting Scroll* reads: "Zhang Qingfu got Mi Xiangyang's *Records of the Treasures to be Visited*

1 E.H. Gombrich, The Museum's Mission, the Enjoyment of Art, the Problem of Critics', *Art News*, January 1974, pp. 54–57; for the Chinese translation, see *Art and Science: Gombrich Talks and Memoirs*, translated by Yang Siliang, Fan Jingzhong, and Yan Shanchun, Zhejiang Photography Publishing House, 1998, p. 121.

with more than four thousand characters, and it is said to be the property of Zhao Wenmin of Sheng State, with the seal of Zhao's son Ang, which in the Ming Dynasty was owned by Lu Zhongzai. His brother–in–law, Qingfu's family had traced Lu's descendants for more than 20 years, invested all the money to buy it back, and then named himself Mi'an."[1] Zhang Chou was a collector of the late Ming Dynasty. He actually named his study after the book *Records of the Treasures to be Visited*, which shows how much he cherished it. This also affected his views on books in Zhao Mengfu's study, allowing him to look at books through an artistic perspective, that is, *Records of the Treasures to be Visited* is a book and an art, and I think it is natural. Especially after this book, there is an epilogue by Zhang Feng (with the courtesy name Bocheng, good at lishu /clerical script) of Ming Dynasty, which is related to the topic here. He said: "Haiyue's small regular script is rare in the world, and this *Records of the Treasures to be Visited* is all out of Taihe's (Li Yong) style, and sometimes mixed with Ou's and Chu's, undoubtedly the genuine work of his prime year."[2] Zhang Qingfu made three consecutive postscripts, also referring to the Ou's and Liu's styles. The nice block–printed version of Song Dynasty has this style and features.

The most direct and important issue related to this topic here is the postscript written by Zhao Mengfu on his other collection "*Annotations of Six Officials*", which does not have his small portrait, or is not as rare as *Hanshu*, but his postscript is of completely new insight.

The frosty moon is like snow at night, and when I read Ruan Sizong's poems, the nine swallows are all cold. However, it is the energetic calligraphy like silver hooks [3] on

1 (Qing Dynasty) Gu Wenbin, *Guoyunlou Painting and Calligraphy*, Vol. 5, *Continuing the Siku Quanshu*, photocopy of Guangxu edition, Shanghai Ancient Books Publishing House, 1994–2002, Vol. 1085, p. 238.

2 See (Qing Dynasty) Bian Yongyu, *Shigutang Shuhui Kao*, Calligraphy No. 4, *The Complete Book of Chinese Calligraphy and Painting*, Shanghai Calligraphy and Painting Publishing House, 1994, vol. 6, p. 118.

3 Silver hooks mean 1. A silver women's ornament. 2. A metaphor for the energetic calligraphy. 3. Metaphorical meniscus. It refers to calligraphy here. —Noted by the compiler.

the Yuchu jade paper[1] that greatly helps me to get the great pure joy of chanting matching with the light and moon. [2]

These few words stand for a major event in the history of book collection. Before him, we can't seem to find such remarks. Lu You is considered to be one of the persons who wrote many inscriptions of books in the Song Dynasty. If you read his *Fangweng Tiba* (*Fangweng's Inscriptions*) once, you can realize how novel Zhao's view of books is. "Yuchu" is the material of books, and "Silver Hook" is completely about a discussion tone in the terms of calligraphy appraisal, which makes Zhao Mengfu the first person with texts available who can appreciate books as works of art. [3]

This inscription on the copy of Guangxu's engraving was made in the second year of Zhizheng (1342), which must be a mistake of the second year of Zhida (1308). Till the second year of Zhizheng, Zhao had been dead for 20 years. Therefore, there must be something wrong with the block–printed copy. If it is faked, it will not be so confused. This book contains postscripts of Wang Shizhen, Dong Qichang, Wang Rangdeng, Zhou Tianqiu, Zhang Fengyi, Wang Yinglou, Wang Chun, Cao Zinian, and Qianlong's officials. It should be a credible collection of the Zhao family.

The editor of *Tianlu Linlang* commented: "Mengfu's postscript is written in small regular script, bringing the best of two Wangs' style into the full play, showing his true love of the book, and it is enough to supplement the

---

1 Chu (chǔ) is the ancient name of Broussonetia papyrifera, and the bark is the raw material for making mulberry paper and rice paper. In ancient times, it was also used as a synonym for paper, with other names Chu Zhibai, Mr. Chu, and Chu Sheng as all aliases for paper. —Noted by the compiler.

2 *Changsha Wangshi Blocked Edition* in the tenth year of Guangxu, 1884, Vol. 3, 24ab.

3 Li Qingzhao's "*Postface to Jinshi Lu*" says: "Every time we get a book, it will be collated together, sorted out, collected and signed the title. If we get the calligraphies, paintings, ritual bronze wares or tripods, we also enjoy and appreciate them, criticizing the defects and flaws under the candle at night. As a result, the paper and letters are exquisite, and the calligraphies and paintings are complete, titled as the best of all collectors." (*Sibu Congkan Xubian*) It can be called a pioneer of book appreciation, but it seems that it was still at the level of craft appreciation. Zhao Mengfu can be said to have entered art appreciation.

entertainment of reading. The best book from the Song Dynasty is rare in the Yuan Dynasty."[1]

In order to illustrate what the book is like in Zhao Mengfu's eyes, I will quote another piece of information. Chen Jiru's *Sixteen Views on Reading* quoted Zhao Mengfu's postscript:

> Collecting books together is not an easy task. Good readers read books, calming and focusing, cleaning the desk and burning incense. Do not curl your head, or do not break the corners; do not invade the characters with your claws; do not expose the page with saliva; do not use it as a pillow; or do not pinch it. Repair it as you damage it; open it reading and close it after your reading. I give this law to those who later got my books to follow. [2]

Regarding the influence of this postscript on the history of book collections, those who are interested can refer to my *Book Collection Inscriptions*. Here I want to compare it with the requirements for appreciation of painting by Tang Hou (1262–1332), who is eight years younger than Zhao Mengfu. One comparison is as the following:

> You can't look at the paintings when you are in hazing or dirty, or drinking under the light. It is firmly to avoid on the paintings the clumsy seal, and the ordinary hand–written inscriptions. Don't copy them; don't modify it to lose the old appearance; and don't decide the authenticity arbitrarily, which makes people short of breath.[3]

These words can be interlinked and intertextualized and discussed together.

---

1 Quoted from *Qinding tianlu linlang shumu (The Imperial Tianlu Linlang Bibliography)*, Zhonghua Book Company, 1995.

2 (Ming Dynasty) Chen Jixin, *Sixteen Views on Reading*, the edition in Daoguang era.

3 See Tao Zongyi (Yuan Dynasty), *Shuofu*, Vol. 13, printed version by Shanghai Commercial Press in the 16th year of the Republic of China.

Only with artworks has one to be so careful and so critical.

Till now, we can briefly conclude that because Zhao Mengfu has two conditions, the fate of books has been changed. One is his appreciative vision and the other is his calligraphy practice. He does not only appreciate books, but also uses books as a model to copy *Ji An's Biography* that we can still see, adding a new one to his calligraphic style. Of course, the most important condition is that Zhao Mengfu is one of the great literati, and only by people like him can books be announced like paintings to help make the reading more interesting, arranged and produced in a study like his. Otto Pächt said something when he was studying the art of book binding during the Renaissance, with the similar rationale. He said:

> No art has a better claim to be called "humanistic" than the book decoration of the early Renaissance. For this art is closely linked with the professional activities of the humanists themselves, in fact the studio of the humanist scholars is its very birthplace.[1]

Just ten years before Zhao Mengfu's death, he made great achievements in small regular script. His *Qiguan Tie (Seven Views Tie)* written by him at 64 years old was three years earlier than *Ji An's Biography*, the fourth year of Yanyou (1317), which, through the lens of such great connoisseurs as Yang Dapiao and Weng Tanxi, represents the peak of his small regular script. Great connoisseurs like Zhang Boying read the copies in the Ming Dynasty, and they admired: "Though many of Songxue's small regular script have been handed down to the world, only this (referring to *Seven Views Tie*) has the legacy style of *Huang Ting* and *Luo Shen*, without usual habit of inclined flattery, allowing for cooperation."[2] In fact, in the rewritten copy most of the spirit of the style has been lost. And

1 Fritz Saxl (1890–1948), *A Volume of Memorial Essays from his Friends in England*, ed., D. J. Gordon, London, 1957.

2 Zhang Boying, *On Rubbings by Zhang Boying*, Hebei Education Publishing House, 2006, p. 312.

Yuan Jue recorded Zhao Mengfu's calligraphy before his death in *The Collection of Qingrong Jushi*, which can further confirm why he used the small regular script similar to Ou's and Chu's brushwork. Yuan Jue said: "At the Emperor's request, Duke wrote the small regular script, with the brush on the paper moving fast like flying, and every time he said those under Ou's and Chu's were not good enough, inadequate to be mentioned. This sutra (*Lingbao Jing*) was finished only two months away from his death. It is so painful as to cry for it!"[1] "Those under Ou's and Chu's were not good enough, inadequate to be mentioned" means Ou's and Chu's in his mind. It just so happens that we also have Zhao's evaluation of Ouyang Xun's style. *Meng Dian Tie*, collected in the Liaoning Museum, is followed by Zhao Mengfu's inscription: "Ouyang Xinben's style of calligraphy is vigorous and distinct, with no parallel in the ancient and modern. Mr. Mi said: 'The quietness is like the supreme; the moving jumps and leaps.' It also seems unknown how magical it is. In the capital, I have seen *Encouraging Learning*, which is a collection of official treasures, and there are complete Kaiyuan inscriptions, and the brushstrokes are the same along with this, but the official copy is on hard yellow paper seemly different. Until the fifteenth of the leap month, the 29th year in the Yuan Dynasty, it was written by Youzhi (Guo Wuxi). Zhao Mengfu from Wuxing." This passage was written by Zhao Mengfu in 1292. The previous year (1291) before this, he wrote the famous "*Guo Xinlun*". Three years (1289) before this, he wrote "*The Preface to Jiang Baishi's Lanting Kao*" (collected by Taipei National Palace Museum), and Jiang Baishi was excelled at a typical small regular script following the Ou's style. Zhao Mengfu had also seen the original piece of "*Lanting Kao*". In his early years, he devoted himself to small regular script, and it is all suggested that he was greatly influenced by Jiang Baishi.

Fuzhou Yong'an Chanyuan Sengtang Ji—The Story of the Meditation Hall in Yong'an Buddhist Temple of Fuzhou—was written a year before Zhao

1 The First Edition of *Sibu Congkan*, Vol. 46, pp. 16–17.

Mengfu's death, and its inscription reads: "On the 24th of the first month of the first year of Zhizhi, the master of Qianjiang passed by Yuxi. When drinking tea, he talked about the Layman Wujin (endless)'s *Yong'an Chanyuan Sengtang Ji—The Story of the Meditation Hall in Yong'an Buddhist Temple*, considering the meaning of the words is exceptional and outstanding, with a profound purpose of emphasizing and encouraging later learning. Because the master asked for my calligraphy, so I wrote this for him." [1]Looking at this epilogue, we can know it must have been written carefully. Unfortunately, no original ink calligraphies were seen. During the Qianlong period, it was collected in Shen Hongping's Chunyu Tower, and also recorded in the third volume of "*Shiqu Baoji*" as one volume, but I don't know whether it is this volume. "*Chunyulou Calligraphy and Painting Catalogue*" records: "This is Wenmin's handwriting in his later years, which was written after getting original scripts of Thirteen Lines. The calligraphy is brilliant and refreshing, removing his cloying and familiar writing habit, and this piece in small regular script should be crowned after the Jin and Tang dynasties." [2] Besides, there is another postscript：

In Wenmin's small regular scripts passed down, there are too many stone rubbing copies. This authenticity is slender, strong and powerful, floating as immortality, which makes someone not seeing it personally doesn't know what Mr. Zhao's calligraphy really looks like. It's a pity that the ink on the paper is dim. How can we find the masters of making fine hooks to engrave a stele of stone to pass it on, having always his cloying and familiar writing flaw habits dispearing engraved by all kinds of vulgar engravings? So treasure it waiting for that.[3]

---

1 See *Shiqu Baoji, Shiqu Treasured Paintings and Calligraphies,* Vol. 3, Photocopy of Wenyuange *Siku Quanshu* by Shanghai Ancient Publishing House, 1987.

2 A transcripted version by Xueyinglu, without page numbers.

3 (Qing Dynasty) Shen Hongping, *Chunyulou Collection*, Vol. 10, engraved edition of Qianlong Era, pages 4–5.

Moreover, "*Dapiao Oubi*" also quoted Zha Yiqu, saying that "Qian from Huzhou has Zhao Chengzhi's calligraphy on 'Subai Tang' plaque, and also a 'Jiezhi' plaque, very slender and strong with bones, different from the popular inscriptions on steles." [1]All these are enough to show that it is difficult to deny "*Ji An's Biography*" only in the style of the calligraphy. If we regard that after the first year of Dade (1297) as the middle period of his calligraphic style, and that after the first year of Yanyou (1314) as the later period,[2] then we can say that he, in his later period, tended to return to the early period, which may be a kind of meaningful vision. We noticed that the "brushstrokes are squarely beautiful and enegetic" or "with structure of squareness and enegy" in "*Ji An's Biography*", no longer winning with side flattery. This can be viewed in a psychoanalytic way, namely: Zhao Mengfu may want to abandon that kind of "a feast for eye", after all, that style tends to be syrupy, saccharined, and cloying, too much tempting to our low–level senses, and too appealing to instant pleasure, but the art of the highest value is solemn, and it requires *ego* to lead the impulse of the *id* in the direction of sublimation, which is the so–called *ego* control in psychoanalysis. In this way, Zhao Mengfu returned to the style of squareness and skillful enegy he had learned in his early years.[3]

Of course, this is just a guess. Even if Zhao Mengfu did have this intention, he would not be able to stop his charming style from spreading in the Yuan Dynasty. "*Ji An's Biography*" is a following block–printed version. What he never expected is that the block–printed version also copied his calligraphy, and it was impossible to end it all at once. It almost changed the appearance of the

1 (Qing Dynasty) Yang Bin, *Dapiao Oubi*, *The Complete Book of Chinese Calligraphies and Paintings,* Shanghai Painting and Calligraphy Publishing House, 1994, Vol. 8.

2 Fu Shen, *Calligraphy History and Calligraphy Marks*, 1996, Taiwan, History Museum, p.184.

3 Fu Shan's famous "*Xunzi Tie*" critisized extremely the softness and beauty of Zhao Mengfu's characters, belittling him and disliking his calligraphy regarding it vulgar. He strongly advocated that It is better to be clumsy than be clever, rather ugly than pretty, rather to be fragmented than be sloppy, rather o be straight than to be arranged. He praised the style of writing of strength and thinness, and believed that this was the only way to "return to the turmoil of the pool", with a strong political implication. That Zhao Mengfu regressed to his early calligraphy style in his later years is also with a hint of repentance. Psychological analysis may be useful here.

engraved script in the Yuan Dynasty and didn't stop affecting until the middle of the Ming Dynasty. Here is an example. Yu Yan (1258–1327) was with the courtesy name Yuwu, about whose residence Zhao Mengfu wrote: "Shiyun Shuyin", and therefore scholars called him Mr. Shiyun. Lu Xinyuan's *Zhouyi Jishuo* in *Bisonglou Cangshu Zhi*, engraved and printed in the Yuan Dynasty, records: "The postscript of the *Shangjing* said: 'Zhongwen, the male heir, had his son Zhen write it. I would like to blockprint it in the Duyi Tower.'" The postscript of the *Tuanchuan* is slightly the same, but changed "had his son Zhen" into "had his sons Zhen and Zhi". [1] Yuwu had no children, and took Zhongwen as his heir. Zhen and Zhi are Yuwu's grandsons, both having titles. Following the family, they handwrote them on the block, so it can be so exquisite." This is a rare historical material since the one hundred and seventy–seven block pages of Yue Ke's handwritten *Manuscripts of Yuchu Poems*. [2] Yu Zhen (1331–1401) was good at small regular script, with his biography in *Shushi Huiyao Xubian – Sequel of the Main Collections of Book History*, whose calligraphy is greatly influenced by Zhao. Why the engraving fonts of the Yuan Dynasty are mostly in Zhao's style is through the actions of people like Yu Zhen that Zhao Mengfu's calligraphy has become the most important typeface in the history of engraving, adding weight to books becoming art.

Speaking of Yu Zhen, we are already talking about Zhao Mengfu's influence. I have to talk about Yu He (1307–1382) who was most influenced by him here. Yu He, with the courtesy name Zizhong, named Zizhisheng, was born in Tonglu, Yanzhou. Yu Zhang, his father, settled in Qiantang and became a native

---

1 The printed version by One Hundred Thousand Volumes Tower in the Eighth Year of Guangxu, Vol. II, p. 1617.

2 The postscript of Yue Ke's *Manuscripts of Yuchu Poems* said: The collection was completed, and had someone to copy it. The writing brushworks were very evil and too vulgar to be seen, so I personally copied several pieces of paper every day. It is unknown whether there was a printed version of the Song Dynasty, or it was not printed to publish. There is "The Sixteenth Grandson Yuansheng, etc" on the first page of each volume of the Wanli Engraved Edition of Yue Yuansheng, which may follow Yue Ke's copies to publish. Even though it is with the same number of boards, there are still some differences between the characters and lines, with the reason unknown.

of Qiantang. Chen Shan (1514–1598) in *Hangzhou Fuzhi* said that he "lives in seclusion, indifferent to fame and fortune, content with pleasure and not willing to be an official, good at poetry and writing. In his early years, he has seen Zhao Wenmin's brushwork, and he practices in large quantities the copybooks of the Jin and Tang dynasties. His running–cursive script looks exactly the same with Wenmin's, so that those who are meddlesome get his calligraphy, they sign Zhao's signature every time, which can't be discerned in a hurry." He can get Zhao's true style, so there are different rumors about him. Feng Daosheng (Jinshi[1] of the second year, Jiajing) thought he was the son of Zhao Mengfu in *Shujue,* and Gu Fu said that he was Zhao Wenmin's nephew in *Spectacular in Life.* No matter who he is, his calligraphy can mess with Mengfu's calligraphy, which all agree with.

In 1986, Mr. Zhang Guangbin published his masterpiece "*Leyi Lun* by Yu He and *Ji An's Biography* of the Han Dynasty by Zhao Mengfu" (pp. 51–60) in the second volume of the 4th issue of *Historical Museum Journal* in Taiwan, and put forward a brand new view: "*Ji An's Biography* is a work by Yu He mimicking Zhao Mengfu." Mr. Zhang's main evidence is the difference in their calligraphy styles. He said:

> The most basic difference between Zhao's calligraphy and Yu He's is that no matter when he writes the dots, the horizontal stroke, the verticals, the left fallings, or the right fallings in Zhao's calligraphy, he starts to move the brush tip back and then moves forward. When he closes and ends, he must have introverted; therefore, his brushstrokes will be even and round, richly strong and powerful, beautiful and mellow, graceful and gorgeous, with a cool air, and in excellent brush and paper, with moderate rigidity and softness. In particular, the learning and cultivated manner is magnificent, showing between the lines, without the appearance of undecentness or engravedness.
>
> In Yu's calligraphy, the brushworks go straight back and forth, starting to cut in,

1 The palace examination for successful candidates in the highest imperial examinations.

lacking variations, closing the brush, and showing the angles sometimes. He is good at imitation, imitating the appearance, but the master's demeanor is difficult to find. The brushes and paper in use are not of good quality, getting used to using strong brush with sharp edges. Regardless of whether it is imitation or self–transportation, although it comes from Songxue's legacy, the difference in style is quite great. The original is not directly following the style of Ouyang, but stern and engraved, with little subtlety. Then it was slightly straight in appearance.

What I'm talking about here is the comparison between the two styles. In fact, it doesn't answer the two questions of *Ji An's Biography*: the issue of calligraphic style and the one of "this engraved version". In particular, it did not explain why Yu He had written such an inexplicable postscript because he was faking. So his conclusion seems too simple. But his conclusion has an advantage, which provides a handed–down example of the style of the calligraphic game described in Yu He's epitaph inscription written by Xu Yikui (1318–ca.1400):

(Yu He's) scripts, like seal script, regular script, running script and cursive script, are all perfect. If a piece of calligraphy is completed and playfully signed by Wenmin with his private seals, no one can discern its authenticity. As for his copying of the calligraphies by people in the Jin and Tang dynasties, it is especially wonderful. When the guests and friends gather in tall magnificent building on sunny days with the wind clear and beautiful, after a few drinks of wine, he drew a brush and spread the paper, waving the brush for dozens of lines. The twists and turns with the rapid conversion were really like the images of the snake startled into the grass and the bird coming out of the forest. Then he stopped the brush, touched the paper, and said shocking all the guests, "What crazy Changshi[1] could do is not as good as what I did." People bid for it,

1 Crazy Changshi is referring to Zhang Xu, a famous calligrapher in Tang Dynasty, what is good at wild cursive script, called "the Sage of Cursive Hand".

regarding his as a treasure.[1]

It is worth noting that some contemporary calligraphy connoisseurs are in favor of Mr. Zhang's conclusions. Mr. Wang Lianqi, one of the Chinese scholars, also concluded in the "Yu He and His Running Script *Lanting Ji*" that the *Ji An's Biography* was written by Yu He, "because there is no emptiness and euphemism of Zhao's calligraphy but Yu He's square severeness and straight sharpness." The reason is similar to Mr. Zhang Guangbin's. Zhang believes that *Ji An's Biography* is not as simple and elegant as Yu's *Leyi Lun*[2], and it is not the work of his later years, while Mr. Wang believes: "*Ji An's Biography* is more sophisticated than *Leyi Lun*. The time when it was written is later." [3]Comparing the opinions of these two experts, it can be known there are great difficulties in calligraphy appreciation.

Mr. Fu Shen, who has spent the most energy in this field, is also an admirer of Mr. Zhang's views. He said that Mr. Zhang "reasoned extremely correctly. Although Yu learned from Zhao, he still had unique personal characteristics. Zhao's brushworks have emptiness in solidness, and he approached the people of Jin, better in rhyme; Yu He's brushworks are all solid, and he approached the people of the Tang Dynasty, better in law."[4]

Mr. Fu's and Mr. Zhang's views are indeed kind of alarming. At this point, I can't help asking myself that I really want to give up this topic, because I really don't have enough ability to distinguish the authenticity of this kind of calligraphy. There are at least two obstacles that I can't overcome here. The first is that I see so few authenticities that I have weak eyesight and no qualifications

---

1 (Ming Dynasty) Xu Yi Rui, *Shifeng Manuscript*, Vol. 13, in *Wulin Wangzhe Yizhu* carved by Jiahui Tang the Ding Family, Qianqiang Jian, in Guangxu Era.

2 It is collected by The Art Museum ot Princeton University, which was writen by Yu He at this age of 54 in the twentieth year of Zhizheng Era, 1360.

3 *Calligraphy Series*, No. 28 issues, Cultural Relics Press, 1991.

4 Fu Shen, *Calligraphy History and Calligraphy Marks*, Taiwan History Museum, 1996, p. 193.

at all. But wandering around, hesitating to go, I always feel it is also a good thing even though my little opinions will become a savage view. I seem to feel vaguely that Mr. Fu's opinions can also be used to prove that the *Ji An's Biography* is genius. The so–called "legacy of the Tang Dynasty" in the epilogue does require "each brushwork is solid, better in law"? To avoid talking about this topic as soon as possible, I just want to quote the opinion of Mr. Huang Dun, another expert on Zhao Mengfu. After careful consideration of Mr. Wang Lianqi's appraisal, he said: "I think that it is lack of evidence to decide *Ji An's Biography of Han* is by Yu He only on the ground of square severeness and straight sharpness, that is, the square trajectory of power as Wen Zhengming said; compared *Leyi Lun* written by Yu He in small regular script with *Ji An's Biography of Han*, not only is it in less exquisitness and skillulness, but also with different spirit and rhythm. So I stick to the old saying." [1]The old saying here includes not only the ancient masters like Wen Zhengming, Dong Qichang and An Qi, but also the modern masters like Xu Bangda. We may still remember the remarks of Xu Bangda's appraisal of *Ji An's Biography* quoted earlier. Both he and An noticed that Yu He forged Zhao's calligraphy, but they both agreed in praising *Ji An's Biography*. Perhaps it was their views of Yu He's forgery that inspired us modern scholars to associate *Ji An's Biography* with Yu He. In this way, the first–rate connoisseurs have divided into two factions on *Ji An's Biography*. Regardless of its authenticity, it has become a deadlock. So we still return to Zhao Mengfu's collection of books.

It may be remembered that in addition to the *Hanshu*, there is also a *Selected Works* in the aforementioned Zhao's collection. What is fascinating is that, like *Hanshu*, *Selected Works* was praised by Wang Shizhen in the Ming Dynasty, but the Wang family was no longer able to collect it, short of money. However, we will not forget his evaluation. He said: "I have seen several versions of *Wenxuan*

---

1 See *Complete Works of Chinese Calligraphy*, Zhao Mengfu, Rong Baogao Publishing House, 2002, Vol. 2, pp. 475–476.

(selected works) from the Song Dynasty. This copy is extremely exquisit, with the paper from Chengxintang, and the ink by Xi." [1] Wang Zhideng also compared this book with the *Hanshu*, saying that it was copied by a good hand with the same paper and ink, absolutely similar to the *Hanshu* in the Wang's collection. These words also make us speculate that Zhao Mengfu's block–printed edition of *Records of History* should be absolutely similar to this one.

In about the fifth year of Wanli (1577), before the book was exchanged from Xu Wenmin to Wang Zhongjia (1544–1613, with the name Daohui), Zhang Fengyi kept it at the desk for several months and proofread *the Annotations to Compilation of Anthology* he was about to publish. About 21 years later, it belonged to Tang Binyin (1568–?, Jinshi in the 23rd year of Wanli, from Xuancheng, leader of the Xuankun Party who attacked Donglin Party members) and Wang Chun once went to look at it and wrote down his impressions and envy feelings:

I know that Zhongjia has the version of *Selected Works* from the Song Dynasty and my heart is shaken desiring it for more than ten years. Arriving at his house, I didn't dare to ask for looking at it personally. Later, the distinguished guest (Tang) in the Xiaoyou Garden of Ruoshan, the Taoist hermit, was shown the ink traces of the Tang and Song dynasties, which are all unprecedented in the world, attracting my soul dreaming for that, and promising me to get a look at the book. Unfortunatly, it was too dark late the day to see it so that I had to leave for home in vain. After I was dreaming for it for several days, I finally got the chance to see it, with paper and ink shining through the eyes, and the characters in regular script well–formed. Actually, I have seen it all day and night to get what I had never done. It is the first pleasure in life to see it with the wind playing through the pine trees and the mountains and the remote black mountains spreading far. [2]

---

1 Quoted from Volume 3 of *The Imperial Tianlu Linlang Bibliography*, the same version as before, p.246.

2 Quoted from Volume 3 of the Imperial Tianlu Linlang Bibliography, the same version as before.

Wang Chun had a little friendship with Qian Qianyi, good at excellent martial arts, and excelled at poems as well, who is recorded in the Ding volume of Qian's *Liechao Shiji Xiaozhuan, A Biography of Poems in the Dynasties.* He became a monk after the end of the Ming Dynasty, and his writings were banned and rarely passed on, and it is only known that the Hangzhou Museum has a copy of *Baoruiqi Poems*, and whoever are interested in it can visit to see it. Most of the above epilogues were written during the Wanli period. Together with my quotation in the first section, one can imagine the attitudes towards books at that time. If that Zhao Mengfu regards *Hanshu* and *Selected Works* as works of art was a unique outstanding individual behavior, it was already a collective behavior of the literati circle in the Wanli period of the Ming Dynasty. We have mentioned Zhang Chou several times. He had taken great pains to record famous paintings and calligraphies. In his *Fashu Minghua Jianwen Biao, List of Famous Paintings and Calligraphies Seen and Heard*, he put the Selected Works, the version of the Song Dynasty, and Wen Tong's *Wan'ai Hengkan, Cijun Tu* juxtaposed with Wang Xian's *Mengyou Yingshan, Dream Tour in Yingshan,* as well as Huang shangu's *Zhu Shangzuo Tie*, etc. (see "Mudu, The Witness Part"). Particularly unbelievable, the *Fashu Minghua Jianwen Biao* also lists the entire text of the *Zuozhuan* copied and the *Collected Works of Li Taibai* by Zhao (the "Diwen, Hearing part").

If we look back a little further and look at Huaxia's Zhenshangzhai Collection, it is even more amazing. The preface of Feng Daosheng's *Zhenshangzhai Fu* describes its collection, including at first the calligraphy by Zhong and Wang, then the paintings from the Tang and Song dynasties such as Wang Youcheng's, with the lists of the collection of inscription rubbings, and finally the collection of books with the most detailed descriptions. The Preface says:

Liu's *Shitong, The History* and *Yutai Xinyong, New Odes to Yutai,* (with the seal of

"Seal of Jianye Study"), are the version of the early days of the Southern Tang Dynasty. Nie Chongyi's *Sanli Tu, Three Ceremony Pictures*, Yu Yan and others' *Wujing Tushuo, Five Classics Illustrated Explanations,* are the excellent version of the Northern Song Dynasty. Xun Yue's *Pre–Han Ji*, Yuan Hong's *Post–Han Ji* (the version of Shaoxing Period, prefaced by Zhi, Prince Ruyin), are beautiful history books of a long legacy; Xu Song's *Jiankang Lu*, and Lu You's *Southern Tang History,* contain greatly amazing records. *Zhou Li* annotated in the Song Dynasty is brand new; *Nine Classics* with the ancient annotation is more lack in the Imperial Academy (collected by Yu Shijian, with Wang Shouxi's postscript). Su Zirong's *Yixiang Fayao, Methods of Appropriation and Imagery,* is aptly called one of the *Zhuzi*; Zhang Yanyuan's *Lidai Minghua Ji, Famous Paintings in the Past Dynasties,* is appraised and collected by Ziang. All passed down from the Song and Yuan dynasties, with a long history, such as Yue's *Zuo Zhuan* of Xiangtai, Huang Shanfu's *Historical Records, Six Officials Annotated Essays* of Jian'an, Guo Zhida's *Annotated Du Gongbu's Poems* (a total of nine schools, proofread by Zeng Yu), *Li Hanlin's Collection* with Zeng Nanfeng's preface (Thirty volumes), *Notes on Han's and Liu's Essays by Five Hundred Schools* (before *Zhu zi*, books in the study; *Selected Works* and *Notes on Han's and Liu's Essays by Five Hundred Schools* are particularly excellent), *Liu Binke's Collection* (a total of 40 volumes, with *Outside Collections* of ten volumes included), *BaiShi Changqing Collection* (seventy–one volumes), *Ouyang Family Collection* (removed and supplemented the missing eighty volumes, the most complete), *The Complete Works of Three Sus, The Collection of Wang Linchuan* (There are in the world only one hundred volumes passed down, but this includes one hundred and sixty volumes), *Guanzi, Han Fei, Three Kingdoms* (large–character edition, published in Yisi Year of Chunxi Period, by Tongzhou Transshipment Division Public Money), *Bao Canjun Collection* (ten volumes), *Huajian Ji* (with good paper and ink), *Yunxi Youyi* (tweleve volumes, written by Fan Fu), *The General Turtle of Poetry Talks* (one hundred volumes, edited by Ruan Yue), *Jingxuetang Zazhi* (eight volumes, written by Ni Si of Jichuan), *Jinshi Lue* (by Zheng Qiao, collected by Da), *Supplements of Baojin Mountain and Forest* (eight volumes, engraved by Sun

Guangxian), *Dongguan Yulun* (with postscripts by Lou Gongkui, etc., engraved rubbings in the early Song, unique good paper and ink, with well prepared volumes, rare in the world), *Tang Minghua Lu* (engraved by Zhu Jingxuan), *Supplement of Famous Paintings of Five Dynasties* (Compiled by Liu Daochun), *Song Famous Paintings Criticism, Lanting Kao* (tweleve volumes, *Sang Shichang Collection*).

After finishing this, he then continued: "The beautiful books are collected, and the ancient books are of the same significance. Therefore Li Wenzheng, Taishiling, an official managing the imperial library and calendaris, wrote in the one–eighth script on the horizontal inscribed board: 'Zhenshangzhai'. The truth is full of insights, and appreciation is the double integration of the magnificent beauty. Hanlin Duke Wenzheng is showing his interest through his inscription and painting. In the past, Zhang Yanyuan was diligent day and night far from his young age to compile the collection, scorned for useless things by others. How could he feel pleased all his life? So was he obsessive and addictive as to loan clothes, reduce food, take a thousand horses as nothing, and take a scoop water as comfortable. Every time Mi Yuanzhang got a book, he was not only exhaustive to enjoy it, but also for days, with hands washed clean totally from the front to the back; he opened it to read after politely bowing his hands, repeated washing hands before exhibiting it, and the strong thunder would not interrupt him when he read it. He could make the correct identification with Chu Zhongling immediatly; and he never missed a point arguing with Huang Changrui. Enjoying this elegant interest is the same symbol for thousands of years. Before sand drowned painfully at the end of lifetime, he would forget his sorrows and happiness, seeing everything without being tired, who is a Special Traveler going beyond the universal.[1]

The allusions of connoisseurs are used here together to create a realm with a strong artistic atmosphere. These words were written in the twenty–eighth year

1 (Ming Dynasty) Feng Fang, *Zhenshangzhai Fu*, in *Ouxiang Lingshi*, printed by Miao Quansun in the twenty–fourth year of Guangxu Era.

of Jiajing (1549), letting us push forward half a century, that is, the tenth year of Hongzhi (1497), when Zhu Yunming (1460–1527) wrote a postscript for a friend's *Wenxuan, Selected Works,* who was Qian Tongai (1475–1549, with his courtesy name Kongtong, and named Yeting):

Since the scholars promoted their fame through classics, Zhaoming's *Selected Works* and the books whose value is not known have been turned over for a long time. If there was a valuable book, of course it must be the case. There had been many literary competitions by scholars for several years in Wuzhong, and the compiled version is to be more expensive. There are three or five types in my collections, all of which are also old carved. Qian Xiucai's is especially good with a high level, and as a talented scholar, he is very competitive; if he is helped by the best version, his literary performance will be promoted particularly. Zhu Yunming wrote this in Dingsi Year, with the brush and ink slab served by the disciple Zhang Lingshi.[1]

By the period of Chongzhen Era, this book seemed to belong to Wang Pingyu. He also wrote a postscript for this when he compiled *Shanhu Wang, Coral Net*, with the tone already like this:

In my family there are still all kinds of books of the version printed in the Song Dynasty such as *Five Classics, Zuo, Guo, Zhuzi, History*, *Han, Tongjian,* and *Collected Works*. They are antique and cute to exhibit for appreciation and enjoyment after cleaning the tables. Later, Tiaoxi engraved the five–color books with red annotations, arranged on the right and left sides alternately, brightly contrasted to the books, which is enough for one hundred cities to follow.[2]

If you read the five–color books with red annotations, they are bad ones,

1 *The Wang Complete Book of Calligraphy,* Vol. 16, *Shiyuan Series,* pp. 1–2.

2 *The Wang Complete Book of Calligraphy,* Vol. 16, *Shiyuan Series,* p. 2.

which the predecessors have already criticized. If you appreciate them, they are pleasant to your eyes. Therefore this has entered the era when books become works of art and are detached from practicality. Xie Zhaozhe gave his grievances in *Wuza Zu, Five Miscellaneous Groups*: "Ling in Wuxing produced various engravings resulting from his eagerness to write a book and gain profit, but also save the labor when they are edited. It is not strange that they are similar of the same quality. Such books as *the Water Margin, the West Chamber, the Lute* and *Moyuan* are focused on the spirits, and beauty eagerly to be stunning. Such spiritual things of the best are a play for the legendary ears and eyes of the clever people, and it is also a pity!"[1] Comparing Ling's block–printed edition with the printed picture books, such a period of time is confirmed from the negative side. Regarding this issue, I have contributed to a dedicated article of discussion, so I won't go into details here. But I want to add a bit about the environment in which Wang Keyu lives. His father was Wang Jimei, with his study named Dongyatang. Li Rihua visited him and wrote down the sights he had seen there: "There are pine trees, rocks, plum trees and orchids in front of the hall, arranged in order. On entering the study, I had a scroll opened to watch, which is a work of the Yuan Dynasty...We climbed into the Mohua Pavilion, with four marble screens showing, a stone couch, with dozens of bookcases of versions printed in the Song Dynasty, and dozens of miscellaneous copybooks, as well as a genus of bronze, porcelains, flower wares and so forth on the table. Wang entertained himself there, refusing the outsiders to get into it."[2]

It seems that the discussion here is getting farther and farther, and I should quickly return to Zhao Mengfu's collection of books and *Ji An's Biography*. It is at this starting point that I put forward a hypothesis; on the basis of this assumption, not only can I judge the *Ji An's Biography* as authentic, but it also

1 *New Century Universal Library*, 13, p. 275.

2 See Li Rihua, *Diary of Weishuixuan*, Vol. 6, the item of December 18th in the forty–second year of Wanli, 1940, *Jiayetang Series*, p. 72.

raises the central question of this section: the book becomes art. I think this hypothesis has a little loophole, because which book "this engraved version" is cannot be implemented in detail. But I also think that this is not a major flaw. It does not hinder my more important thesis. In general, my hypothesis has more advantages than judging whether *Ji An's Biography* is simply true or false. In my opinion, one hypothesis is better than the other, which can be compared with the following three points:

1. Simplicity: the more concise and clearer a hypothesis or a theory is, the easier it will be understood, and more importantly, the easier it will be refuted.

2. Inclusiveness: a hypothesis with a larger package capacity, that is, a hypothesis with more content that can be explained is more advantageous.

3. Creativity: it seems very important to be able to raise new interesting and creative questions. For the humanities scholar, his main task is, after all, to bring the static records and documents of the past to life.

In view of the above, we have not only solved the two seemingly difficult problems of *Ji An's Biography*, not easily pushing it out of the ranks of masterpieces, letting it still shine, but also explained Zhao Mengfu's postscript inscriptions on the *Selected Works* and his book collection instructions with a new perspective. Besides that, more importantly, the history of books can be viewed from a new perspective. The clues to revisit the history of books are roughly as follows:

First of all, Zhao Mengfu viewed books through the lens of his unique appreciative eyes, just like the full-fledged appraisal eyes on calligraphies and paintings at that time. They are a natural extension of the elegant tastes of people in the Song Dynasty, which has been explained by *Jinshi Studies of the Song Dynasty* published by Mr. Wang Guowei in *The Collection of Chinese Studies* as early as in 1928 (Vol. 1, No. 3).

Then there is the atmosphere of the times constructed by the *Preface to Zhenshangzhai Fu* quoted above. At that time, in the middle of the Ming Dynasty, a wave of retro was popular, including literature, paintings, bronzes, and ceramics, and of course, books were the most important item. There are not only bronzes, porcelains, jade, scrolls of calligraphies and paintings, but also books painted on *Playing with the Antiques* by Du Jin (ca.1465–1509), collected in the National Palace Museum in Taipei, with the inscriptions as these: "the Antiques are common but it is a great ambition to collect them largely. Another name is viewing where rituals and music are located. There is no ritual and music every day and people are ashamed. If they are done right, I have something to look forward to." This can be regarded as a sign of the beginning of this trend. In this fashionable atmosphere, not only the books printed by the blockboard in the Song Dynasty become antiques, but its reprinted editions have also formed a new typeface—Imitation Style from the Song.

At this point in writing, we might as well look to the West to see how Westerners in the same period view books. Antonio Averlino Filarete (ca. 1400–1469) described a portait in hard pen by Piero Medici (1414–1469) in *Trattato d'architettura*, saying: "Looking at the books in that room, as if they were a pile of gold.... Let's not talk about his reading activities. Sometimes, his pastime teisure may be to let the eyes scan over these books, killing the time and providing pleasant entertainment for the eyes."

This precious material was quoted by Gombrich, although all the books are still written by hand. But in Europe, as early as in the 12th century, decorating handwritten scripts of the Bible became an important work for artisans, especially the initial letters of each chapter, sometimes in a variety of colors and quite gorgeous. [1]Such splendid handwriting books themselves are works of art, and their appreciation value is far greater than their practical functions. They often took months or even years to complete, and the price was even

1 Cf. Christopher de Hamel, *The Book: A History of the Bible*, London, 2001, pp. 83–84.

more expensive. This was probably the case for the expensive rare collection of books by Duke of Berry, the most important book lover of the 15th century. [1]The Florentine writer Vespasiano da Bisticci's *Live of Illustrious Men* has a passage about the Duke of Ubino's Library: "His library only collects handwritten books. If there is a printed book, he will feel ashamed."[2] At that time, printed books had just appeared in Europe. In any case, these stories give us the opportunity to think about the general human psychology. Gombrich commented:

> We don't always get into the happiness of people in remote ancient times, even in imagination. However, Filarete's account of Piero's collection can still be translated into visual terms. Many books clearly marked as written or illustrated for Piero are still hidden in the Laurenziana Library in Florence, including illustrations of the works of Cicero, Plutarch, Josephus, Pliny and Aristotle. These books "provide material entertaining eyes" for those who find them. [3]

There is an epilogue of a man of the Ming Dynasy on the protective leaf of *Caochuang Yunyu* blockprinted in the Song Dynasty, which can be regarded as a model for people in that fashion to treat the books blockprinted in the Song Dynasty: "On Duanyang in Gengyin Year of Wanli Era, I made a trip to Qilu, and visited Mr. Mingfu's Office passing by Xia Town, where there is this excellent engraving of the Song version, which is rare in the world and should be quested as a copybook, which is recorded here for joy. Luo Wenrui from Xindu."[4]

Taking books as calligraphic copybooks is the distant reverberation of Zhao Mengfu's "Silver hooks on Jade paper", which is entirely artistic. At this time,

---

1 Cf. L. Febvre and H. Martin, *The Coming of the Book*, London, 1993, p. 27.

2 E.H. Gombrich, The Museum's Mission, the Enjoyment of Art, the Problem of Critics', *Art News*, January 1974, pp. 54–57.

3 (England) E.H. Gombrich, The Renaissance: The Great Age of Western Art, ed. by Li Benzheng & Fan Jingzhong, China Academy of Art, Hangzhou, 2000, p. 164.

4 See the Song edition by the Jiang's Milou in Wucheng in the Republic of China.

during the Wanli period, new types of books that became independent works of art finally appeared. The *Hushan Shenggai,* now collected in the French National Library, is the most representative. It combines poetry, calligraphy and painting into one and is published in four–color overprinting, in the Wanli period between 30 and 40 years (1602–1612),[1] a masterpiece of Hangzhou engraving and printing. *Wenzi Huibao* was also published at this time, and it is a selection of calligraphy works printed on the board including various calligraphic works. By the autumn of the thirteenth year of Chongzhen, the engraving publications of "Huizheng Tu" (1640) by Min Yuwu had reached the peak of Chinese printmaking art. Du Jin's so–called "playing with the antiques and becoming great" also formed the climate at that time, Books to form encyclopedic knowledge and cosmic landscapes through images are also published in time, with the best–known *Sancai Tuhui, Three Talents Drawing* (1609), as the most famous.

We can re–evaluate, with this view of history, Xu Zonglu's (1490–1559) engraved books, who was a calligrapher. His engraved *Guoyu* (the fourth year of Jiajing) and *Lüshi Chunqiu* (the seventh year of Jiajing) are all in characters of ancient Chinese styles, and there was an impact in the middle and late Ming Dynasty, although Cha Tashan later criticized: "It was because he didn't know *Six Books*.For this reason, if you can explain the *Shuowen*, never will you dare to use it." But if it is placed in the retro atmosphere, it may be another explanation, from which you can also deduce some traces that Feng Daosheng made counterfeit books in crooked and twisted posture, and that Fu Shan wrote calligraphy with many strange characters.

By the Qing Dynasty, people's eyes on books, especially the ones of Qianjia scholars, were very different from those of the Ming Dynasty, but the influence could not disappear. Jin Dongxin played with ancient books and finally wrote a

1 See my essay "Overprints and Block–prints as well as Their *Huizhen Paintings*", in *New Art*, 2005, Issue 4, pp. 77–82.

new style of calligraphy, which he was in the same tune with Zhao Mengfu, both inspired by engraved books.

Books can become a kind of art, and in turn influence other kinds of art. This process is, not done overnight, as what Gombrich remarked, which is not just a matter of recruiting it, and has gone through a long and special history. As Johan Huizinga said, the special history is: the reason why something becomes art is not because of people's desire for beauty, but because of its excess development, when it is piled up as treasures in the treasure house of the palace and nobles. It is no longer applied to real life, but becomes a luxury and rare object when it is viewed and developed its artistic style.

Though the above outline is only a sketch, it suffices to explain what we have researched on the relationship between books and calligraphy, the relationship between books and paintings, especially books as the destiny of books themselves, is really too shallow, which is still a piece of history to be explored.

Of course, the ancients did not have the concept of art or a fine arts. For them, they were just antiquities or antiques, but the language of the ancients describing books was so exquisite, such as Sui Jiangzong's (519–594) *Huangtaizi Taixue Jiangbei, Crown Prince's Lectures on Tablet in Imperial College:* Secret Classics in the palace, wonderful texts in the green scroll, old books stored, incomplete bamboo–slip books from Songshan, Foreign non–orthodox history books outside, books in the imperial library, are all printed without decoration, carved with silk",[1] that the seeds of beauty have long been planted, and even the appreciative vision beginning from Zhao Mengfu, in the twentieth century, has finally been expressed in modern terms, which is the passage I quoted at the beginning of the article, and now we are back to the starting point.

Looking back again at Mr. Zhang Guangbin's theory on fakes, I think,

---

1 See *Jiang Lingjun Collection*, Vol. 1, republished by Xinshutang in the fifth year of Guangxu Era, *Han, Wei and Six dynasties Baisanjia Ji*, p. 18.

although it can satisfy the first point of a good hypothesis, it has almost nothing to do with the other two points. So without conclusive credible evidences, I abide the old saying and don't want this treasure to be degraded. Originally, we don't have many treasures, so we must use Occam's razor with caution not reducing the entity. This is the second reason why we don't get involved in the discussion of identifying works purely through eyesight.

Before closing this, I would like to talk about another anecdote related to Zhao Mengfu's collection, which happened around 1600 and was recorded in Zang Maoxun's (1550–1620, Jinshi in the eighth year of Wanli) "Postscript of Selected Works of Six Ministers" in *Selected Works of Fu Baotang*, with the locations in Nanjing and Hangzhou:

> Traveling in Baixia, I visited Kaizhi with guests[1]. In the office, at the time, the shade by sycamore trees was filled with seats, breezing cool. He showed us *Selected Works* on the table, it was appropriate to recite and satirize a few articles, which might be Kaizhi's secret rare Song edition cherished. One of the guests took Yang Yongxiu (Yang Shen, 1488–1559) for an example, saying: "'Ancient books are not only infallible, but also have ancient fragrance. 'I don't know where the fragrance is from?" I said, "Don't you feel the smell of ink and paper in the new book?" Kaizhi agreed absolutely. By the autumn of Gengzi (1600) I visited Kaizhi on the lake, and the version of *Selected Works* with Li's annotation was just engraved, quite exquisit, and so I asked for the former book for a look. Kaizhi, picking it up by hand to show me, said: "This is safe alone. Although poorer, I am fortunate not to make it be Wang Yuanmei's *Hanshu*." I once saw Yuanmei's *Hanshu* with Zhao Wenmin's postscript. I was ashamed that I couldn't write such excellent calligraphies as Wenmin even though I was also from Wuxing, that I could make *Selected Works* more important for this. Just write a few to remember the lifetime. [2]

1 Feng Mengzhen (1546–1605), Offering Wine of Imperial academy, convicted, bought a land from Wang Zhongjia in Gushan to build Kuaixuetang.

2 (Ming Dynasty) *Futang Selected Works, volume of Continued Revision of Siku Quanshu*, photocopy of Erbing in the first year of Tianqi, Shanghai Guji Publishing House, 1994–2002, Vol. 1361, p. 91.

This anthology is not the one in the collection of Zhao Mengfu. It was in the fifth year of the Wanli Era (1577) of Feng Kaizhi's honoring as Jinshi that *Selected Works* collected by Zhao entered Wang Zhongjia's study. By chance, it was Wang Zhongjia that sold the land to Feng Kaizhi and allowed him to build the famous Kuaixuetang in Gushan. Like *Hanshu,* this book was transferred to Tang Binyin by Wang Zhongjia, and finally entered the imperial court. Emperor Qianlong wrote:

> This book (*Selected Works*) is also known as one of the three most important books, a parallel to *Hanshu* and *Dushi* in China honored by Dong Qichang. In the Yuan Dynasty, Zhao Mengfu, and Wang Shizhen, Dong Qichang, Wang Rangdeng, Zhou Tianqiu, Zhang Fengyi, Wang Yinglou, Wang Chun, Cao Zinian, and the elites of the South East in the Ming Dynasty, all of them left their inscriptions and postscripts about it. There is also the inscription by Li Kai at the beginning of our country's establishment. The paper is as smooth as jade, with the method of Chengxintang of Southern Tang Dynasty as well. The handwriting is exquisite, with the masters' brushwork of the Northern Song Dynasty. *Hanshu* can be seen in the imperial court, and it is connected with *Dushi* as two treasures, with the latter's where abouts located unknow. The one as great as this in the Tianlu Linlang is also rare.[1]

None of The Three Treasures of Song Version called by Dong Qichang can be seen now. Today's talk about book art can't help but feel melancholy, a reminder of Qian Qianyi's emotions: Gossip from water and sky, fallen in the world long; News about flowers and the moon has become a story.

---

1 It is quoted from the third volume of *the Imperial Tianlu Linlang Bibliography*, in the same edition as the former.

Word bank

1.anthology n.（诗、文等的）选集

2.appreciative adj. 感激的；欣赏的；赏识的；有欣赏力的

3.epilogue n. 结尾部分；尾声；收场白

4.protective adj. 保护的；防护的

5.calligraphic adj. 书法的；美术字体的

6.reverberation n. 反响；反射；回响

7.overprint v. 在……上加印；加盖

8.masterpiece n. 杰作；代表作

9.encyclopedic adj. 百科全书的；知识广博的

10.hypothesis n. 假设；前提

11.loophole n. 漏洞；射箭用小窗口

12.implement n. 工具；器具

13.flaw n. 瑕疵；缺陷

14.hinder v. 阻碍；打扰

15.allusion n. 影射；典故

16.connoisseur n. 鉴赏家；鉴定家

17.authentic adj. 可信的；真正的

18.simplicity n. 简明；简易

19.refute v. 驳斥；反驳

20.inclusiveness n. 包容性

21.advantageous adj. 有利的；有益的

22.creativity n. 创造力；创造性

23. appraisal n. 估量；估计

书 法

The Chinese Calligraphy

帝王父子书

宋代是中国历史上崇文尚艺的时代。在北宋皇帝赵佶（1082—1135）身体力行的影响下，许多帝王都爱好书画艺术。

赵佶即宋徽宗，他自己就是书画家和鉴藏家。[1] 他在位时广聚历代文物、书画，极一时之盛，亲自主持翰林图画院，指导编辑《宣和书谱》和《宣和画谱》，甚至堪称主持中国首届大型书画展的策展人，他甚至以九五之尊的身份亲自担任展览解说员，在这样盛大的展览活动期间，宋徽宗会将御笔书法赐予众大臣。[2]

伊佩霞在《文化积善：宋徽宗的收藏》中有极其详尽的论述：[3]

这不是宋徽宗唯一一次让他的官员观赏他的财富。在另一段中，蔡絛言道，他展示他获得的古青铜器：

---

1 ［美］伊佩霞著，殷凌云、毕夏译：《文化积善：宋徽宗的收藏》，将由上海书画出版社出版。

2 同上，第125页。

3 同上，第122页。

尝有旨，以所藏列崇政殿暨两廊，召百官而宣示焉。当是时，天子尚留心政治，储神穆清，因从琐闼密窥，听臣僚访诸左右，知其为谁，乐其博识，味其议论，喜于人物，而百官弗觉也。[1]

伊佩霞书中还描述了另一展览的事件：

宋徽宗也向一群精选的高级官员展现宝物，把这作为宴会和派对的一部分。根据蔡京撰写的记录，1112 年，宋徽宗在太清楼安排了一次盛宴，他说，他希望它能够像《诗经》中提到的周朝皇家宴会。4 位资深宦官掌管准备事宜，11 位重臣受邀为客人。当他们抵达宣和殿时，"至宣和殿，止三楹，左右挟，中置图书、笔砚、古鼎、彝、罍、洗。陈几案台榻，漆以黑"。

这种活动常常举办：

宋徽宗展示他的收藏品的另一场合是在 1119 年保和殿的一次私人聚会上，蔡京对此也做了回忆。[2]客人中包括数位宋徽宗自己的亲戚——他的两位兄弟、他的三儿子楷（他曾通过了前一年的进士考试，擅长绘画和书法），以及远亲族人赵仲忽（他是文物收藏家）。此外，宋徽宗邀请了蔡京以及蔡京的几个儿子和孙子，包括蔡絛，他前年娶了宋徽宗的第五个女儿（蔡絛此时 22 或 23 岁，他是否被邀作客还不清楚）。[3]蔡京连续数年处于半退休状态，每五天上朝一次。其他嘉宾包括重臣王黼，他在军机处供职一年有余，和自 1116 年以来就在军机处掌权的检校太尉童贯。

客人们穿过美丽的花园，来到保和殿，随后他们发现，宋徽宗为他们的到访做了充分准备。宋徽宗的龙椅御榻已被放置在大殿中央，大殿东西两侧都摆放着图籍、青铜器、绘画和书法等珍玩。在蔡京的记述中，他描绘了宋徽宗

1 （宋）蔡絛著：《铁围山丛谈》，卷四，第80页。

2 这个故事的来源是《挥麈录》"余话"，卷一，第276—279页；通过《续资治通鉴长编》"史部"卷40，第1251—1252页为辅；和《说郛》"函"114，第5238—5239页。

3 《挥麈录》中没有列出他，《续资治通鉴长编拾补》版本也没有，不过《说郛》中一章做了收录。

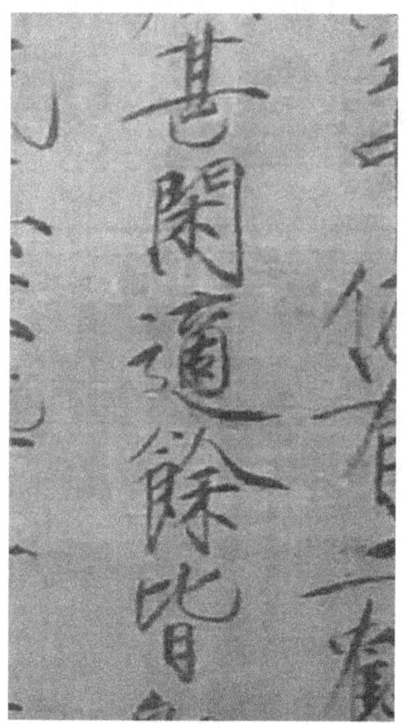

瘦金体
Slender Gold Style

为他们充当导游的状况：

令我们惊讶的是，“上亲指示，为言其概。因指阁内：‘此藏卿表章字札无遗者。’命开橱，橱有朱隔，隔内置小匣，匣内覆以缯绮，得臣所书撰《淑妃刘氏制》。臣进曰：‘札恶文鄙，不谓袭藏如此。’念无以为报，顿首谢”。[12]

由此可见，宋徽宗时代的艺术鉴藏何其兴盛。宋徽宗的书法初学薛稷，变其法度而自号“瘦金体”[3]。宋徽宗的瘦金体楷书较多见，草书流传绝少，辽宁博物馆藏赵佶书《草书千字文卷》为纸本，纵 35.1 厘米，横 1172.1 厘米，颇

1 《挥麈录》“余话”，卷1，第276—277页。

2 ［美］伊佩霞著，殷凌云、毕夏译：《文化积善：宋徽宗的收藏》，将由上海书画出版社出版。

3 瘦金体是中国书法史上一种独特的书体，由北宋徽宗赵佶所独创，与晋楷、唐楷等传统书体区别较大。瘦金体运笔灵动快捷，笔迹瘦劲，瘦而不失其肉。

为壮观。此卷书于十一米的描金云龙笺上，笔势洒脱劲利，变幻莫测，一气呵成，有如疾风骤雨，气魄非凡。此作书于宣和壬寅(1122)，宋徽宗时年40岁。

宋徽宗的艺术收藏成为北宋亡国的部分原因。宋徽宗的儿子赵构（1107—1187）却没有因为北宋的灭亡而完全放弃书画艺术。赵构即南宋高宗皇帝，字德基，北宋宣和三年（1121）封康王，靖康二年（1127）于临安即皇帝位，在位36年。他留心书画，对书法用功尤勤，初学黄庭坚，后学米芾，进而上溯晋唐，其对南宋君臣书法影响尤大。辽宁博物馆藏赵构《章草书洛神赋卷》为绢本，纵27.9厘米，横398厘米，意义重大。

此卷以章草书曹植《洛神赋》全文，格调古朴，运笔沉稳圆厚，草法谨严又富于韵致。字间不互相连接而各自成形，但笔意贯通，仍有浑然一气之感。卷末落“德寿殿”款并钤“德寿殿御书宝”印，可证为他退位后隐居德寿殿所书。[1]

父子既是皇帝又是书法家，世间罕见。

1 此处参考了辽宁博物馆的展览介绍。

Calligraphies by Father–and–Son Emperors

The Song Dynasty of China was an era of advocating literature and art in Chinese history. Under the personal influence of Emperor of the Northern Song Dynasty, Zhao Ji (1082–1135), many emperors liked painting and calligraphy.

Zhao Ji, Emperor Huizong of the Northern Song Dynasty, was a prominent calligrapher and painter in his own right. During his reign, he was an avid collector of old calligraphies, paintings and other relics and unsurprisingly he had built up an unprecedented large collection.[1] He personally supervised the activities of the Academy of Painting and compiled the *Xuanhe Catalogue of Calligraphy* and *Xuanhe Catalogue of Painting*. Song Huizong can even be called the first curator who presided over China's first large–scale painting and calligraphy exhibition. He personally served as the interpreter as the distinguished emperor, during such a grand exhibition, and would give away the imperial calligraphies by himself to the ministers. [2]

Patricia Buckley Ebrey detailed in her book *Accumulating Culture: The Collections of Emperor Huizong*:

This was not the only occasion on which Huizong let his officials see his treasures. In another passage Cai Tao reports his display of the ancient bronzes he had acquired:

Once Huizong issued an order that the antiquities in the collection be displayed in the two side chambers of Promoting Governance Hall and have the officials summoned

---

1 (America) Patricia Buckley Ebrey, *Accumulating Culture: The Collections of Emperor Huizong* (translated into Chinese by Yin Lingyun and Bi Xia, to be published by Shanghai Calligraphy and Painting Publishing House), Seattle & London, University of Washington Press, 1984.

2 id., p. 125.

to view them. At that time Huizong was attentive to government matters, concentrated and serene. He would secretly peek through the cracks in the inner doors to hear his officials discuss the objects with each other. He could recognize each one and enjoyed listening to their displays of broad knowledge; he savored the flavor of their discussions, and appreciated their eminence, all without the officials knowing he was there.[12]

In the book, another event is also described by Patricia Buckley Ebrey:

Huizong also showed treasures to select groups of senior officials as part of banquets and parties. In 1112, according to the record Cai Jing wrote, Huizong arranged a grand banquet at Grand Clarity Edifice, saying he wanted it to be like the royal banquets of Zhou times mentioned in the *Book of Songs*. Four senior eunuchs took charge of the preparations and eleven senior officials were the guests. When they arrived at Harmony Revealed Hall, "paintings and calligraphy, brushes and inkstones, ancient cauldrons, libation cups, tall jars, and washpans were displayed on black lacquered tables and stands. "[34]

This type of events often happened:

Another occasion when Huizong displayed objects in his collection was a private party at Harmony Preserved Hall in 1119, which Cai Jing also recounted. [5]Guests included several of Huizong's own relatives—his two brothers, his third son Kai (who had passed the jinshi examination the year before and was skilled at painting and calligraphy), and

1 id., p.122.

2 (Song) Cai Tao, *Tieweishan Congtan(Collected Talks from My Little World)*, 4.80.

3 (America) Patricia Buckley Ebrey, *Accumulating Culture: The Collections of Emperor Huizong* (translated into Chinese by Yin Lingyun and Bi Xia, to be published by Shanghai Calligraphy and Painting Publishing House), Seattle & London, University of Washington Press, 1984, pp. 122–123.

4 *Huichen Lu,the remaining chapter* 1.274.

5 (America) Patricia Buckley Ebrey, *Accumulating Culture: The Collections of Emperor Huizong* (translated into Chinese by Yin Lingyun and Bi Xia, to be published by Shanghai Calligraphy and Painting Publishing House), University of Washington Press,Seattle & London, 1984, pp. 122–123.

the more distantly related clansman Zhao Zhonghu (who was a collector of antiquities). In addition, Huizong invited Cai Jing and several of Cai's sons and grandsons, including Cai Tiao, who the year before had married Huizong's fifth daughter (whether Cai Tao, then twenty–two or twenty–three, was among the guests is not clear). [1]Cai Jing had for several years been semiretired, coming to court only once every five days. Other guests included the senior official Wang Fu who had been on the Council of State for over a year, and the eunuch military commander Tong Guan, on the Council of State since 1116.

After the guests passed through beautiful gardens and arrived at Harmony Preserved Hall, they found that preparations had been made for their visit. Huizong's seat had been placed in the center of the hall which had the side rooms holding books, bronzes, paintings, and calligraphies. Cai Jing, in his account of this occasion, portrayed Huizong as acting as the tour guide:

To our surprise the emperor personally pointed to different works of art and told us about them. Then he pointed to the studio where every one of the memorials in my hand had been stored. He ordered someone to open the case. In it was a red divider and behind the divider a small box, and in the box was something covered in silk, which turned out to be the appointment paper I had written for the Pure Consort Miss Liu. I said to the emperor, "My calligraphy is poor and my prose is bad. I didn't think you would have kept it". Not knowing how else to respond to him, I bowed my head deferentially. [23]

It can be seen that how grand the art collection was in the era of Emperor

1 The source for this story is the first chapter on page 276–279 in the remaining chapters of *Huichen Lu*; supplemented by the 40 chapter on page 1251–1252 in the History Part of *Xu Zi zhi Tong jian Changbian*; and letter 114. 5238–5239 of *Shuofu*.

2 He isn't listed in *Huichen Lu,* nor is he listed in Supplementary Supplements of *Xu Zizhi Tongjian Changbian*, although in a chapter in *Shuofu.*

3 (America) Patricia Buckley Ebrey, *Accumulating Culture: The Collections of Emperor Huizong* (translated into Chinese by Yin Lingyun and Bi Xia, to be published by Shanghai Calligraphy and Painting Publishing House), University of Washington Press, Seattle & London, 1984, p.123.

Huizong of the Song Dynasty. Emperor Huizong learned calligraphy first from Xue Ji, but changed his style into what he himself called the "Slender Gold Style".[1] His works, *Thousand–character Classic in Cursive Script*, collected in Liaoning Museum, quite spectacular, is written on paper, with the size of 31.5 cm in length and 1172.1 cm in width. Though the emperor's slender gold in regular script is commonly seen, his cursive script is really a rarity. This scroll is eleven meters in length, decorated with patterns of gold clouds and dragons. Accomplished at one stretch, the brushwork reflects a torrent of unpredictable changes, as if there were a rainstorm. It was executed in the fourth year of Xuanhe (1122) when the emperor was forty.

Song Huizong's art collection became part of the reason for the demise of the Northern Song Dynasty. However, Zhao Gou (1107–1187), Song Huizong's son, did not completely abandon the art of calligraphy and painting because of the demise of the Northern Song Dynasty. Zhao Gou, Emperor Gaozong of the Southern Song Dynasty, with the courtesy name Deji, was granted the title of Prince Kang in the third year of Xuanhe in the Northern Song Dynasty (1121), and enthroned in Lin'an in the second year of Jingkang (1127). During his reign for 36 years, he paid great attention to painting and calligraphy and was particularly diligent in calligraphy spending a considerable amount of time practicing calligraphy. Initially he learned from Huang Tingjian and then from Mi Fu, and went back to the masters of the Jin and Tang dynasties. His calligraphy had a tremendous influence on the kings and ministers of the Southern Song Dynasty. His works, *Ode to the Goddess of the Luo River*, collected in Liaoning Museum was written on silk with the size of 27.9cm in length and 398cm in width, of significance.

This scroll is a text reproduction of Cao Zhi's "*Ode to the Goddess of the*

1 Slender Gold Style: It is a unique style in the history of Chinese calligraphy, created by Zhao Ji, Huizong of the Northern Song Dynasty, and quite different from traditional styles such as regular script of Jin and Tang Dynasties. Writing Slender Gold Style, the brush movement is smart and fast, and the handwriting is thin and slender without losing its flesh.

Luo River." Executed in early cursive script, its brushwork displays an ancient simplicity with calmness and dignity. The layout is designed with precision and elegance. Though each character as an independent form is disconnected, there is a hidden link to impress it as a connected whole as if it is completed at one stretch. At the end of the scroll the signature characters of "Morality and Longevity Hall" are seen alongside a seal of "Morality and Longevity Hall of the Imperial Calligraphy Treasure", indicating that the work was completed in the Moral and Longevity Hall where Zhao Gou lived in seclusion after his abdication. [1]

It is rare in the world that the father and son are both emperors and calligraphers.

---

1 Referred to the introduction of the works in Liaoning Museum.

师徒授业谈

吴敢[1]

情景：2021 年 4 月 15 日深夜，吴敢教授在家中现场批阅外籍学生迪米的书画作业，直至 16 日凌晨约 2 点。下文中“吴”指吴敢教授，“赵”指赵子峰。

吴：你看，像你这里，就是你转时，因为你不知道怎么写，就特别生硬。然后，实际上，这几个圈圈是特别难的。

迪米：嗯！

吴：到最后这一点，点都是很实的，他用的是实笔，就像今天子峰说的，他觉得黄宾虹比我画得实，确实，他用实笔，都是吃住；那我呢？我有些地方用虚的，这样变化就多一点，更虚灵一点，像吴镇，他就基本上都是实笔；但是，倪瓒，他里面就有很多虚的地方。

赵：吴镇也是用秃笔。

吴：秃笔，顶得很牢。

赵：看他那个竹子，一笔一笔。

吴：是的。所以我都觉得你要有一点虚的东西。中国画，虚的东西就有很多，你如果虚的东西不知道，实际上你也不太能把握到位。譬如，临摹黄公望，就很难，黄公望他是实中虚，实里面带点虚的东西，又很潇洒。但是你完全用这种实的，你是达不到他那么潇洒的效果的。你一定要懂得，实里面怎么使它虚起来。（笑）所以，这个是很微妙的，真的。如果你能够用虚了，那你又跨进了一大步。

---

1 吴敢，祖籍浙江浦江，现居杭州，出身艺术世家，为中国美术学院书画鉴定专业教授，著名学者，硕士、博士研究生导师，中国美术学院书画鉴定中心主任，善于艺理，工于书法。此文为吴敢教授指导外国学生的现场教学谈话录，生动真实且极富洞见，他提倡“以书入画，书为画源”的高妙艺理。

我上次看西泠那个展览，有董其昌的那一张；然后，黄宾虹有两套册页，很好，但是看了董其昌那件，你就觉得董其昌还是更厉害，他有很多虚的地方，黄宾虹，如果，我觉得，再给他多少年，就像他自己说的，再有几十年的话，我觉得他可能会更好。

赵：实中虚，跟太极里面的图案很像，黑里面有白点，白里面有黑点。

吴：实中虚，虚中实。就是中国真正好的东西为什么要阴阳完美的平衡，就是因为，它可以长久，只有这样它的能量才能长久保持。阴多或者阳多，它都不能保持这么长久。所以，为什么好的艺术品你觉得到现在都还可以这么打动你，就是因为它里面的平衡。王羲之为什么好，品评里面说他是千古书生，说起来，他功夫不如张芝，天然不如智永，但是他两者都有啊！是吧？他这天然和功夫，这也是阴阳啊！他这两者结合的最好。

迪米：嗯！

赵：就像和珅与刘罗锅的关系。相互制衡。

吴：嗯！所以，（指着字帖）你如果知道它有一些哪里刻得不好，虽然像这样刻手已经走了很多，但是因为你有点知道了，你把它写出来的话，你会觉得，譬如说它里面还有许多虚的，你这个“尔”字可以比它写得更好，因为它这个里面还是都是实的。但是，实际上，你在里面可以看到这里面有很多虚的东西，因为这个里面藏有很多变化，你不是很使劲，这个就把笔按死了，你到这里面，哎！我往上再去一点，虚一点，再实一点，再虚一点，再实一点。然后，实际上，这一笔里面，你有很多虚实的变化，所以，你就比它丰富，比它好看美观。[1]

赵：我觉得吴老师在写这个的时候，他其实手很放松，其实只是用了很小的力，然后往下走，你也在顺着笔锋的力。

吴：其实也不是。其实如果你没有控制对，使这种蛮力，只能使这种关系更不对。虽然你看我没有使什么劲，但是实际上，我要比那种要使劲大得多得多，所以你听我写字的时候，就会有声音，就是像黄宾老说的，对的笔就像蚕食叶一样，有这种“嚓、嚓、嚓、嚓的声音”，因为你的笔是顶住的。若那个关系是对的，就有这种摩擦变化。反正这个里面很好玩的。（指字帖）这个里面完

1 临帖之高妙论。

全是实的，但实际上没有这笔好看（指吴自己的书法），因为它这笔有变化。[1]

赵：刻完之后拓出来就是黑的，没有墨韵。

吴：我觉得，迪米，就从这一笔里面，就可以看出你真正自然书写，你怎么在这里加一点虚的东西，然后会比这笔好，这笔完全用实的，但没有变化。你要知道如果是真正这些高手自然写出来，这一笔会是什么样的关系。[2]

迪米：嗯！

吴：所以说看古帖，你要在很多方面能够知道，那些刻工毕竟不是那些书手，因为那些刻工有刻不好的地方，但是你要知道，如果是那些高手的墨迹的话，它是会怎样，就是你不能完全按照它这个来。[3]

赵：吴老师讲得很透。

迪米：嗯！谢谢吴老师！

吴：哪里！画那些画，包括你即使画那种，你随便勾几笔的，那种笔墨的功夫都不是一般人能达到的。实际上还是就是在实践当中，还是有感觉的，像毕加索那样。

赵：用那个线。

迪米：这个是一样的。

吴：对，我那天看毕加索画的。他有好几个视频，我看了一下，我觉得还不错，但是，按照中国的要求，他还不够好。

迪米：哦！

吴：他还是用笔什么的，可能跟他的工具有关系。所以，他会显得那个动作稍微简单了一点。但是好看，他那个也还好看。但是，它里面，就是说中国画的里面，笔和笔之间的那种关系更复杂。可能因为毛笔比较软吧，比他那个硬，感觉他用的稍微简单一点。我估计可能就是。迪米，你就是拿笔，或者真正那个的时候，有些地方，你到这种地方（指作品），你的手腕已经是很不舒服了。

迪米：就是！

---

1 临帖之高妙论。

2 临帖之高妙论。

3 临帖之高妙论。

吴：像这种属于那个转得都卧在那里，怎么可以使这笔“咔”（示范动作）很舒展。然后，到这种地方，你笔不能偏，要始终是，譬如说：你什么时候拿起笔来画一个圆圈，笔都是能够知道的，这就说明你婉转就有点厉害了。

迪米：我试试！

吴：要不然，你画一个圈到这里，你的手就像这种一样，你的手腕就很不舒服了。你可以去试试看。

迪米：我回去试试！

吴：也可以多画几个圈，所以像什么以前说达·芬奇画蛋什么的，这是有道理的，道理一样。用笔是转了。怎么使画这种婉转的线条，你的笔在一个对的关系当中。

迪米：都一样吧，应该是，吴老师。

吴：好像你还不太能控制这种长锋，像这种哈（指作品）。

赵：确实，有时想想人和笔、笔和人就是相互磨合，控制不好笔就很野。

吴：笔不在正确的关系上去发展就会野。你像这种就是，写到这里时（指作品），笔已经塌掉了，吃掉了。你不要这样去用手腕去写它，这一笔不是这样的，你如果是这样去写的话，到这里你的手就锋又失掉了。你这笔就是。你的身体有多长全部都可以就“踏、踏”（动作示范），你不要这样去用手腕去写，这样去用手腕去写到这里你的手腕已经别扭了；而且，偏掉了，到这里就偏掉了。你看，我如果这样写，我的手又轻松，而且这个关系始终是对的，我没有说我的手腕会到这样的程度，到这样的程度，你经常这样写的话，一个你坚持不长久，另外一个，你的手腕经常处在很别扭的位置，就是要始终在对的关系中。

你如果书法里面的点能够写好，一个三点水“氵”你能够写对，那你要去画这种苔点那太容易了，因为“氵”好难啊，第一点还好一点，到第二点，尤其是第二点到第三点这个关系，第三点要往上提的，你的笔还不实，那你已经是高手了，你如果能把这个“氵”写好，你要去打这种苔点，那基本上已经不太有敌手了，真的（笑）。[1]

赵：感觉像练式功绝学，需要第几层第几层。

---

1 笔法之妙论。

吴：我跟你说，你真正明白这非常清楚的，谁好，他到底厉害在哪里，你很清楚了。你跟那种一比，你自己怎么样，就是一样的，很清楚的。你的笔墨功夫到一个什么样的境地，好不好？你是不是真的厉害，跟他们比还差多少，很清楚的。这种实际上就是标准还是很客观的。所以为什么像这些人，他对自己，很多人那个时候也不承认他，但为什么这些人对自己会这么自信，他觉得自己的画 50 年之后，就是会有知音的。就是因为他懂啊，他跟前面比，他知道自己的高度已经在那里了，他不需要一般的这种人的认可，对自己，他是很清楚的。我已经在哪里了，这些人很懂美术史的。前面的那个高度在那里，最根本的东西是什么，我有没有达到，都是在我们学校讲过中国画学，不是一般的小画家，真的。像这些人都是很清楚的，历史。

赵：吴镇当时也是啊。没有人买他的画。

吴：他们心里都太清楚了。这种实际上他自己到什么份上，前面的东西都有。他是很清楚的。迪米，先去找到楷书帖啊，因为最基础的东西，是最难的。而且你那个东西不明白，你后面是不能有太大自己的发展。

迪米：你建议我什么样都可以吗？

吴：就是你要去找一本你觉得比较喜欢的。

迪米：好的。

吴：多宝塔这种呢比较好入门，相对来说，因为颜体一开始你要写太难，它难的，颜柳都太难，初唐这几家比较容易入门。你要在那个基础上以后，你才可以去写颜真卿的那种小蘑菇后的这种东西。因为他那个全是用笔。很难。那个柳公权全是用笔，很难。所以欧啊宇啊褚啊，包括颜真卿早一点的这种都可以。就找一本帖，你把那个最基础的这些东真正就是抓握住了，你“永”字八法里面，至少你比如说有点啊、横啊、竖啊；那个比如说，撇笔难一点，那至少你那笔基本上能够写对，那你有个“永”字八法里面有个 4、5 法基本上能够写对以后，慢慢地，那就可以不断地再往上。[1]

实际上就是，中国画的基础是书法，你如果没有书法的话，一开始很容易落到形式上去。你的那种对中国画的认识就不对。你如果是从书法进入，以书入画的，它很多关系就容易理清。你字一旦写好了，要画点画很容易。只不

1　临帖之高妙论。

是抓握的形有点不一样。然后，你字的形能够把握好，你要抓握点画的形，有什么难的。画偶尔有什么地方你稍微率意一点，不到一点，没有问题的，字总共只有这么几笔，有一笔不到，就马上不能看了。所以像张彦远说：为什么以前的大画家都是大书家，道理就是这样。所以，迪米你如果能把中国毛笔字写到一定程度，你回去画那种画，那他们都膜拜了。（笑）[1]

迪米：我先去把字写写好。有意思嘛。

吴：对。我觉得你还是要在中国再待一段时间，然后把这一场你真正有时候有东西到一定高度，然后就不会退。就真正明白了，能够经常把握住它，这样才可以。你的资质，我觉得，实际上是很不错的，因为你有非常质朴、非常天真的这一块。

迪米：慢慢来。

吴：你不能慢慢来。有时候要有勇猛精进。好玩啊！

迪米：是很好玩。

吴：无穷尽。想想黄宾虹，如果他能再有几十年的话。如果能把普通人浪费掉的时间给这些人就好了哈！（笑）所以你在书法上能达到那样的高度，你要来画一点文人画，那是一点问题都没有，对他们来说，黄宾虹这种写字和画画会有区别吗？没有区别。

赵：以前字图一体的嘛，后来半图案半文字，然后就纯文字，分开了。

吴：（字）既是书又是圆形。它在那个情景里面。等到后面你脱离了那个情景了，再去琢磨那个支字，就感觉没这么有意思了。

赵：容易落到了另一个套路里吧。

吴：对。就是活泼的东西没了。这个写字、画画却是一样的。还是要气韵生动。要活的。文字也是这样。王羲之脱离当时那个情景也不行。迪米，不错的，还是很用功的。

迪米：好玩啊！我觉得很开心，我觉得不管怎样，好玩。

吴：对！很好玩！但是如果等到你（动作），这笔基本上能把握了，那这种好玩又会更好玩。

迪米：不一样。

---

1 书画关系论。

吴：就是。这个就是有时候，你把握住了以后，真的有一点那种、就是那种明道的这种喜悦。就是好像在很多那种物质的那种满足之上。

赵：但是还有那种状态，眼光和认识提高了，但是手上跟不上去。

吴：那会比较痛苦。手跟上了那就好了。如果你眼光永远在手之上，那里很好的。手可以不断进步的。所以他们很多人，他没有什么认识，他的手在他的心之上，这样就不行。

赵：弘一的悲喜交加，悲和喜相互转换。人生也是这样。

吴：大部分人都是这样，只有极少数人可以止于自善。一直保留，停留在那样的悟道的那种状态里面。大部分人都会退转，哎呀！这笔我碰到了，写对了，然后下一笔又不行了，对不对？你笔笔（笑）都写对的人到底少的。所以要止于自善很难的。就是大部分人都会只是偶尔的触碰到那个点。然后就马上又退步了（笑）。

赵：确实，很多艺术都要综合的，多练。悟性。

吴：确实很难啊！不练也不行，乱练也不行。往往就是，乱练后面改不过来了。好像你一点不练吧，你怎么会到对的路上去呢？所以好像这个也蛮难的。可能有时候就是，要有机缘，碰到好的东西，好老师，如果能碰到一个好的老师，或者，朋友当中突然在某个方面能够提供你跟你相互切磋，提供你进步的这种契机，或者偶然一个什么机会，你突然通过别的东西顿悟。

赵：某种现象，就像以前很多人。

吴：对的。公孙大娘舞剑悟道，张旭两个帖子写得真好。那是顶尖的水平。而且，他在二王的基础上，又有更多的变化。他有很多的变化又出于二王之外。所以他的那个有很多很奇异的、鬼形异状的那种东西，比较典雅。但是到了张旭，他有很多没有那么典雅，但是他的变化更加出人意表。二王有很多用圆的地方，张旭有很多用方的地方。

赵：方？

吴：对。他是以方来求圆圈的。你去看帖里面，张旭的那两个帖写得太好了。就是跟二王比，形没有二王那么典雅，那么好看，但是他的那个用笔直锋功夫多变，还在二王之上。

赵：怀素听嘉陵江水而悟道。黄宾虹看雨淋墙头悟道。自然界有很多东西可以去发现。

吴：你要有很多积累，才可以通过这样悟道。看到这种现象的人多了，有几个能够悟到那个道理，是吧。（取出一轴画）这个黄宾虹把它临过，把它临成了一套册页。上次美术馆展过。我也想来临一下。（这里）都是硬折的，是不是？像这种都写的不对，那张写得好一点。但是，按理说，像他们这种，只要把握应该就不会，这说明他的动作，包括像这种都还是有问题。就是可能他写这一笔的时候，他的手腕确实还没有完全把握住。才会有这样的问题。你看，实际上，这笔也都是不对的。这笔也都不对。这种、这个形，还是很尖翘，它不是那种正确的笔势带过来的。但是，他就是把"尖翘"作为他的特色的话；这一片写得特别好，他就把它的……这一片马一浮和他写的、跟他写得特别像。是吧？特别像马一浮写的。然后，他露锋就露锋了，有什么关系呢？这就变成他的特点了。这也蛮好看的。这里失掉了，好像每个人都有一两笔把握不太好的。

就是"永"字八法，每一笔都写好的人还是很少的。这个确实有点难。所以，像他们写这种笔，我就不太喜欢的。好像太露，我还是觉得要写的、要把锋含一点，吃进去，像这种方，我不会把笔这样露着。我肯定要把这个笔顶住，收进去，这样我觉得含蓄一点，好看一点。我觉得，你只要把你的特色发挥了，也就没有问题。他自己这样，另有一番面貌，各自审美观可以有不同，就把你的魅力发挥出来就行了，没有一定之规。[1]

1 笔法之妙论。

The Teaching Conversation

Wu Gan[1]

Scenario: Late at night on April 15, 2021, Wu Gan was reviewing his foreign student Dimi's calligraphic and painting homework at home, which ended until about 2 a.m. on the morning of the 16th. In the following, Wu stands for Professor Wu Gan, with zhao referring to Zhao Zifeng.

Wu: Look, here, it's very blunt, because when you turn you don't know how to write. Then, in fact, these circles are particularly difficult to write.

Dimi: Hmm!

Wu: We can see that the last points are very solid. He, Huang Binhong, used the solid brushstroke. As Zifeng said today, in his view of point, Huang Binhong painted more solid than me. Indeed, he used solid brushstrokes. All are steady and concrete against the paper; what about me? I use vacant and feeble brushstrokes in some places, so that there will be more changes with a little more ethereal spirit. Like Wu Zhen, he basically uses solid brushstrokes; however, Ni Zan is on the contrary, and there are many vacant and ethereal things in his works.

Zhao: Wu Zhen also uses bald brushes.

Wu: Bald brushes are very strong and steady against the paper.

---

1 Wu Gan, is from a family of artists, a native of Pujiang, Zhejiang Province, now living in HangZhou. He is a famous professor and scholar of Calligraphy and Painting, in China Academy of Art, He is excelled at art theory and calligraphy. This article is an on–site teaching conversation record by Professor Wu Gan, instructing his foreign students. It is full of deep insights, vivid and true. He advocates the brilliant art theory of "Painting starting with calligraphy, with calligraphy as the source of painting".

Zhao: Look at his bamboo, stroke by stroke.

Wu: Yes. Therefore, I think you need something blank and ethereal. There are many ethereal and imaginary things in Chinese paintings. If you don't know the ethereal things, you will actually not be able to grasp them well. For example, it is very difficult to copy Huang Gongwang's works. Huang Gongwang's is ethereal in the solid, very concrete, and very unrestrained. There is something in his, and there is something vacant in the solid. It looks like a solid brushstroke, but if you are completely to write in this kind of solidness, you can't achieve such an unrestrained effect as his. You must understand how to make it ethereal in the solid. (Laughs) So, this is very subtle, really. If you can use the ethereal, which means you have taken another big step forward.

Last time I visited the exhibition by Xiling, where there was the one by Dong Qichang; two sets of albums by Huang Binhong, very good. However, after seeing Dong Qichang, you think Dong Qichang is still more powerful. He has a lot of emptiness. If Huang Binhong, I think, is given more years to, as he said by himself, if there are more decades, I think, he might be better.

Zhao: The relationship between solidness and the emptiness is very similar to the patterns in Tai Chi, where are white dots in the black and black dots in the white.

Wu: The solidness is in the emptiness and the emptiness in the solidness. This is why the real good things in China need the perfect balance of Yin and Yang, because it can last for a long time, and only in this way can its energy be maintained for a long time. If there is too much yin or yang, it cannot last so long. So, why do you think a good artwork can still move you so much till now? It is because of its balance inside. Why is Wang Xizhi good? It is said in the review that he was a scholar of thousands of ages. Speaking of it, his skill is not as good as Zhang Zhi's, and his nature is not as good as Zhong Yong's, but he had both! Right? His nature as well as skill from diligence is also something of yin and yang! He is the best combination of both.

Demi: Hmm!

Zhao: It's like the relationship between He Shen and Liu Luoguo, restraining and balancing each other.

Wu: Yes! So, (pointing to the copybook) If you know some of it is not well engraved, although you have already lost a lot like this, but because you know a little bit, if you write it out, you can feel, for example, it, there are many vacant things in it. You can write the character "er 尔 " better than it, because it is all still fully solid inside. However, actually, you can see a lot of emptiness in it, because there are many variations in this. You are not writing very hard, and if so, this will press the brush to death. You are moving to here, hey! My brush goes up a little bit more, a little more emptily, a little more solidly, a little more emptily, a little more solidly. Then, in fact, in this brushstroke, you have a lot of changes, solid and vacant, so yours are richer than it, and more beautiful and better–looking than it.[1]

Zhao: I think when Master Wu is writing this, he actually is in a very relaxed hand. In fact, you use a very small amount of force and then go down, and you are also borrowing the force of the brush.

Wu: Actually not. In fact, if you can't control the brush right, using this kind of brute force, you only make this kind of relationship worse. Although you see that I don't exert much effort and power, I actually spend much more effort than that, so when you listen to me writing, you can hear a sound, just as Huang Binhong said, the right brushstrokes are just like silkworms nibbling on leaves, there is this kind of sounds "cha, cha, cha, cha," because your brush sticks to resisting the paper. If the relationship is right, there is this kind of friction changes. Anyway, this is very fun.

This (Pointing to the copybook) is completely true, but in fact it is not as good–looking (Pointing to Wu's own calligraphy), because it has variations. [2]

1 This is the sublime remarks of copying the copybook.

2 This is the sublime remarks of copying the copybook.

Zhao: After the engraving, it will be black without any ink rhyme.

Wu: I think, Demi, from this brushstroke, you can see that you really write naturally. If you know how you can add a little vacant feeling here, then it will be better than this brushwork. This brushstroke is completely solid with no changes. You need to know what kind of relationship this brushstroke would be like if it were written naturally by these masters.[1]

Demi: Hmm!

Wu: So when you read ancient copybooks, you need to be able to know in many ways that those carvers were not those of calligraphers after all, because those carvers were not good at carving, but you have to imagine that if it is a master, if it is really written in ink, what it will be like, that is, you can't copy it completely. [2]

Zhao: Master Wu explains it very thoroughly.

Demi: Hmm! Thank you Master Wu!

Wu: Welcome! To draw those paintings, even if you draw the kind you just stretch a few brushstrokes, the skill of that kind of brushstrokes is not something ordinary people can achieve. Right! In fact, it is still in practice that it can be felt, as Picasso did.

Zhao: Use that line.

Demi: The same.

Wu: Yes, I saw Picasso painting that day. He has several painting videos, I watched them, and I think it's not bad, but according to Chinese requirements, he is not good enough.

Demi: Oh!

Wu: He still uses a brush or something else, which may have something to do with his tools. Therefore, he will appear to be a little simpler in that action. But it looks good, also good–looking. However, in it, that is, in Chinese painting,

---

1 The sublime remarks of copying the copybook.

2 This is the sublime remarks of copying the copybook.

the relationship between brushstroke and brushstroke is more complicated. Maybe it's because the Chinese brush is softer and harder than his. It feels that he uses a little easier. I guess it might be so. Demi, when you just hold the brush, or when it is at that moment, in some places, when you go to this kind of place (pointing to the work), your wrist is already very uncomfortable.

Demi: Exactly!

Wu: Like this kind of turning brushstroke you turn it lying there when you turn, how can you make this brushstroke "Ka" (demonstration movement) very stretching. Then, to such a place, your brush can not be deflected, but always be controlled; for example, when you pick up the brush to draw a circle, you can know where the brush can go, which shows that you are a little good at turning the wrist.

Demi: Let me try!

Wu: Otherwise, if you draw a circle here, your hands goes like yours, and your wrists will be very uncomfortable. You can try it.

Demi: Going back, I'll try!

Wu: You can also draw a few more circles, so it makes sense Da Vinci painted eggs and the same is true of that. The brush is turned. How can you draw such tactful lines that your brush is in a right relationship?

Demi: It's all the same. It should be, Master Wu.

Wu: It seems that you still can't control this kind of long brush tip, such as this kind (pointing to works).

Zhao: Indeed, sometimes thinking about the writer and brush, the brush and writer, there is just an adaption to each other. If you don't control the brush well, it's very wild.

Wu: If the brushstroke is not developed in the right relationship, it will be wild. Like this, when you write here (pointing to works), the brush has collapsed and was eaten up. Don't write it with your wrist like this. This brushstroke is not like this. If you write like this, your hand will be lost again, as is this. You can stretch your brush just "Ta, Ta" (action demonstration) as long as your body is. Don't use your wrist to write like this. If you use your wrist to write here, your wrist is already awkward; moreover, it's off and lost deflected. It's off and lost deflected here. You see, if I write like this, my hands are relaxed, and the relationship is always right. I don't say that my wrist will reach such an extent. To such an extent, if you often write like this, you won't hold on for long. Another, your wrist is often in a very awkward position, that is, your brush must always be in the right relationship.

If you can write the dots in calligraphy well, and you can write a three–point radical " 氵 " correctly, then it is easy enough for you to draw this kind of moss dots, because " 氵 " is so difficult to write well. The first point is better; to the second point, especially the relationship between the second to the third point, the third point is to be raised; your brushstroke is not solid. You are already a master, if you can write this " 氵 " well, if you are going to paint this kind of moss dots, and you basically have no rivals anymore, really (laughs). [1]

Zhao: It feels like practicing kungfu, needing levels.

Wu: Let me tell you that if you really understand this very clearly, you know very well who is good, and where he is really good. Comparing you with that, how you yourself is, the same, it's very clear. What kind of situation is your brush–and–ink skill? Are you truly skillful? How much are you shorter than them compared with them? It's very clear. This kind of standard is actually very objective. So why do people like these guys, he treats himself, many people didn't recognize him at that time, but why were these people so confident in themselves? He felt that after 50 years he would have a friend knowing well his paintings. It's because he understood these. Compared with the previous ones, he knew where his height is already. He didn't need the recognition of ordinary people. He knew himself very well: Where I am already; and these people know art history very well. The height ahead is there, what the most fundamental

1 Wonderful theory of brushwork.

thing is, whether I have reached it or not. All these are what I have talked about Chinese painting in our teaching. Not an ordinary little painter, really. People like these are very clear about history.

Zhao: Wu Zhen was also the same at that time. No one bought his paintings.

Wu: They are all extremely aware of these in their hearts. In fact, where he reached can be seen in everything in front of him. He was very aware of that. Demi, find the regular script to copy first, because the most basic things are the most difficult. And if you don't understand that, you can't have much of your own development in future.

Demi: Can you suggest me something?

Wu: You are going to find a copybook you think you prefer.

Demi: Ok.

Wu: Duobao Pagoda is a better way to get started. Relatively speaking, it is too difficult for you to practice Yan Style at the beginning; it is difficult. Yan and Liu styles are too difficult, and the styles of the early Tang Dynasty are easier to learn. You have to build on that foundation before you can write things like Yan Zhenqing's little mushroom. Because that is all about the skills how he only uses brushstrokes, which is very hard. In Liu Gongquan's style, that is all about the skills how he only uses brushstrokes, which is very difficult. Therefore, Ou, Yu, Chu, including the early style of Yan Zhenqing, these can be followed. Just find a copybook. You try to have grasped the most basic elements. In the Eight Methods of the character "Yong 永 ", you at lease grasp a dot, a horizontal, and a vertical. For example, it is more difficult to write the brushstroke of left falling. At least your brush can basically be moved correctly, then you have grasped 4 and 5 methods that can basically be written correctly in the eight methods of a "Yong", and you can slowly continue to improve more. [1]

As a matter of fact, the basis of Chinese painting is calligraphy. If you don't have calligraphic skills, it is easy to fall into the form in painting at first;

---

1 This is the sublime remarks of copying the copybook.

your understanding of Chinese painting is wrong. If you enter painting from calligraphy and use calligraphic skills to paint, many of the relationships will be easy to sort out. Once you have written your handwriting well, it is easy to draw little dots. It's just that the shape to be held has a bit differences. Then, if the shape of your character can be grasped well, you have no difficulty grasping the shape of the painting at all. Occasionally, there are some places in the painting that you are a little rash, a little lost, and there is no problem. The character is only made up of a few strokes in total, and if there is a stroke lost, it will be terrible immediately. As Zhang Yanyuan said, that's why the great painters in the past are all great calligraphers. That's the truth. So, Demi, if you can write Chinese calligraphy to a certain extent, and you go back to draw that kind of painting, then they will all worship you. (Laughs) [1]

Demi: I'll go and write the characters first. It's interesting.

Wu: Yes. I think you still have to stay in China for a while, and then you really have something to a certain high level in this, and then you will not retreat, really understanding it, and can grasp it often, so you've got it. Your aptitude, I think, is actually very good, because you have a very simple and innocent one.

Demi: Take my time and slowly.

Wu: You can't take your time and slowly. Sometimes you have to be courageous and diligent to go forward. It's fun!

Demi: It's fun.

Wu: Endless. Think of Huang Binhong. Only if he could have a few more decades! It would be great if the time wasted by ordinary people could be given to these people! (Laughs) So you can reach that height in calligraphy. If you want to paint a little literati painting, there is no problem at all. For them, is there any difference between Huang Binhong's writing and painting? There is no difference.

Zhao: In the past, the character and picture were integrated, but later half

1 On the relationship between calligraphy and painting.

pattern and half character, and then pure characters, separated.

Wu: (Characters) are both calligraphy and circles. It is in that scene. When you get out of the scene later, then ponder the separated character, it doesn't feel so interesting.

Zhao: It's easy to fall into another routine.

Wu: Yes. The lively spirits are gone. The writing and drawing are the same. Still have to be vivid. To be live. The same goes for the character. If Wang Xizhi departed from the context at the time, it is not good, either. Demi, very good, and still very hardworking and diligent.

Demi: It's fun! I think it's fun, I think it's fun anyway.

Wu: Yes! It's fun! But if you wait until you (action) can grasp this brushstroke, then this kind of fun will be even more fun.

Demi: It's not the same.

Wu: Exactly. This is sometimes, after you grasp it, there is really a bit of that kind of joy, which is the kind joy of awareness of the essence, seeming to be beyond the top of the satisfaction of a lot of that kind of material.

Zhao: But there is still a state where the vision and understanding have improved, but your hand can't keep up with it.

Wu: That will be more painful. Just keep your hands up with that. If your eyes are always beyond your hands, it's great on earth. The hand can continue to improve. So, many of them don't know much, and his hand is above his heart, and then it won't work.

Zhao: Hongyi's sorrow and joy mixed? Sadness and joy are interchangeable. Life is the same.

Wu: Most people are like this, and only a very small number of people can stop at self–improvement, keeping it all the time, and remaining in that state of enlightenment. Most people will retreat, oops! I happen to catch this brushstroke, which I write right, and then the next one won't work. Right? How few are people who write correctly (laughs) every brushstroke. So it's hard to stop at self–improvement. That is, most people will only touch that spot occasionally, then immediately regressed (laughs).

Zhao: Indeed, many arts need to be integrated and practice more. Savvy realization.

Wu: It's really hard! It's not good if you don't practice and you can't practice indiscriminately. Often, it is impossible to change after random training. It seems that if you don't practice at all, how can you get on the right path? So it seems to be quite difficult. Maybe sometimes, you have to have chance to meet good things, and good teachers; if you can meet a good teacher, or suddenly in some aspect among friends, you can learn from each other and provide you with this kind of improvement. By chance, or by accident, you suddenly have an epiphany through something else.

Zhao: A certain phenomenon, just like many people before.

Wu: That's right. Aunt Gongsun by dancing her sword enlightened Tao; Zhang Xu wrote two copybooks really well. That is the peaking level. Moreover, he has more changes on the basis of the two Wangs. Many of his changes came from outside of the two Wangs. So his has a lot of weird, ghost–shaped features, which are more elegant. However, speaking of Zhang Xu, many of his were not so elegant, but his changes were even more unexpected. The two Wangs has many features using circles, and Zhang Xu has many using squares.

Zhao: Squares?

Wu: Yes. He pursued the round through the square. Look at the copybooks. Those two copybooks by Zhang Xu are extremely exquisitely written. Compared with the two Wangs', his shape is not as elegant and beautiful as the two Wangs', but his straight–forward brushstroke skill moving the brush tip is changeable, going still beyond the two Wangs.

Zhao: Huai Su understood the Tao by listening to the Jialing River. Huang Binhong watched the rain shower on the wall and got enlightened. There are many things to discover in nature.

Wu: You need a lot of accumulation before you can enlighten the way through this. There are more people who see this phenomenon, and a few can realize the truth, right? (Take out the one painting handscroll) This, Huang Binhong copied it and turned it into a set of albums, which last time was exhibited at the museum. I want to copy it, too. (Here) are all straight folds, right? Features like this are all written wrong, but that piece is better. However, logically speaking, like them, as long as you grasp it, you shouldn't. This shows that his actions, including those like this, are still problematic. It is possible that when he moved this brush, his wrist hadn't fully grasped it. There will be such a problem. You see, in fact, this brushstroke is also wrong. This brush is also wrong. This and this shape is still very sharp, because it is not brought by the correct gesture. However, if he just made the "pointed clevis" his characteristic, this piece is particularly well written, so he wrote it... This piece, is very similar to the style that Ma Yifu wrote. Isn't it? Especially like the style that Ma Yifu wrote. Then, he will show up, what does it matter? This became his characteristic. This is also pretty good–looking. It's lost here. It seems that everyone has one or two strokes that are not very good at.

It is the eight methods of the character "Yong 永 ", and there are still very few people who write each stroke well. This is really difficult. Therefore, I don't like them very much when writing brushstrokes are like this, seeming to be too exposed. I still think that if you want to write, you need to include a little bit of the front and eat it in, like this kind of square, I will not expose the brushstroke like this. I will definitely hold this brush and put it in, so that I feel a little more reserved and better–looking. I think that as long as you give full play to your characteristics, there will be no problem. He is like this, with a different feature, and one's own aesthetics can be different. Just show your charm, because there are no certain rules. [1]

---

1 Wonderful remarks of brushwork.

Word bank

1.scenario n. 脚本；剧情概要；梗概

2.blunt adj. 钝的；不锋利的；直率的；生硬的；耿直的 v.(使)变钝；使减弱

3.solid adj. 固体的；实心的

n. 固体；固体食物；立方体

4.brushstroke n. 一笔；一画；笔法

5.steady adj. 稳固的；固定的

6.vacant adj. 未被占用的；茫然的；空(着)的

7.feeble adj. 虚弱的；衰弱的

8.ethereal adj. 轻飘的；飘逸的

9.imaginary adj. 想象中的；假想的

10.unrestrained adj. 无节制的；不受限制的；放纵的

11.album n. 相册；集邮簿；画册；册页

12.copybook n. 临摹本；描红簿

13.engrave v. 雕刻；在……上雕刻；镌

14.sublime adj. 崇高的；高尚的；令人崇敬的；壮丽的

15.calligrapher n. 书法家

16.adaption n. 适应；适应性变化过程

17.horizontal adj. 水平的；横向的；统一的；一致的；地平线的

18.vertical adj. 垂直的；竖的

19.regress v. 退回；倒退；退化

20.savvy n. 智慧；实际知识 v. 知晓；懂 adj. 聪慧的；具有实际知识的

21.indiscriminately adv. 任意地；差别地；无例外地

22.epiphany n. 耶稣显现；显现节；神灵的显现；顿悟的时刻；大开眼界的时刻

23.enlighten v. 启发；启迪；开导

24.accumulation n. 积累；积聚；堆积

25.handscroll n. 手卷

中国书法[1]

林语堂[2]

中国书法的地位在世界艺术史上确实无足与之匹敌者。因为中国书法所使用的工具为毛笔，而毛笔比之钢笔来得潇洒而机敏易感，故书法的艺术水准，足以并肩于绘画。中国人把“书画”并称，亦即充分认识此点，而以姊妹艺术视之。然则二者之间，其迎合人民所好之力孰为广博，则无疑为书法之力。书法因是成为一种艺术，使有些人费绘画同样之精力、同等之热情，下功夫磨炼，其被重视而认为值得传续，亦不亚于绘画。书法艺术家的身份，不是轻易所能取得，而大名家所成就的程度，其高深迥非常人所能企及，一如其他学术大师之造诣。中国大画家像董其昌、赵孟頫同时又为大书法家，无足为异。

赵孟頫（1254—1322）为中国最著名书画家之一，他讲他自己的绘画：“石如飞白（笔触中带有空心笔画）木如籀（笔画相对均匀且扭曲），写竹还于八法通。若也有人能会此，方知书画本来同。”

据我看来，书法艺术表示出气韵结构的最纯粹的原则，其与绘画之关系，亦如数学工程学天文学之关系。欣赏中国书法，意义存在于忘言之境，它的笔画、它的结构只有在不可言传的意境中体会其真味。在这种纯粹线条美与结构美的魔力的教养领悟中，中国人可有绝对自由贯注全神于形式美而无庸顾及其内容。一幅绘画还得传达一个对象的物体，而精美的书法只传达它自身的结构与线条美。在这片绝对自由的园地上，各式各样的韵律的变化，与各种不同

1　本文摘录自林语堂著名的论文集《吾国与吾民》，访问时间2022年1月2日，https://www.haoshuya.com/11/8288/565700.html#headid。

2　林语堂（1895—1976），原名和乐，出生于福建龙溪，在香港逝世。他毕业于莱比锡大学，中国著名作家、学者，新道家代表人物。其曾创办《论语》《人间世》等刊物，代表作品有《京华烟云》《东坡诗文选》等。

的结构形态都经尝试而有新的发现。中国之毛笔，具有传达韵律变动形式之特殊效能，而中国的字体，学理上是均衡的方形，但却用最奇特不整的笔姿组合起来，是以千变万化的结构布置，留待书家自己去决定创造。如是，中国文人从书法修炼中渐习的认识线条上之美质，像笔力、笔趣、蕴蓄、精密、遒劲、简洁、厚重、波磔、谨严、洒脱；又认识结体上之美质，如长短错综、左右相让、疏密相间、计白当黑、条畅茂密、矫变飞动，有时甚至可由特意的萎颓与不整齐的姿态中显出美质。因是，书法艺术齐备了全部完美观念的条件，吾们可以认作中国人审美的基础意识。

书法艺术已具有两千年的历史，而每一个作家都想尽力创造独具的结体与气韵上的新姿态。是在书法中，我们可以看出中国艺术精神的最精美之点。有几种姿态崇拜不规则的美，或不绝的取逆势却能保持平衡，他们的慧黠的手法使欧美人士惊异不置。此种形式在中国艺术别的园地上不易轻见，故尤觉别致。

书法不独替中国艺术奠下审美基础，它又代表所谓“性灵”的原理。这个原理倘能充分了解而加以适当处理与应用，很容易收得有效的成果。上面说过，中国书法发现了一切气韵结体的可能的姿态，而它的发现系自然界摄取的艺术的灵感，特殊是从树木鸟兽方面——一枝梅花，一条附有几片残叶的葡萄藤，一支跳跃的斑豹，猛虎的巨爪，麋鹿的捷足，骏马的劲力，熊罴的丛毛，白鹤的纤细，松枝的纠缠盘结，没有一种自然界的气韵形态未经中国画家收入笔底，形成一种特殊的风格者。中国文人能从一枝枯藤看出某种美的素质，因为一枝枯藤具有自在不经修饰的雅逸的风致，具有一种含弹性的劲力。它的尖端蜷曲而上绕，还点缀着疏落的几片残叶，毫无人工的雕琢的痕迹，却是位置再适当没有，中国文人接触了这样的景物，他把这种神韵融会于自己的书法中。他又可以从一棵松树看出美的素质，它的躯干劲挺而枝杈转折下弯，显出一种不屈不挠的气派，于是他把这种气派融会于他的书法风格中。吾们是以在书法里面有所谓“枯藤”、所谓“劲松倒折”等等名目喻书体者。

有一著名的高僧曾苦练书法，久而无所成就，有一次闲步于山径之间，适有两条大蛇，互相争斗，各自尽力紧挣其颈项，这股劲势显出一种外观似觉柔和纡缓而内面紧张的力。这位高僧看了这两条蛇的争斗，猛然而有所感悟，从一点领悟上，他练成一种独有的书体，叫做“斗蛇”，乃系模拟蛇颈的紧张纠曲的波动的。是以书法大师王羲之（321—379）作《笔势论》，亦引用自然界之物象以喻书法之笔势：

> 划如列阵排云，挠如劲弩折节，点如高峰坠石，直如万岁枯藤，撇如足行趋骤，捺如崩浪雷奔，侧钩如百钧弩发。

The Chinese Calligraphy[1]

Lin Yutang[2]

The position of Chinese calligraphy in the history of the world's art is truly unique. Owing to the use in writing of the brush, which is more subtle and more responsive than the pen, calligraphy has been elevated to the true level of an art on a par with Chinese painting. The Chinese are fully aware of this when they regard painting and calligraphy as sister arts, *shu–kua*, "calligraphy and painting," forming almost an individual concept and always being mentioned in the same breath. Should there be a question as to which has a wider appeal, the answer would undoubtedly be in favour of calligraphy. It has thus become an art cultivated with the same passion and devotion, dignified by as worthy a tradition, and held in as high esteem as painting itself. Its standards are just as exacting, and its masters have reached heights as unattainable by the common run of men as the masters in other lines. The great Chinese painters, like Tung Gh'ich'ang and Chao Mengfu, are usually great calligraphers also.

Chao Mengfu (1254–1322), one of the best known of Chinese painters, said of his own painting: "Rocks are like the *feipo* style of writing (with hollow lines in the strokes), and the trees are like the *chuan* style of writing (with relatively even and twisted strokes). The method of painting lies yet in the 'eight

---

1 The article is an excerpt from Lin Yutang's famous essay collection *My Country and My People*, accessed on January 2, 2022, https://www.haoshuya.com/11/8288/565700.html#headid.

2 Lin Yutang (1895–1976), formerly known as Hele, was born in Longxi, Fujian province and died in Hong Kong, China. He graduated from The University of Leipzig. He is a famous Chinese writer, scholar and representative of new Taoism. He once founded *the Analects of Confucius, the World*, and other publications, with representative works are *Beijing, Dongpo Poetry* and so on.

fundamental strokes' of writing. If there is one who can understand this, he will realize that the secret of calligraphy is really the same."

It seems to me that calligraphy, as representing the purest principles of rhythm and composition, stands in relation to painting as pure mathematics stands in relation to engineering or astronomy. In appreciating Chinese calligraphy, the meaning is entirely forgotten, and the lines and forms are appreciated in and for themselves. In this cultivation and appreciation of pure witchery of line and beauty of composition, therefore, the Chinese have an absolute freedom and entire devotion to pure form as such, as apart from content. A painting has to convey an object, but a well–written character conveys only its own beauty of line and structure. In this absolutely free field, every variety of rhythm has been experimented upon and every type of structure has been explored.

The Chinese brush makes the conveyance of every type of rhythmic movement possible, and the Chinese characters, which are theoretically square but are composed from the oddest elements, present an infinite variety of structural problems which every writer must solve for himself. Thus, through calligraphy, the Chinese scholar is trained to appreciate, as regards line, qualities like force, suppleness, reserved strength, exquisite tenderness, swiftness, neatness, massiveness, ruggedness, and, restraint or freedom; and as regards form, he is taught to appreciate harmony, proportion, contrast, balance, lengthiness, compactness, and sometimes even beauty in slouchiness or irregularity. Thus the art of calligraphy provides a whole set of terms of aesthetic appreciation which we may consider as the bases of Chinese notions of beauty.

As this art has a history of well–nigh two thousand years, and as every writer tried to distinguish himself by a new type of rhythm, or structure, therefore, in calligraphy, if in anything, we are entitled to see the last refinement of the Chinese artistic mind. Certain types, such as the worship of beauty of irregularity or of a forever toppling structure that yet keeps its balance, will surprise the Westerners by their finesse, all the more so because such types are not easily seen in other fields of Chinese art.

What is of significance to the West is the fact that, not only has it provided the aesthetic basis for Chinese art, but it represents an animistic principle which may be most fruitful of results when properly understood and applied. As stated, Chinese calligraphy has explored every possible style of rhythm and form, and it has done so by deriving its artistic inspiration from nature, especially from plants and animals – the branches of the plum flower, a dried vine with a few hanging leaves, the springing body of the leopard, the massive paws of the tiger, the swift legs of the deer, the sinewy strength of the horse, the bushiness of the bear, the slimness of the stork, or the ruggedness of the pine branch.

There is thus not one type of rhythm in nature which has not been copied in Chinese writing and formed directly or indirectly the inspiration for a particular "style." If a Chinese scholar sees a certain beauty in a dry vine with its careless grace and elastic strength, the tip of the end curling upward and a few leaves still hanging on it haphazardly and yet most appropriately, he tries to incorporate that into his writing.

If another scholar sees a pine tree that twists its trunk and bends its branches downward instead of upward, which shows a wonderful tenacity and force, he also tries to incorporate that into his style of writing. We have therefore the "dry–vine" style and the "pine–branch" style of writing.

A famous monk and calligraphist had practised writing for years without result, and one day walking on a mountain path he chanced upon two fighting snakes, each straining its neck, which showed strength in apparent gentleness. From this inspiration he developed a most individualistic type of writing, called the "fighting–snakes" style, suggesting the tension and wriggling movement of the snakes' necks. Thus Wang Hsichih (321–379), China's "prince of calligraphists," spoke about the art of calligraphy in terms of imagery from nature:

Every horizontal stroke is like a mass of clouds in battle formation, every hook like a bent bow of the greatest strength, every dot like a falling rock from a high peak, every turning of the stroke like a brass hook, every drawn–out line like a dry vine of great old age, and every swift and free stroke like a runner on his start.

Word bank

1.subtle adj. 微妙的；细微的；难以描述的

2.in the same breath 相提并论

3.appeal v. 呼吁；吁请；恳请

4.undoubtedly adv. 确实地；毋庸置疑地；无疑

5.calligraphist n. 书法家

6.cultivation n. 耕作；教化；培养；栽培

7.witchery n. 巫术；魔法；魅力；魔力

8.conveyance n. 运送；载送；运输

9.rhythmic adj. 有节奏的；与节奏有关的

10.infinite adj. 无限的；无穷的

11.suppleness n. 顺从；柔软；易弯曲

12.exquisite adj. 极美的；美的；精致的

13.tenderness n. 柔软；亲切；柔和

14.swiftness n. 迅速；敏捷

15.neatness n. 整洁；干净

16.massiveness n. 沉重

17.ruggedness n. 坚固性；险峻

18.compactness n. 紧凑；小巧

19.slouchiness n. 懒散

20.irregularity n. 不规则；无规律

21.well–nigh adv. 几乎；差不多

22.distinguish v. 识别；区分

23.entitle v. 给……权利；给……题名

24.refinement n. 精炼；精制

25.worship n./v. 敬神；拜神；崇拜

26.topple v. 失去平衡；不稳而缓慢倒下

27.finesse n. 灵巧；精妙

28.animistic adj. 万物有灵论的

29.inspiration n. 灵感；吸气

30.plum n. 李子；梅子

31.vine n. 藤本植物；葡萄

32.leopard n. 豹

33.paw n. 爪子；手

34.sinewy adj. 肌肉发达的；多腱的；有力的

35.bushiness n. 繁茂

36.slimness n. 细长

37.stork n. 鹳；赐儿白鹳

38.elastic adj. 有弹性的；有弹力的

39.haphazardly adv. 偶然地；随意地

40.tenacity n. 固执；坚韧

41.strain v. 竭尽全力；使 (身体部位) 充分发挥功能

42.wriggling adj. 蠕动的；扭动的

绘　画

The Chinese Painting

奕奕欲生

中国美术史上有许多精于笔墨、善写生的画家，据传，画史尊称“画圣”的唐代著名画家吴道子笔画颇为传神，每次在龙兴寺绘制壁画时，寺里都挤满人观看他的现场创作。再譬如黄筌，据载，他字要叔，成都人。黄筌幼有画性，长负奇能。善画花竹翎毛，兼工佛道人物，山川龙水，全该六法，远过三师。[1]

花鸟师刁处士，山水师李昇，人物龙水师孙遇也。刁处士蜀，授而教之竹石花雀，又学孙位画龙水、松石、墨竹，学李昇画山水、竹树，皆曲尽其妙。

筌早与孔嵩同师，嵩但守师法，别无新意；筌既兼宗孙、李，学力因是博赡；损益刁格，遂超师之艺。

后唐庄宗同光年，孟令公知祥到府，厚礼见重。建元之后，授官职，赐紫金鱼袋。至少主广政甲辰岁，淮南[2]通聘，信币中有生鹤数只，蜀主命筌写鹤于偏殿之壁。警露者、啄苔者、理毛者、整羽者、唳天者、翘足者，精彩体态，更愈于

1　此部分由编者编写自《图画见闻志》《益州名画录》。
2　淮南：杨隆演为淮南节度使，后改称吴王建国，为五代十国之一。

生。往往生鹤立于画侧。蜀主叹赏，遂目为六殿鹤焉。先是蜀人未曾得见生鹤，皆传薛少保画鹤为奇，筌写此鹤之后，贵族豪家，竞将厚礼请画鹤图。少保自此声渐减矣。时人谚云："黄筌画鹤，薛稷减价。"广政癸丑岁，新构八卦[1]殿，又命筌于四壁画四时花竹、兔雉鸟雀。其年冬，五坊[2]使于此殿前呈武军进者白鹰，误认殿上画雉为生，掣臂数四。蜀主叹异久之，遂命欧阳炯撰《壁画奇异记》以旌之。又写《白兔》于缣素，蜀主常悬坐侧。有《四时山水》《花竹》《杂禽》《鸷鸟》《狐兔》《人物》《龙水》《佛道》《天王》《山居诗意》《潇湘八景》[3]等图传于世。石牛庙画龙水一堵见存。[4]

按故宫博物院藏、黄筌所画《写生珍禽图》，乃为其子所作，画稿极为精彩，画题为"珍禽"。其实为杂画，包括鸟雀、乌龟及昆虫数十种，无不奕奕欲生。此图为手卷，绢本，设色，纵 41.5 厘米，横 70.8 厘米，是黄筌传世的重要作品。画家用细密的线条和浓丽的色彩描绘了大自然中的众多生灵，尺幅不大的绢素上，画了昆虫、鸟雀及龟类共 24 只，均以细劲的线条画出轮廓，然后赋彩。24 只小动物均匀地分布在画面中，它们之间并无关联，亦无统一的主题。画幅左下角有一行小字："付子居宝习"，由此可知，这样一幅精妙的《写生珍禽图》只是作者为创作而收集的素材，是交给其子黄居宝临摹练习用的一幅稿本。[5]

1　八卦：传为伏羲氏所创。乾、兑、离、震、巽、坎、艮、坤分立八方，分别代表"天、地、雷、风、水、火、山、泽"八种事物与自然现象，世间万物皆可分类归至八卦之中，它亦是二进制与电子计算机的古老始祖。

2　五坊：唐代为皇帝饲养猎鹰猎犬的官署。

3　潇湘八景：《梦溪笔谈》："宋迪工画，其得意者有平沙雁落、远浦归、山市岚、江天暮雪、洞庭秋月、潇湘夜雨、烟寺晚钟、渔村夕照，谓之景。"按黄筌已有潇湘八景，可见不始于宋迪。

4　（宋）郭若虚著：《图画见闻志》，（宋）黄休复著，俞剑华注释，《益州名画录》，江苏美术出版社，2007年，第83—84页。

5　聂崇正，见故宫博物院官网，https://www.dpm.org.cn/collection/paint/228361.html。

As Vivid as Live

There are many artists who excel at meticulous painting with wonderful brush stroks, good at depicting things as vivid as live. It is legend that Wu Daozi, a famous painter in the Tang Dynasty, honored as "the Sage of Painting" in the painting history, was so expressive in his painting that every time he painted murals in LongXing Temple, the temple was packed with people watching his live creating attracted by him. Another example is Huang Quan, according to the records, whose courteous name Yaoshu, a native from Chengdu. Huang Quan has a gift of painting, always with a unique talent. He is good at drawing flowers, bamboo, and feathers, as well as Buddha and Taoist figures, mountains, rivers and dragons, in all the six methods, far beyond his three teachers.[1]

He learned to draw the flower and bird from his teacher Diao Chushi, landscape from Li Sheng, the figure, dragon and water from Sun Yu. Diao Chushi, from Shu, taught him to paint the bamboo, rock, flower, and finch. He also learned under Sun Wei to paint dragon, water, pine, rock, ink bamboo; and under Li Sheng to paint landscape, mountains, rivers, bamboo, trees, all to the best of its wonderfulness.

At first he studied with Kong Song under the same teacher, but Song only obeyed the rules with no new ideas. Because Quan concurrently learned from Sun and Li, he had a broad knowledge; he improved Diao's style, and therefore he was more excelled than his teacher in art.

---

1 This refers to (Song) Guo Ruoxu, *Tuhua jianwen zhi* annotated by Yu Jianhua. *Tuhua jianwen zhi*, Phoenix Publishing and Media, Inc, Jiangsu Fine Arts Publishing House, Nanjing, 2007, pp. 83–84. Besides, it also refers to *Yizhou Minghua Lu* by Huang Xiufu of the song Dynasty.

In the Tongguang Year of Zhuangzong of Later Tang Dynasty, Zhixiang, Duke Mengling, visited him to the house with great gifts. After the Jianyuan, he was granted to the official rank, given the Purple Fish Bag. Till the Jiachen Year reign of the Young Ruler Guangzheng, the Huainan[1] State made friends with others through messengers, and several living cranes were in the gifts, so the ruler of Shu ordered Quan to paint cranes on the wall of the partial hall. The ones, alarming, pecking moss, combing feathers, tidying the feathers, crying to the sky, skipping the foot, were in wonderful gestures, more vivid than the living. Cranes often stood by the side of the paintings. The Lord of Shu sang high praise for that, hence named it Six–Hall–cranes. Because the people of Shu had never seen living cranes before that and it was said that the cranes Xue Shaobao painted were wonderful. After Quan painted the cranes, the noble rich families would all offer generous gifts to get the crane painting by him. Since then, Shaobao's fame had faded. As the saying went at the time, "Huang Quan painted cranes, and Xue Ji discounted." In the Guichou Year of Guangzheng, a new structure Eight Diagrams[2] Hall was constructed, and Quan got the order to paint murals on the four walls with flowers, bamboo, rabbits, and pheasant birds. In the winter of that year, an official of the Wufang five–lane [3] palace presented the white eagle from Wujun in front of this hall, and the eagle mistook the painted pheasants for living ones, tugging the arm flying to them four times. The Lord of Shu was greatly amazed at that for a long time, and hence ordered Ouyang Jiong to write "The Record of Mural Singularity" to memorize it. He also depicted *White Rabbit* on white silk, which the Lord of Shu often hung by his seat. There were some paintings surviving such as *Landscapes of Four Seasons, Flowers and Bamboo, Miscellaneous Birds, Birds, Fox and Rabbit, Figures, Dragon with Water, Buddha, The Heavenly King,*

1 Huainan: Yang Longyan was the Military Governor of the Huainan garrison, and later he founded his own state and became the King of Wu, one of the Five Dynasties and Ten States.

2 Eight Diagrams: It is said to be created by Fuxi. Dry, Dui, Li, Zhen, Xun, Kan, Gen and Kun were in eight directions separately. They respectively stand for the eight objects and natural phenomena of "heaven, earth, thunder, wind, water, fire, mountain and swamp". Everything in the world can be classified into the Eight Diagrams, which is also the ancient ancestor of binary and electronic computers.

3 Wufang: an official workshop in the Tang Dynasty that raised falcon hounds for the emperor.

Poetic Life in Mountains, Xiaoxiang Eight Sights,[1] spread all over the world. Such a mural as the one on a wall of Shiniu (Stone Cattle) Temple painted as *Dragons with Water* survived.[2]

It is said *Rare Birds from Nature* portrayed by Huang Quan, collected in the Palace Museum in Beijing, is done for his own son, which is wonderful. Though it is titled as "rare birds", it is actually a painting with kinds of motif, including dozens of miscellaneous paintings, such as birds, turtles and insects, all alive and sound. This picture is a handscroll, on silk, in color, 41.5 cm×70.8 cm. It is an important work by Huang Quan handed down till now. The painter depicted many creatures in nature with fine lines and rich colors. On such a small piece of silk, he painted as many as 24 insects, birds and tortoises, all of which were outlined with fine lines and then endowed with color. The 24 animals are evenly distributed in the picture, but they are not related to each other, with out a unifying theme. There is a line of small characters in the lower left corner of the painting: "Fu Zi Jubao Xi 付子居宝习 (For my son Jubao to exercise)", from which we can know that such an exquisite painting as *Rare Birds from Nature* is only the materials collected by the artist for his creation, and it is a manuscript given to his son Huang Jubao for copying exercises.[3]

---

1 Xiaoxiang Eight Views: *In Mengxi Bitan* (*Brush Talks from Dream Brook*): "Song Di was good at painting, and his masterpieces included *Wild Geese Fall on the Flat Sand, The Sails Return from the Far Water, Sunny Haze around Mountain City, Evening Snow along the River, Autumn Moon above Dongting Lake, Night Rain in Xiaoxiang, Evening Bell Rings in Smoking Temple, Sunset in Fishing Village*, that is the Eight Views." According to this, Huang Quan already had Xiaoxiang Eight Views, it can be seen that it does not start from Song Di.

2 (Song Dynasty) Huang Xiufu, *Yizhou Minghua Lu* annotated by Yu Jianhua, Phoenit Publishing House, Nanjing, 2007, pp. 83—84.

3 Nie chonyzheng, see the official website of the Palace Museum, Beijing, https://www.dpm.org.cn/collection/paint/228361.html.

早期人物画

高居翰[1]

约公元100年，中国首部字典《说文》的作者写道："画，界也。"他把"画"字解释为，表示一只手执记号笔，画出田野的四条边界，也就是画出田野（"画，界也；象田四界；聿，所以画之"）。16世纪以降，个性独特的伟大画家石涛在其文章开篇中把一笔说成"万物之源"——我们几乎可以适其意地译为："笔画乃始"。

是始也是终；在中国绘画史上，以毛笔绘线，一直是核心事实。欧洲绘画也起源于一种线性艺术，但随着画家们的注意力从勾勒轮廓转向它们所封闭的东西，集中再现光影、体量和纹理，软化或模糊轮廓，从而降低了线条的重要性，绘画就失去了它的线性特性。中国画的过程则引向了一个不同的方向；中国艺术家从未特别在意忠实地再现表面的颜色和纹理或物质，而是更加强调笔墨本身，把它作为他们主要的描述和表达手段。风格运动倾向于打破个性独特的笔触的完整性，或从属于表面处理的线描，人们通常视之为非正统，认为这背离了主要传统。

中国现存最早的真画出现在两块大约公元前3世纪的丝绸碎片上，它们出土于现在湖南省长沙墓。这些画笔法精细，在墨笔线画定的区域里平填色彩，这已经体现了这种技法，甚至部分体现了在许多世纪里将一直保持着基本和正统的风格。它们是人类、恶魔、动物和植物的象征性代表，通过它们的轮廓，在中性的丝绸底面作为独立图像呈现。这种古老的再现方式对应着一种更为古

1　高居翰（James Cahill，1926—2014），生卒于美国加州。曾长期担任加州大学伯克利分校艺术史和研究生院的教授，以及华盛顿弗利尔美术馆中国书画部顾问。他的著作主要通过风格分析研究中国绘画史，成为经典，因而他享有世界范围的学术声誉，乃当今中国艺术史研究的权威之一。本文节选自《中国绘画》，第11—14页。

老的思维模式，其中“象”扮演着重要的角色，它是对自然现象、物体和世界各方面的抽象概括，与语境隔离开来，被概念化。最早的文字形式“象形文字”就是一种形象；另一个例子是被称为《易经》的古代占卜卦象，被认为是源于物质宇宙的视觉图案。画家所创造的形式也是另一种。当组成一个场景时，它们相互并置而不是整合。十之八九是虚空的；除了把一种形象与另一种形象分开，空间根本不存在。

这些人物画在一块泥板上，这块泥板出自汉末（公元前206年—公元22年）的一座墓穴，现庋藏波士顿美术馆，仍然单独矗立在一块形状不定的地面上。然而，这位艺术家已经发现了两种方法可使他的画统一：通过暗示的动作，人物似乎被一种共同的节奏所左右；通过绑定他们的眼神交流所显示的相互意识。这样一幅小画当然不能代表汉代绘画的最高成就，然而即使是这样一幅小画，也已经开始超越真正概念艺术的限制。它展示了观察的结果，尽管几乎可以肯定画家不是创作写生画（中国画家很少如此）。其中的男人是自给自足的，有意识的个体，而不仅仅是象征或刻板印象。此外，他们现在是宇宙戏剧中的小角色，因为无论这幅画主题为何（这还没有被明确确定），它显然无无宗教色彩。据当时的文献记载，这幅最伟大的汉代绘画是关乎世俗生活的。儒家思想代表了中国思想的理性主义和以人为本的一面，在国家和社会中占据了主导地位，它的影响延伸到绘画：儒家保持着陶冶情操的主题绘画，在社会中发挥着道德功能，净化了精神，升华了心灵。历史轶事和经典文献中图释的往昔名人画像最受尊敬。

波士顿瓷砖上绘制的人物容貌轮廓表明画家可能已经在试验惯用的笔法，虽然尚未意识到中国毛笔的全部潜力——也许是人类设计的最多才多艺、反应最快的绘画工具。以线条的宽度呈现出波纹状，这样以一种自发性的气氛来活跃画面，强调轮廓，加强动感，这似乎是许多汉代艺术的目标。纵观中国绘画史，衡量优秀作品的主要标准之一就是笔墨品质。同样的毛笔被用于写字，而自汉朝以降艺术或书法的辉煌兴起最终深刻地影响了绘画技法，但并未持续很

1 《易经》是阐述了天地世间关于万象变化的古老经典，包括《连山》《归藏》《周易》三部易书，现只有《周易》现存于世。该书从整体角度去认识和把握世界，把人与自然看做是一个互相感应的有机整体。其内容涉及哲学、政治、生活、文学、艺术等诸多领域，是儒道两家共同的经典。

久。波士顿瓷砖画的轻松笔法只在类似的非正式草图中保留下来，而几乎没有书法特征的最古老风格的纤细匀称线条，在更多的成品中仍然是几个世纪以来的标准。

公元 3 世纪初，汉朝解体，随后很长一段时间内中国分裂为数个小国，直到 6 世纪末，没有一个国家成功地征服了其他国家，统治整个中国。我们知道许多活跃在六朝时期的艺术家的名字，也知道他们的同时代人对他们的看法，因为正是这个时代产生了第一部关于绘画的品评文献。然而，在现存的所有真正的古画上都有这一时期唯一一位艺术家的名字，他就是约 345 年出生的顾恺之。他不仅因他的绘画而出名，而且因他古怪的言行而著称。时人称赞他“三绝：才绝、画绝、痴绝”。

The Early Figure Painting

James Cahill[1]

"To paint is to draw boundaries," writes the author of the *Shuo wen*, the first Chinese dictionary, around the year A. D. 100. He explains the character for hua, "to paint", as representing a hand grasping a marker and drawing the four boundaries of a field, that is to say, delineating a field. Sixteen centuries later, the great individualist painter Tao–chi was to open his theoretical treatise by speaking of the Single Brushstroke as "the origin of all existence, the root of the myriad phenomena" —one might almost, without violating the sense, translate: "In the beginning was the Brushstroke."

In the beginning and also in the end; the line drawn by a brush remains the central fact of Chinese painting throughout its history. Painting began in Europe also as an art of line, but lost its linear character as painters turned their attention from the outlines to what they enclosed, concentrating on the rendition of light and shadow, mass and texture, softening or obscuring contours and so lessening the importance of line. The course of Chinese painting led in a different direction; its artists, never so concerned with reproducing faithfully the color and texture of surfaces or the corporeality of mass gave ever greater emphasis to the brushline itself, taking it as their primary descriptive and expressive

1 James Cahill (1926–2014) was born and died in California, USA. He was a longtime professor of Art History and graduate school at the University of California, Berkeley, and a consultant to the Chinese Painting and calligraphy Department at the Freer Gallery in Washington. His works on the history of Chinese painting through style analysis have become classics, and he enjoys a worldwide academic reputation as one of the authorities in the study of Chinese art history today. This excerpt is taken from *Chinese Painting,* Rizzoli International, Inc., New York, 1977, pp. 11–14.

means. Stylistic movements that tended to destroy the integrity of the individual brushstroke, or to subordinate linear drawing to surface treatment, were generally regarded as unorthodox departures from the main tradition.

The earliest surviving examples of true painting in China are on two fragments of silk, dating from around the third century B.C, which were excavated from tombs at Ch'ang–sha in present–day Hunan Province. The pictures, drawn in fine, black ink brushline, with flat washes of color filling the areas thus bounded, exemplify already the technique, and even something of the style, that was to remain basic and orthodox for many centuries. They are symbolic representations of humans, demons, animals and plants, set off as separate images by their outlines from the neutral silk ground. This ancient mode of representation corresponds to an even more ancient mode of thought in which "images" (hsiang) played an important role as abstractions of natural phenomena, objects and aspects of the world isolated from context and conceptualized. The characters of the written language in their earliest form as "pictograms" were images of one kind; another was exemplified by the hexagrams of the ancient divination text known as the *Book of Changes*,[1] thought to be derived from the visual patterns of tie physical universe. The forms created by the painter were still another. When composed into a scene, they were juxtaposed without being integrated. Between and around ten was void; space had no existence except as that which separated one image from another.

The figures painted on a clay slab from a tomb of the latter part of the Han dynasty (206 BC–221 AD) now in the Museum of Fine Arts, Boston, still stand isolated against an amorphous ground. But already the artist has discovered two means of unifying his picture: through suggested movement, the figures seeming to be swayed by a common cadence, and through the mutual awareness revealed

1 *Book of Changes*: It is an ancient classic about the changes of the world, including the *Three Books of Changes, Lianshan, Guicang and Zhouyi.* Only *Zhouyi* exists today. The book, from a holistic perspective, understands and grasps the world, human and nature as a mutual induction of an organic whole. Its contents involve philosophy, politics, life, literature, art and many other fields. It is a common classic of Confucianism and Taoism.

in the exchange of glances that binds them. Even a minor drawing such as this—it certainly does not represent the highest achievements of Han painting—already begins to transcend the limitations of a truly conceptual art. It shows the results of observation, although the artist almost certainly did not paint from life (Chinese painters very seldom did). The men in it are self–sufficient, conscious individuals, not merely symbols or stereotypes. They are now moreover, minor players in a cosmic drama, for whatever the subject of the painting may be (it has not been clearly identified) it is apparently not in any way religious. The greatest Han painting, as reported in the literature of that period, was secular. Confucianism, representing the rationalistic and human–centered side of Chinese thought, had become dominant in state and society, and its influence extended to painting: pictures of edifying subjects, the Confucianists maintained, performed a moral function in society, refining the spirit and elevating the minds of men. Portraits of eminent personages of the past illustrations to historical anecdotes or classical texts were most esteemed.

The lineament in which the figures on the Boston tile are drawn, while it has not yet realized the full potentialities of the Chinese brush—perhaps the most versatile and responsive drawing implement devised by man—suggests that painters may have been experimenting already with idiomatic brushwork. Fluctuations in breadth of line serve to enliven the drawing with an air of spontaneity, to accent contours, to intensity that sense of movement which seems to have been the objective of much of Han art. One of the chief criteria of excellence in Chinese painting throughout its history is quality of brushline. The same brush was used for writing, and the brilliant rise of the art or calligraphy in the Han and later dynasties was eventually to affect profoundly the technique of painting. But not until much later; the relaxed brushwork of the Boston tile persists only in similarly informal sketches, while the thin, even line of the most ancient style, with little of calligraphic character, remains standard for centuries in more finished works.

The disintegration of the Han empire in the early third century A.D. was followed by a long period of division into smaller states, none of which succeeded in conquering the others and ruling the whole territory of China until the end of the sixth century. We know the names of many artists who were active during the intervening Six Dynasties period, and a little about what their contemporaries thought of them, for this is the age that produced the first critical literature on painting. The only artist of the period whose name is attached to any surviving pictures of real antiquity, however, is Ku K'ai–chih, born around the year 345. He was famous not only for his painting, but also for his eccentric speech and behavior. His contemporaries credited him with "pre–eminence in three fields: wit, painting and foolishness."

Word bank

1.boundary n. 分界线；边界；界限；击球超过边界线得分

2.delineate v. 准确描述；准确标出

3.individualist adj. 个人主义的 n. 个人主义者；利己主义者

4.theoretical adj. 理论的；理论上的；由理论得出的

5.treatise n. 论文；专著

6.brushstroke n. 一笔；一画；笔法

7.existence n. 存在；生存；实体；生活；存在物

8.myriad n. 无数；极大数量；一万 adj. 无数的；数量极大的；包罗万象的

9.phenomena n. 现象；phenomenon 的复数

10.violate v. 违反；违背；性侵犯；扰乱

11.linear adj. 摆成直线的；沿直线的；线形的

12.outline n. 轮廓画；略图；草图；提纲；速记形式 v. 描出……轮廓；概述；概括

13.enclose v. 围住；包围；随信附上；使(修道会或其他团体)与世隔绝

14.rendition n. 演绎；诠释；秘密引渡；译文；直译；视觉形象；视觉再现

15.obscure v. 隐藏；掩盖；使……模糊不清 n. 某种模糊的或不清楚的东西

16.obscuring adj. 隐晦的

17.contour n. 轮廓；周线；围线；等高线 v. 使与某轮廓吻合；在(地图、图表)上标等高线

18.lessen v. 变少；缩小

19.corporeality n. 肉体的存在

20.brushline n. 笔触

21.descriptive adj. 描述的；客观描述的；描写性的

22.expressive adj. 富于表情的；富于表现力的；表达的；表现的

23.stylistic adj. 风格的；文体的；讲究文学风格的

24.integrity n. 诚实；正直；完整；完全；完整性

25.subordinate adj. 下级的；级别低的；次要的；第二位的

n. 部属；下级 v. 使成为次要；使居于第二位；使隶属；使服从

26.unorthodox adj. 非传统的；非正统的；异端的

27.departure n. 出发；启程；离开；背离；横距

28.fragment n. 碎片；碎块；破片；片段；不完整的部分 v. 裂成碎片；使裂成碎片

29.excavate v. 挖掘；挖；在……发掘；把(地面)挖开

30.tomb n. 坟墓；冢；葬身之地

31.bound v. 跳动；跳跃着前进；形成界限；关；n. 跳跃；界限；边界；限制；限制范围；界 adj. 正在到……去的；准备到……去的；限制在某个场所的

32.exemplify v. 是……的例证；举例说明；作为……的例证

33.orthodox adj. 正统的；正宗的；普通的；正常的；正统派犹太教的；正教的

34.symbolic adj. 作为象征的；使用象征的；象征主义的

35.representation n. 代表；有人代表的状况；描述

36.demon n. 魔鬼；恶魔；精灵

37.neutral adj. 中立的；确定的；不带电的；中立国的；公正的 n. 中立者；中立国；非彩色；

38.mode n. 方法；做法；方式；模式

39.correspond v. 相似；相符；一致；通信；相当

40.image n. 形象；比喻；像；镜像；相似；幻象 v. 作……的像；描绘……的形象

41.abstraction n. 抽象；出神；心不在焉；孤立的考虑

42.isolate v. 使隔离；使孤立；使脱离；孤立处理 n. 被隔离的人；分离菌；隔离群

43.conceptualize v. 使概念化；使形成概念

44.pictogram n. 象形文字

45.hexagram n. 六线形；六角星形；卦象

46.divination n. 占卜；预测

47.derive v. 从……中获得；源自；来源于；从……得出；推导自

48.compose v. 创作；组成；构成；

49.juxtapose v. 并置；并列；并排摆放

50.integrate v. 使结合；使合并；使平等进入

51.void adj. 无效的；空的；空缺 n. 真空；空处；空虚；v. 宣告……无效；排泄；疏空

52.clay n. 黏土；泥土；陶土

53.slab n. 厚平板；石板；混凝土板料；案板；砧板；厚桌面 v. 去掉……膘皮

54.amorphous ad. 无固定形状的；不规则的；无组织的

55.sway v. 摇摆；摆动；管理；控制；统治 n. 有节奏的摇摆；统治；控制

56.cadence n. 声音的起落；终止式；终止；节奏；节律；抑扬顿挫；降调

57.bind v. 紧系；紧拴；固定；装订；给……镶边；n. 恼怒；法律约束；困境；尴尬的处境

58.transcend v. 超出；超越；胜过；超过

59.limitation n. 限制性规定；限定；追诉时效；限制

60.conceptual adj. 概念的；概念上的

61.observation n. 观察；言论；评论

62.conscious adj. 清醒的；感到的；意识到的

63.symbol n. 象征；符号；标志 v. 象征

64.stereotype n. 陈规；老套；铅版；铅版印刷；陈俗的人 v. 使成为老一套；使成为陈规

65.cosmic adj. 宇宙的；无比巨大的

66.secular adj. 尘世的；世俗的；不受教规约束的；在俗的

67.Confucianism n. 孔子学说；儒学；儒教

68.rationalistic adj. 理性主义的；理性论者；纯理论的

69.dominant adj. 最重要的；最有影响的；n. 占优势的事物；显性基因；属音；音阶第五音

70.edify v. 教诲；开导；启迪；教化

71.Confucianist n. 儒家

72.moral adj. 道德的；能尊奉道德规范的；有道德观念的；n. 道德教训；寓意；

73.elevate v. 举起；抬起；使上升

74.eminent adj. 卓越的；出众的；显赫的

75.personage n. 大人物；要人；人物

76.illustration n. 插图；说明

77.anecdote n. 轶事；趣闻；传闻

78.esteem n. 尊敬；敬重 v. 尊敬；敬重

79.lineament n. 特征；线性构造；线状行迹

80.tile n. 瓦；瓷砖；花砖；软木片 v. 用瓦盖；铺瓦于

81.potentiality n. 潜力；可能性

82.versatile adj. 多功能的；多才多艺的

83.responsive adj. 反应迅速的；积极反应的

84.implement n. 工具；器具；履行 v. 贯彻；实行；履行

85.devise v. 策划；发明；想出；遗赠

86.idiomatic adj. 习语的；符合语言习惯的

87.brushwork n. 笔法；绘画风格

88.fluctuation n. 波动；起伏；踌躇

89.breadth n. 幅度；宽度；广度；广泛性

90.enliven v. 使更有趣；使更吸引人

91.spontaneity n. 自发性；自然发生

92.accent n. 口音；腔调；重音；强调；高光 v. 强调；突出；以重音演奏

93.intensity n. 强烈；剧烈；强度

94.objective adj. 客观的；宾格的；客观存在的；真实的 n. 目的；目标

95.criteria n. 标准；准则

96.excellence n. 优秀；卓越；杰出

97.brilliant adj. 有才能的；聪明的；灿烂的

98.calligraphy n. 美术字；书法

99.profoundly adv. 深深地；深刻地

100.persist v. 坚持；执意；持续

101.informal adj. 不拘礼节的；轻松的

102.sketch n. 素描；速写；草图；短剧 v. 作素描；画速写

103.calligraphic adj. 书法的；美术字体的

104.disintegration n. 分裂；解体；瓦解

105.empire n. 帝国；天下；商业王国

106.division n. 部门；分开

107.conquer v. 击败；征服；攻占

108.territory n. 领土；版图；领地

109.intervene v. 插入；插手

110.antiquity n. 古代；古时；古迹

111.eccentric adj. 不合常规的；古怪的；怪僻的；偏心的 n. 古怪的人；怪僻的人

112.eminence n. 著名；卓越；出众

九鬲房读画札记

王超[1]

引言

人类对色彩的感知与其自身历史一样漫长，而有意识地应用色彩则是从原始人用固体或液体颜料涂抹面部与躯干开始的。在新石器时代的陶器上已经可见到原始人对简单色彩的自觉运用。

中国传统绘画中使用的颜料，按其原料不同，分为矿物和植物两种。植物性颜料又叫水色，色彩透明，可以相互调和使用，覆盖力较弱，色质不稳定，容易褪色，包括花青、藤黄、胭脂等。矿物性颜料又叫石色，是用矿石磨制加工而成，色彩厚重，相互不能调和使用，覆盖力强，色质稳定，不易褪色，有石青、石绿、石黄、朱砂、赭石等。敦煌壁画中就曾大量使用矿物性颜料，虽然历经千年，色彩依旧浓重艳丽。

中国古代文献中有许多关于绘画使用颜料的记载，南朝画家谢赫（479—502）提出“随类赋彩”的理论；唐代张彦远（618—907）在其成书于唐大中元年（847）的著作《历代名画记》中，叙述了当时绘画颜料的产地、使用以及各种颜料的性能等；唐代敦煌文书中有关于当时颜料价格的记述；[2]清初《小山画谱》《绘事琐言》两部书中，详细地描述了中国画颜料从选择原料、研磨、处理和使用的方法。但是，在绘画作为一项技艺的时代，绘画颜料的配方和制作被视为秘技，并不对外传授。各自不同的配方，造成颜料名称相同但色相上会有一些区别，直至20世纪初，中国绘画颜料的制作还一直保持着家庭作坊生产

1　王超，现为中国美术学院绘画艺术学院版画系教授，硕士研究生导师，版画系第一工作室主任兼传统木版水印工作室负责人；1974年生于山东，2021年毕业于中国美术学院，获艺术学博士学位。

2　王仲荦：《金泥玉屑丛考》，中华书局，1998年，第209—210页。

和画家自行加工的方式。由于矿物颜料的原料大多来自中亚，来之不易，使得矿物颜料的价格比植物颜料昂贵许多。“唐代以前以矿物颜料为主，唐以后因植物颜料随着染织业的发展而逐渐利用于绘画之中”[1]。

中国古代版画深受中国传统美学思想的影响，所使用的颜料和设色方法与传统绘画相同。中国绘画在唐宋以前，基本以重彩设色为主流；自从元代水墨画盛行，大青绿、重着色的绘画被文人墨客斥作院体而不加重视，文人画主流以水墨为主，色彩在中国绘画中的使用逐渐变少，即便画中出现颜色，也要求能达到清淡、幽雅的气质。植物性颜料因其易溶于水而且透明度高于矿物质颜料，较适合表现淡雅的审美品位。

美术史与书籍史家范景中先生将古籍彩色印本按照印刷的版次和版数，分为一版多色本（如印于1600年前后的《花史》）、一版多次本（如元刻《金刚般若波罗蜜经注解》）、多版套印本（如闵刻本）和饾版套印本（如《十竹斋书画谱》）。“从印刷技术上讲，一、二项要容易些，三、四项实为一项，较难也较为复杂；前两项反映了较早较粗糙阶段的技术，后两项则是成熟阶段的产物。但从套印的角度来看，第一项只是彩印，而不是套印。”[2]范景中比照哈斯克尔（Francis Haskell）描述18世纪早期艺术书籍出现的《美术书籍的艰难诞生》（*The Painful Birth of the Art Book*），进而认为，“明代万历期间兴起的单纯为观赏而出版的书籍”，是中国书籍史上的大事，可在晚明整体艺术气氛特别是赏古、鉴古的艺术气氛中去研究。[3]同一时期发明的“饾版”和“拱花”两种技法，又使套色彩印更上层楼，成就了中国版画史中的一批杰作。至此，中国古代版画已不只是书籍艺术的一部分，亦可视为独立的艺术门类。

文人趣味的古代版画（如套色书籍、画谱、笺纸）沿袭文人绘画的淡雅审美，多使用植物性颜料，除线条主版大多刷印黑（墨）色，使用最多的是花青、朱砂、藤黄和赭石色。由于受到套版数量的限制，中国古代通过“版”这一媒介印刷形成的版画，并不同于中国古代手绘图画中的设色方法。版画用色屈指可数，通过交叉组合使用单色、混合颜色与依靠套色“版”的重合叠压产生的

---

1 蒋玄佁：《中国绘画材料史》，上海书画出版社，1986年，第95页。

2 范景中：《序言：套印本和闵刻本及其〈会真图〉》，载董捷：《明清刊〈西厢记〉版画考析》，河北美术出版社，2006年，第1页。

3 同上，第5页。

叠印色，再加上自一版多色发展而来的“掸色”技术，丰富了画面色彩。

自清代以后，色彩浓艳的年画版画兴起，织物染料也加入了版画颜料家族。民间世俗的色彩美学与文人幽远淡雅的审美趣味并行，套色版画走向更多元的趣味呈现。

颜色：徽墨与苏作颜料

17 世纪、18 世纪，徽墨称雄中国，迄今亦然。墨有松烟、油烟之别，色相上亦有相应的冷暖和神采差异。水印木刻工作者对徽墨别有一种亲近感：首先，套色版中的主版往往即是墨版；其次，首次成书于 1588 年的《方氏墨谱》和 1606 年的《程氏墨苑》既是徽州制墨史上的要籍，也是版画史上的杰作。我个人于此更有一层绮想遐思，总觉得是徽州制作墨模的工艺直接启发了日后的版画拱花技法。我偏好徽州油烟墨，日常使用的是 20 世纪 70 年代胡开文出产的“铁斋翁书画宝墨”。这种墨的原型为富冈铁斋（Tomioka Tessai，1837—1924）20 世纪初在曹素功墨厂所制定的版墨。

同一时期最好的颜料，我以为是出自经济、文化重镇苏州。直至今天，“苏作”依然代表着中国最高的工艺水平。我本人整个职业生涯都使用始创于 17 世纪的苏州姜思序堂出产的颜料。植物颜料有色膏状态的成品，使用方法如下：首先取一小片色膏，浸入温水泡半小时，水量依需要的颜色浓度而定；然后以毛笔搅拌，再调入适量鱼鳔胶即可使用。备制时限遵循“现用现调，隔夜弃之”的原则，故同一批版画的色彩可能有一定的随意性，无法保证完全一样。朱砂虽然是矿物颜料，仍有色膏成品。同为矿物颜料的石绿是我常用的唯一一种色粉介质颜料，备制方法与色膏略有差别：先用指腹研磨，调入适量温水，调匀后再加入适量鱼鳔胶，继续用指腹研磨，达到一定黏稠度即可。17 世纪、18 世纪的版画制作，有多少径用色膏，有多少用色粉，尚待美术史家考证。在古版画中，尚有一类为境外销售而制作的画作，其中不乏使用西洋颜料的可能。

设色：单色、混合色与叠印色

中国传统版画中，为使色彩变淡，并不是往其中加进白色，而是兑入清水，所谓“色薄即淡”（西方的湿壁画和水彩也是兑水调和。油画也有薄涂法，水彩也更是如此。虽然趣味不同，但视觉效果上基本相似），这不同于西方绘画的色彩经验。也因为这种用薄色、淡色的习惯，颜料中一定的色相差异可以忽略不计。譬如，在传统中国工笔重彩画中，石绿颜料根据细度有头绿、二绿、三绿、四绿之别，以头绿最浓、最粗，讲究的画家选购颜料时会作区分。传统版画中，石绿用量很少，且以淡雅效果为上，故不作区分。但在对朱砂颜料的使用中，传统中国画、篆刻与版画有一致的色相区分。对国画家和印人而言，朱砂颜料可细分为朱磦、头朱、二朱、三朱，粗分也可分为漂制后处于上层的朱磦与底层的朱砂。朱磦粒细、色暖、价昂，而朱砂粒粗、偏冷、稍廉。在以画谱、画传、笺谱、笺纸形式传世的 17 世纪、18 世纪的版画中，印章也是画面的一部分，印色呈现出深浅、冷暖之不同，无法一概而论。在篆刻史的讨论脉络中，同一时期印色的地域、时期特征研究，目前几近空白，古版画中的印色材料，或可旁参。实践中，缘于个人之色彩偏好，我的调色盘中只有朱磦，未曾用过朱砂。

传统版画的调色，除了兑入清水，还利用已有色彩相互混合，如赭墨即为赭石与墨的组合、暗红为胭脂调墨所得、草绿出自藤黄和花青的混合等。新的色彩是由画中主版——墨、花青以及其他配色掺杂而成，本身即拥有画面中已有的色彩元素，所以和其他颜色相搭配显得非常协调。调色之外，与画面上渐变、退晕效果相关的操作术语叫“掸色”，是一种一版多色的彩印设色方法：印工用毛笔在版上色彩变淡或色相转化的一端快捷地加上清水或相应的较深的色彩，覆纸刷印时借助纸张的渗化性，形成渐变效果。如果印版较小，也可以手指直接点些清水或别的颜色。清水“掸色”类似于工笔画中的“分染”。这样的处理自然有相当的即兴意味，在整个印制过程中亦不失为兴到意足的华彩篇章。郑振铎先生曾考证印于 1600 年前后的《花史》“是用几种颜色涂在一块雕版上，如用红色涂在花上，绿色涂在叶上，棕色、黄色涂在树干上，然后覆上纸张印刷出来"[1]。《花史》作为一版多色的早期例证，其设色是写实的；"掸色"技法的出现为一版多色又注入了"墨分五色"的流动与变化趣味，更适合再现富有表现意味的文人画线条与着色。

另外，中国传统画注重的是对象的固有颜色，而光源以及环境色在中国画家的眼中显得并不重要，甚至为了某种特殊需要，有时也会采用夸张或假定的色彩。

用版：小叶黄杨、梨与枣

版画用版的选择，需要综合考虑木材产地、生长周期、刻画精度与价格等因素。就地取材总是一个方便的原则。原木须泡在水中一年，脱胶（去蛋白质）后晾干一年，方可完成防裂处理，锯为板材。刻书以小叶黄杨木为上选，因其质地紧密、细腻，尤其能传达插图本精微的线条的细节趣味。晚明巨制《环翠堂园景图》与《人镜阳秋》画面中的线条纤毫毕现，用版当为小叶黄杨木。流传下来的 17 世纪、18 世纪的版画作品，梨木版为多，虽精度稍逊于小叶黄杨木，但胜在经济易得。亦有使用枣版的情况，相较梨木，其质地稍嫌粗糙。"灾梨祸枣"，作为对出版物的批评或是谦逊说法，仍保留在现代汉语中。

对 17 世纪、18 世纪的版画而言，从经济和画面表现角度揣度，一幅套印版画中所有印版的板材当是一致的。这一情形在现代有了突破，典型的例子即荣宝斋在 20 世纪五六十年代以木版水印方式复制的《韩熙载夜宴图》，全图主要使用梨木版，而在表现眉毛、胡子的地方则用小叶黄杨饾版。

另外，值得一提的是，套色版中存在双面刻版的情形。紫竹斋藏有 19 世纪的年画版片，其中即有正面刻线版、背面刻色版的情况。饾版因雕刻精细，为保护雕面，不适用双面刻版。

1 转引自范景中：《序言：套印本和闵刻本及其〈会真图〉》，载董捷：《明清刊〈西厢记〉版画考析》，河北美术出版社，2006年，第1页。

水印台：压杆的妙用

对 17 世纪、18 世纪的套色版画的制作来说，水印台是重要的工具。它的巧妙之处在于压杆及垂纸用空洞。压杆是通过两个固定点压住一叠纸，方便印工顺次刷印。

水印台的发明，其最大的贡献或许不在版画，而首先是书籍印刷。它的出现，保证了书籍印刷事业的生产效率和标准化程度。以我的亲身实验为例，使用水印台，6 小时可刷印 1000 张单色线版，或者说，1000 张书页。并且，不同印张的纸张边距的大小之差异微乎其微。

紫竹斋水印台长 180 厘米，宽 100 厘米，高 80 厘米，较普通书桌稍高。我的工作凳高 65 厘米，方便伏案工作；如果印制大幅版画，也方便左右移动身子。工作时面对水印台，右首可见一根突起于桌面的压杆，通过两个间距为 80 厘米的可调节螺丝与桌面相连，松开螺丝，即可将一叠纸的右边夹在压杆之下，再拧紧螺丝，就固定好了整叠纸。压杆之右为宽 15 厘米、长 80 厘米的空洞，待刷印完成，将纸张往右一掀，纸张即自然覆过压杆，垂入空洞中。我琢磨过固定点间距的选取，80 厘米恰巧稍大于四尺全开纸的宽度（接近 70 厘米），古制取值虽不用公制整数，但实际长度很可能相当接近。

印台还有一神奇的活动部件，功用为纸面绷直用校准板，并有两个高度，用于协调不同的雕版厚度，正式的部件名未见诸文献。

紫竹斋水印台承袭自荣宝斋，是我日常使用的画案。我在别处——从古至今仍以传统方法印行古籍的广陵古籍刻印社，到一间间年画艺人的作坊，都看到过使用压杆的类似的印台。如果说紫竹斋的水印台与 17 世纪的水印台有什么区别的话，我想就是固定压杆的部件：现在用两个螺丝固定，而当年用的该是两根绳子。2005 年，欧洲木版基金会据紫竹斋水印台复制了一张水印台，现藏欧洲木版教育信托的伦敦办公室。

工作流程

说起水印木刻，人们常用的步骤是勾描、刻版、水印、装裱。就水印部分，我再分解一下制作流程。

首先是备制颜料，上文已详述。然后是备纸：用刀口宽 5 厘米的马蹄刀切纸，将整叠纸正面朝下，右边夹于压杆之下。接下来是固定印版。首先拉出最下方的纸，根据幅面位置（如用饾版，还需依幅面上的线描稿）确定印版位置。我用杭州胡庆余堂产的中药膏药，用膏药灯加热、软化膏药（膏药灯出现之前大概是将一片片膏药放于手心，以体温软化膏药吧），再分别堆到印版边缘与桌面结合处，黏合印版与桌面。在室温中，膏药又会恢复硬度，即可充分固定印版。使用膏药的好处是不伤版，但是膏药较贵。我在年画艺人的作坊中见过用蜂蜡固定印版的做法，蜂蜡较膏药易得，也可能为古人所使用。印版固定之后，用湿布盖上，俗话叫“闷”，半小时后取下。这一步骤使木纤维中的水分充分饱和，避免前后印张的画面干湿不一。

接下来是刷色。以毛笔蘸色，涂到要印制的版上。用棕皮做的圆刷，左手持刷，顺时针方向划圈，将颜料扫匀。如需掸色，则以毛笔或手指在需要的部分点染。

然后就是拓印了。拓印工具叫“耙子”，是底部包覆了一层棕皮的木块。紫竹斋旧藏中有马尾所制、尺寸相同的同类工具，惜今已无存。棕材纤维非平行排列，而是彼此叠压，故施压后刷行平面中纤维兼有叠合、松开，凹凸参差，刷动时往往有颗粒感，刷痕明显。耙子使用一段时间后，刷行平面棕材的交叠之处被磨平，滑顺感会取代颗粒感，刷痕隐去。再用一段时间，棕材刷行平面出现新一轮凹凸参差，刷痕复现。马尾制耙子，因纤维平行顺列，可有效避免刷痕，但因取材、制作不易，今日罕见使用。

右手从压杆处取纸，纸张正面贴合已刷色的印版，眼观覆于校准板断面部分的纸面是否绷直，随后右手持耙子在纸张背面施压自下而上一次一次拖动，此步骤称“背拓”或“透印”。如耙子过新或过旧，或刷印过快过重，都可能在印张上留下刷痕。在中国传统中，这样的刷痕并不受欣赏，而被视为是作业中的偶然无奈之物。在不少 17 世纪、18 世纪古籍尾页留黑中亦可见类似背拓刷痕，而非刨木不平所致。

为应对耙子生命周期中的颗粒感变化，今日印工往往在纸张背面另覆衬纸，通常为较光滑的熟纸，以弱化摩擦效果，避免在纸张正面暴露刷痕。日本的浮世绘画家，着迷于这样的刷痕（日文：摺り迹），放大这种排线趣味和过程趣味，刻意展现，影响及今。与“背拓”、“透印”相对应的日语术语“裏摺”也因此多一分对表现性（而不只是过程性的）刷痕的侧重[1]。

刷印单版，直接以耙子背拓即可。如涉及多版，则还有套版的步骤。套版顺序遵循先线版（墨版）、后色版及色版由浅入深的原则。饾版对版有别于普通套版，需先行勾画白描线稿，并将此线稿正面朝下夹入压杆，置于压杆下整叠纸的最下方。然后依此白描线稿逐步套版。

整叠纸依序印完，再用马蹄刀切纸，即可得成品。相同图像不同印张之间的差异，色彩是很重要的考察角度。因为调色的随意性、掸色的即兴意味和颜料“隔日弃之”，不同印张在色彩上可能呈现一定的差异。而更大的差异则在水印之后的装裱环节，不同的刻书家或藏家对不同装裱形式的偏好——或册页、或蝴蝶装、或线装，甚至立轴——在同一批印张数百年的流传生命中，赋予其多样的面貌。

大英博物馆藏17世纪、18世纪套色版画示例

现举大英博物馆藏版画数例，并谈一下我对其色彩处理的心得。明崇祯胡正言（1580—1671）刊彩色套印本《十竹斋书画谱》，是以“饾版”印制成的具有教材性质的画册，融诗、书、画、印艺术为一体，是木版水印史上的巨制鸿构，有“画苑之白眉，绘林之赤帜”之誉。凡书画、竹、墨华、石、翎毛、梅、兰、果八谱，每谱两册，全帙共十六册，蝴蝶装。

翎毛谱，画、题各二十幅，有杨文骢于“天启丁卯立秋日”所题《翎毛谱小序》，非常精彩地评介了胡氏所施饾版之法：“胡曰从氏巧心妙手，超越前代，以铁笔作颖生，以梨枣代绢素，而其中皴法、染法、点法，及着色之轻重、浅深、远近、离合无不呈妍曲致，穷巧极工。即当行作手观之，定以为写生妙品，不敢作刻画观。”此翎毛谱二十图，画上无名款，从印鉴来看，应全为凌云翰一人所作。凌云翰，字五云，万历、崇祯时人。《明画录》说他善画山水，其实凌氏亦善花鸟，尤工画石，为胡正言所推许。

---

1 感谢上海图书馆梁颖先生出示上海图书馆藏笺，此引发了我对刷痕的思考。

此幅版画为翎毛谱之一（图 1）。首先印制的是表达竹竿、石和雀鸟的外轮廓的淡墨版，清水掸色；其次为表达鸟眼、鸟喙、石上苔点和竹叶勾线的浓墨版，亦有部分清水掸色。再次，补两个饾版，即表达雀鸟的头、背及翅梢的赭石色版，与表达雀尾、翅的花青版。最后以藤黄、花青调草绿色刷版，清水掸色，部分以极淡的赭石掸色，完成竹叶填色。左侧朱文印，印文为“五云”，可能为钤印所得。整幅灵活使用掸色技法，设色富于浓淡、冷暖变化，传神地再现了绘画的笔墨趣味。

图 1 《十竹斋书画谱》之《翎毛谱》 大英博物馆藏

Feather in *Calligraphies and Paintings Categories of Ten Bamboo Studio*, collected by the British Museum.

画中描绘的内容是两人因赌局而争执，后有一人作调解（图 2）。这张版画由七种不同颜色的套版印刷而成：分别是作为主版的墨色，首先印制完成画面的白描稿、后面一个人物的上衣和前面两个人物的鞋子；赌桌、圆凳、远处围栏的底部用较纯净的花青色；竹子搭建的围栏、立屏的边框是灰暗的藤黄色；立屏的内框、屏风山水里面的远山、左边两个人物的服饰印有明亮的藤黄色。三个人物的帽缨、腮红和左边人物的上衣、长衫是用胭脂红色；凳子面、桌子边框、立屏的脚、右边人物的上衣用较重的蓝灰色；前面两个人物的长衫是较淡的蓝灰色。最后用刷色后水分自然减少的毛笔，在左前人物的蓝灰衣裳上，晕染出富有动态的衣褶效果，并用同样的方法晕染左前人物的上衣轮廓，

图 2　清早期（约 1700）苏州套色木版画　汉斯·斯隆藏品　大英博物馆藏
Suzhou chromatic woodblock prints, the early Qing Dynasty (ca. 1700), Hans Sloan's collection, collected by the British Museum.

表现出裘皮的质感。

在此幅画中，围栏、立屏的边框，是用藤黄色加少许墨调制成微微有些绿色倾向的灰暗色调；左边人物的衣服先印较淡的花青色，然后在上面套版上红色，所以叠印产生了另外一种紫色；左下角凳子面、桌子边框、屏风脚和右边人物的上衫的灰蓝色，是由花青添加墨色调和而成。

此画设色稳重古拙，因花青、藤黄、胭脂及墨，均是植物性颜料，较矿物性颜料便宜，取之容易，在中国早期民间版画中大量使用。

如果说上一幅是"掸色"的示范之作，这一幅设色的特殊之处在于叠印与最后的干笔晕染。在 20 世纪的山东高密年画中，最后一步称"扑灰"，即以干毛笔扫碳粉，在画面上擦出需要强调的部分。1700 年前后的苏州，这类似的一步，我只能用国画术语"干笔晕染"或"干笔皴擦"表达，当时的术语是什么是个值得探究的课题。

图 3　清早期（约 1700 年）苏州套色木版画
汉斯·斯隆藏品　大英博物馆藏（画中题“飞入花丛似粉台，姑苏，瑞林写”，并钤印两枚）
Suzhou chromatic woodblock prints, the early Qing Dynasty (ca. 1700), Hans Sloan's collection, collected by the British Museum. (In the painting, the "fly into the flowers like a pink table, Gusu, Ruilin wrote", with two seals).

此幅（图 3）与上一幅同属一套版画，应是当时的年画。这张画由六块套版印刷。浓重的墨色作为主版印出梅花的枝干和双燕；稍微淡一些的两种墨色印双燕翅羽和树干中间的部分；绽放的梅花花蕊是藤黄色，蓓蕾是石绿色；树干根部的草丛和绽放梅花的轮廓是赭石色加入了少量的墨调制成的一种暖灰色。印制顺序大体依次为：墨版、深浅两种淡墨版、藤黄版、石绿版、暖灰版。

画中（图 4）人物具红脸特征，通行的说法认为其是关羽（约 160—220）。人物所持之长柄斧头又是另一位历史人物程咬金（589—665）的惯用兵器。或许可以这么说，这是一幅挪用了部分程咬金特征（attributes）的关羽像。

此版画采用套印和手工彩绘相结合的方法，先用木版雕出画面的主要线条，淡墨印刷，再以颜色填绘。此画所用颜色亦为染衣的染料，故比较鲜艳、透明。颜色无法一概以国画颜料名目名之，姑且说有朱红、胭脂、明黄、嫩绿、深蓝和浓墨。特别要指出的是，门神的脸部使用了铅白色，因时间久远而变黑。全幅设色单纯艳丽，装饰性强，用线率真洗练，有较强的节奏感。综合以上风格特征，与存世 19 世纪四川绵竹年画接近，为少见的 18 世纪存世之作。

此画所用颜料，颜料备制方法当于上文所述有异，具体俟考。今天民间年画依然常以染料为颜料，因为染料比较便宜。

图 4　清早期（约 1700）套色门神木版画　汉斯·斯隆藏品　大英博物馆藏
A chromatic woodblock print of Door–god, the early Qing Dynasty (ca. 1700), Hans Sloan's collection, collected by the British Museum.

此图（图 5）以鸢尾花为主要描绘对象，后面衬托山石、樱草，画法精细，设色典雅。墨色印制花卉及山石轮廓；浓淡两色草绿印成花叶；花青、清水掸色印花瓣，藤黄色印花蕊和后面的樱草花；花青添加墨调和成蓝灰色，清水掸色，印制山石的底色。形象精确工细，色彩含蓄蕴藉，色调淡雅清丽，构图巧妙。

这是一批画（二十八幅）中的一幅（图 6），这批画在日本、中国都有广泛的著录，泷本弘之、德力富吉郎、薄松年、范景中都曾述及。薄松年先生在《苏州年画的兴衰和收藏》一文中对于这批版画有这样的记述："花卉画的套色较为丰富明丽，雕印手法也多种多样，有的瓜果不印墨线而纯以大片套色表现，如国画中的没骨法。更有的花卉运用了拱花技术，使花朵突出纸面，

图 5 清康熙四十年（1701）木版彩色套印《芥子园画传》第三册《翎毛花卉谱》之一 大英博物馆藏。《芥子园画传》，其用色优雅，镌绘雅致，刊刻精美，是清代彩印本的典范，亦是中国古代印刷史上的经典之作。

One of the third volume of *The Manual of Feather and Flowers in The Mustard Seed Garden*, woodblock color overprinted in the 40th year of Emperor Kangxi of the Qing Dynasty (1701), collected by the British Museum. *Jieziyuan Huazhuan*, with its elegant color, elegant and exquisite engraving, is the model of color print in the Qing Dynasty, and also a classic work in the history of ancient Chinese printing.

图 6 明万历三十年（1602）刊印套色木版画 汉斯·斯隆藏品 大英博物馆藏

chromatic woodblock print, the 30th year (1602) of Wanli, Hans Sloan's collection, collected in the British Museum

显出层层的立体效果，非常别致……其印刷年代至少在康熙中期以前，是苏州地区较早的套色木版画。”[1] 范景中先生指出，这套画为“Kämpfer 版画”，得名于 Engelbert Kämpfer（1651—1716），他在 1690 年至 1692 年间从长崎购买，并于 1693 年带回欧洲。[2]

此画以胭脂红、花青、藤黄、草绿、赭石、墨六色分版套印。居中的牡丹，先印满铺整朵花的色版，并在局部作清水掸色；然后叠印位于花朵中心的饾版，塑造深浅层次。画中右侧的玉兰或辛夷，不取固有色白或紫红，而为草绿色，或许一则为了省版，二则为了强调整幅画面的红绿对比。画面左上方题字“千红万紫斗精神，采得芳菲色色新”，款署“金阊丁氏写”，未用印鉴。整幅画面雕版印刷极为精美，饾版套色准确，是稀有的早期木版画珍品。

《百子图》（图 7）的作者为筠谷，关于筠谷其人，目前有黄增和张述渠两说。[3] 印工为张星聚。画面上，元宵之夜，梅雪争艳，张灯结彩，孩童嬉戏。画面包含两个场景：下方为一处装饰华美的宅院，孩童们或骑小马，或扮将帅，或拉兔子灯，以类似轴侧的传统办法表达空间关系。上方展现了一处面山临水的庭院景象，左边是一组攀阶去往赏景亭的孩童，右边是一处厅堂，另一组孩童与女眷们正为攀阶的孩童鼓劲。赏景亭取仰视视角，而右边的厅堂则用了单点透视表现（左上假山庭院墙的透视不在一个透视点上，稍稍展开，画工随意性？）。绘画技法极其精湛，画中题跋有“仿泰西笔意”，当是受到自西洋传入的“透视法”和铜版画的影响。最有特色的是其建筑、风景的描绘，运用铜版画似的线条细密而规整地平行排列，混杂使用传统空间表达与西洋透视方法，以大幅画面表现庭院楼阁、山川明月的情景交融，不失为清早期姑苏版画的创制。

此图画幅较大（98.2 厘米 × 53.5 厘米），或为取三段分别制版印刷[4]。最上方为字版，其次为表现登临赏玩之乐的中段，然后是表现宅院嬉戏的下段。中段与下段分别套版印刷。主体建筑及人物轮廓使用的是墨和花青调和成的蓝黑

---

1 《中华文苑》中的《文物天地》，见www.china—culture.com。

2 Basil Gray, “Sloan and the Kämpfer Collection,” in The British Museum Quarterly, London, 1953, 18; Joseph Vedlich, The prints of the Ten Bamboo Studio followed by Plates from the Kämpfer Series and Perfect Harmony. Fribourg/Geneve, 1979; Wolfmar Zacken, Die Kämpfer Drucke, Wien, 1995.

3 Clarissa von Spee, *The Printed Images in China*, British Museum Press, 2010, p. 41.

4 *The Printed Images in China Catalogue*, p. 40，图录称此图由三块版印成。

图 7 《百子图》(1743) 苏州地区印套色木版画 大英博物馆藏

One–Hundred Children, Suzhou chromatic woodblock print, 1743, collected by the British Museum.

色。因木版雕刻大面积交叉线困难，在每一段，作者用浓淡两块线条方向不同的蓝黑色线板，交叠成排线效果。人物服饰、屋檐取朱砂，另一些人物服饰取藤黄，分别套色印刷。这样，中段与下段就要分别用四块版，加上上段的字版，总计九块版。这对一幅年画来说是否过于费工？如果大版不易得，刷印时将上中段、下段或上、中、下段拼接固定，则 9 次套印可省为 5 次甚至 4 次。另外，我在金陵刻经处见过高 180 厘米的大版，刻的是观音像，当时是否也可能存在足够大的版呢？

这幅画虽有浓淡变化，但不涉及撣色。因印版较大，如做撣色，单板作业时间延长，恐怕一部分版面已刷颜料会失去应有的水分。

Jiugefang's Notes of Reading Engravings

Wang Chao[1]

Introduction

Humans have been perceiving color for such a long history as humans themselves, and the conscious use of color began when primitive human beings used solid or liquid paint on their faces and bodies, whose conscious use of simple colors can already be seen on neolithic pottery.

The pigments used in traditional Chinese painting are divided into mineral pigments and plant ones according to their different raw materials. Plant pigments, also known as water color, transparent color, can be used in harmony with each other, with weak covering power and unstable color quality, easy to fade, including flower green, gamboge, rouge and so on. Mineral pigments, also called stone color, are made of ore grinding and processing. They have thick color, but cannot be used in harmony with each other, with strong covering force and stable color quality, not easy to fade. There is lazuli, stone green, stone yellow, cinnabar, ochre and so on. Mineral pigments were used extensively in Dunhuang frescoes in China, and their colors are still strong and gorgeous after over millennia.

There are many records about the use of pigments in ancient Chinese

---

1 Wang Chao is a professor of China Academy of Art, a PH. Doctor of Engraving, born in Shandong in 1974. In 1998, he graduated from China Academy of Art; in 2021, he received a Ph.D. from China Academy of Art. He is a master supervisor of the Printmaking Department of the School of Painting and Art, the director of the first studio and the head of the traditional woodblock watermarking Studio.

literature. Xie He (479–502), a painter in the Southern Dynasty, proposed the theory of "giving colors according to the class". Zhang Yanyuan (618–907) described the original places, uses and properties of various pigments in his famous *Lidai Minghua Ji* (*Famous Paintings of the Past Dynasties*) written in 847 in the first year of Dazhong in the Tang Dynasty. Dunhuang documents of the Tang Dynasty have descriptions of the price of pigments at that time;[1] in the early Qing Dynasty, in the two books *Hill Painting* and *Details of Painting,* there were detailed descriptions of the methods of selecting raw materials, grinding, processing and using the colors of Chinese painting. However, in the era of painting as a skill, the recipe and production of painting pigments were considered secret skills and kept inside. Different recipes result in pigments with the same name but some differences in hue. Until the early 20th century, the production of Chinese painting pigments has been kept in the family workshop and the painter's own processing. As the raw materials of mineral pigments mostly come from Central Asia, not easy to obtain, the mineral pigments are much more expensive than the plant pigments. "Before the Tang Dynasty, mineral pigments were mainly dominant. After the Tang Dynasty, plant pigments were gradually used in painting with the development of dyeing and weaving industry."[2]

Because ancient Chinese printmaking was deeply influenced by traditional Chinese aesthetic thought, the pigments and colored methods used were the same as those used in traditional paintings. Before the Tang and Song dynasties, Thick–colored Chinese Painting was basically the mainstream. Since the popularity of ink painting in the Yuan Dynasty, large blue–green and thick colored paintings have been criticized by literati as the court style, without paying attention to them. The mainstream of literati painting is mainly in ink

1 Wang Zhongluo, *Jinni Yusui Congkao*, Beijing, Zhonghua Book Company, 1998, pp. 209–210.

2 Jiang Xuanyi, *History of Chinese Painting Materials, Shanghai*, Shanghai Painting and Calligraphy Publishing House, 1986, p. 95.

and monochrome, and the application of color in Chinese painting has gradually decreased. Even if the color appears in the painting, it is required to achieve a light and elegant temperament. Because they are soluble in water and more transparent than mineral pigments, plant pigments are more suitable for the expression of elegant aesthetic taste.

Fan Jingzhong, a famous historian of Art history and book history, has divided the ancient color printed books in accordance with the printed edition and version number, into multi–colored version of one print (e.g. Huashi/*the History of Flower* printed before and after 1600), a multi–time printed version (such as *Jingang Prajnaparamita with Annotations* carved in Yuan Dynasty), multiple overprinted version (such as photocopies by Min) and embossing edition overprint this (such as *Shizhuzhai Shuhua Pu/Calligraphies and Paintings Categories of Ten Bamboo Studio*). "In terms of printing technique, the first and second items are easier while the third or fourth items are actually one item, more difficult and more complex. The first two reflect an earlier, more crude stage of technology, while the last two are products of a mature stage. But from the overprint point of view, the first item is just colored printing, not overprint." [1]Compared to Francis Haskell's *The Painful Birth of The Art Book* (1987), which describes the emergence of Art books in the early 18th century, Fan Jingzhong argues that books published for appreciation only during the Wanli Period of the Ming Dynasty is an important event in the history of Chinese books, which can be studied in the overall artistic atmosphere of the late Ming Dynasty, especially in the artistic atmosphere of appreciating the antiquity.[2] The other two techniques invented at the same time like the "Multicolored printing" and "embossing" made multicolor printing even better, creating a number of multicolor masterpieces in the history of Chinese printing. So far, Chinese

1 Fan Jingzhong, "Preface: Overprint and Min's Prints and Their *Huizhen Tu*," in Dong Jie's *An Analysis of Printmaking Xixiang Ji in the Ming and Qing Dynasties,* Hebei Fine Arts Publishing House, 2006, p. 5.

2 id., 2006, p. 1.

ancient printmaking is not only a part of book art, but also an independent art category.

Ancient literati prints (such as colored books, painting copybooks, and notepaper) followed the elegant aesthetic of literati painting, and mostly used plant pigments. In addition to the black (ink) color of the main plate of lines, the most used colors were floral blue, cinnabar, gamboge and ochre. Due to the limitation of the number of sets of plates, prints by the medium of "plate" in ancient China were different from the color setting method in ancient hand–painted pictures. There are only a few colors used in prints. The color of the picture is enriched by the use of monochrome, mixed colors and overprint colors produced by superimposed pressure relying on chromatism "plates" and the "light color brushing" technique developed from one plate with multicolor.

Since the Qing Dynasty, colorful New Year prints rose, and fabric dyes also enlarged the printmaking pigment family. The color aesthetics of the secular folk goes hand in hand with the quiet and elegant aesthetic taste of the literati, making it develop into diverse tastes.

Color: Huizhou Ink and Pigments Made in Suzhou

In the 17th and 18th centuries, the ink made in Huizhou was the dominant ink in China, and it still is. There are different ink pine smoke and lampblack, and their color also has the corresponding coldness and warmth as well as appearance difference. Watermarking woodcarving workers have a sense of kinship with Huizhou ink: firstly, the main version of the color plates is often the ink plate; Secondly, *Fang's Mo Pu* (1588) and *Cheng's Mo Yuan* (1606) are both important books in the history of ink–making in Huizhou and masterpieces in the history of printmaking. Personally, I think it is the technique of making ink mold in Huizhou that directly inspired the technique of arch flower in prints later. I prefer Huizhou lampblack ink, and use commonly the ink named Tiezhaiweng

Painting and Calligraphy Treasure Ink produced by Hu Kaiwen in the 1970s. The prototype of this kind of ink is formulated version ink made by Tomioka Tessai (1837–1924) at the beginning of the 20th century in the Cao Sugong Ink Factory.

At the same time, the best pigment, I think, is from the economic and cultural city of Suzhou. Until today, "Made in Suzhou" still represents the highest level of craftsmanship in China. During my entire career I have been using pigments from Jiang Sixu Hall in Suzhou, which was first created in the 17th century. There are the finished products of plant pigments made into the paste state. when used the preparation method is as follows: first take a small piece of color paste, and immerse it in warm water for half an hour, with the amount of water according to the required color concentration. Stir it with a brush, and add the right amount of fish glue, and then you can use it. The preparation time follows the principle of "mix and use it instantly; abandon it overnight", so the colors of the same batch of prints may have a certain arbitrariness and cannot be guaranteed to be exactly the same. Although cinnabar is of mineral pigment, it still has colored paste finished products. The Stone green, also a mineral, is the only one pigment as powder medium I commonly use, whose preparation method is slightly different from that of color paste: first grind it with the fingers, mix evenly into the appropriate amount of warm water, add the appropriate amount of fish glue, continue to grind it with the fingers, and stop to an extent of a certain viscosity. Art historians have yet to prove how many in prints were made in pastes or in toners in the 17th and 18th centuries. Among ancient prints, there is also a category of paintings made for sales oversea, among which there is the possibility of using Western pigments.

Coloring: Monochrome, Mixed Color and Overprint Color

In traditional Chinese printmaking, water is added instead of white pigment to make the color diluted light. The so–called "thin color is light" (western frescoes and watercolors are also mixed with water. Oil painting also has thin coating method, and watercolor is also close. Although the interest and taste is different, they have the similar visual effect, basically.), which is different from the color experience of Western painting. Also, because of this thin, light color habit, a certain hue difference in pigments can be ignored. For example, meticulous heavy–colored in traditional Chinese paintings, stone green pigments are divided into the first green, the second green, the third green and the fourth green according to their fineness. The first green is the thickest and coarsest, and the exquisite painters with high requirements will distinguish them when choosing pigments. In traditional printmaking, stone green is used very little to mainly achieve the elegant effect, so there is no distinction. But in the use of cinnabar pigment, traditional Chinese Painting, seal carving and prints have consistent color distinctions. For Chinese painters and printers, cinnabar pigment can be subdivided into zhubiao, the first red, the second, the third, or at least can be divided into the upper layer of zhubiao and the bottom layer of cinnabar after bleaching. Zhubiao is expensive, with fine pieces and warm color, and cinnabar is slightly cheap, coarse and colder. In the prints from the seventeenth and eighteenth century handed down from generation to generation in the form of painting categories, painting biographies, notepad and notepaper, with the seal as also a part of the picture, the color of the print is varied in darkness and lightness, in coldness and warmth, which cannot be generalized. In the discussion of the history of seal engraving, the research on the regional and period characteristics of the printing fashion in the same period is almost blank at present, and the printing pigment materials in ancient prints may be taken as a reference. In practice, due to my personal color preference, my color palette only contains zhubiao, and I have never used cinnabar.

In the traditional color palette of prints, in addition to adding water, the existing colors are mixed with each other, such as ochre ink, which is the combination of ochre and ink, dark red, the blend of rouge ink, and grass green, the mixture of gamboge and indigo. The new color is from the main color version of the painting—ink, indigo and other colors mixed together, it by itself has the existing color factors in the picture, so it is very harmonious with other colors. Besides mixing color, the term relevant to the operation of the gradient change and fading halo effect in the image, called "dan se", is a kind of a multicolor printing method: printers quickly add clean water or darker colors at the end of the plate with the writing brush where the colors become lighter or the hue transforms, to form a gradient effect brushing coated paper for printing with paper's infiltration capacity. If the printing plate is small, you can also directly point on water or other colors with your fingers. Clean water dusting is similar to "separate dyeing" in fine brushwork. Such treatment naturally has a considerable sense of improvisation, and in the whole printing process also can yet be regarded as a splendid festivity with meaningfully sufficient color.[1] Mr. Zheng Zhenduo once proved that *the History of Flowers* printed around 1600 was "painted with several colors on a block of engraving, such as red on flowers, green on leaves, brown and yellow on tree trunks, and then printed on paper". As an early example of polychromatism, the color of *the History of Flowers* is realistic; the appearance of the dusting technique injected the flow and change interest of "five colors of ink" into a multi–color version, which is more suitable for reproducing the lines and coloring of literati paintings with rich expressive meaning.

In addition, the inherent color of the object is paid attention to in traditional Chinese painting, while the light source and environmental color are not important in the eyes of Chinese painters, and even for meeting some special needs, sometimes exaggerated or assumed color will be used.

---

1 Quoted from Fan Jingzhong, "Preface: Overprint and Min's Prints and Their Huizhen Tu," in Dong Jie's *An Analysis of Printmaking Xixiang Ji in the Ming and Qing Dynasties*, Hebei Fine Arts Publishing House, 2006, p. 1.

Plate Materials: Boxwood, Pear and Jujube Wood

The selection of printmaking plate materials needs to consider the factors such as origin, growth period, engraving accuracy and price. It is always a convenient principle to use local materials. Log must dip in water for a year, and after degumming (removing protein) dry for a year, then it just can complete the anti–cracking treatment, and be sawed for a plate material. Lobular boxwood is the best choice for the book engraving, because its texture is close and delicate, especially to convey the subtle line details of the illustrated book interest. The grand works of the late Ming Dynasty, *Landscape Map of The Garden of The Huancui Tang* and *The Human Mirror in Autumn*, show fine lines meticulously carved, employing certainly the boxwood as the printing plate. Most of the engravings handed down from the 17th and 18th centuries are made from pear wood blocks, which are less delicate than small–leaved boxwood, but are easier to obtain economically. There is also the use of jujube wood, whose texture is slightly rough compared to pear wood. "Unlucky pear, disastrous jujube" remains in modern Chinese, either as a criticism of the publication or as a modest way of remark.

From the point of view of economy and picture performance, the wood material for an overprint of all plates should be the same for the prints in seventeenth and eighteenth century. There has been a breakthrough of this situation made in modern times and a typical example is the woodblock watermarking copy of *Han* Xizai's *Banquet* in The 1950s and 1960s, whose whole picture was mainly made from pear woodblock, but for the eyebrows and beards, boxwood block was used as well.

In addition, it is worth of mentioning that there is a double–sided version of the color plate. Zizhu (Purple Bamboo) Studio contains the print plate pieces of New Year pictures in the 19th century, including the front line–engraved plate and the back engraved color plate. Multicolor plates are engraved meticulously, and in order to protect the embossing surface they are too fine to be carved on both sides.

Watermarking Table: the Wonderful Use of Pressure Rod

The watermarking table was an important tool for the multicolor prints of the seventeenth and eighteenth centuries. The clever thing about it is that the lever and the paper are using empty holes. The pressure bar presses a pile of paper through two fixed points for printers to facilitate the printing process in order.

Perhaps the greatest contribution of the invention of the watermarking table was not in printmaking, but in the first place in the printing of books. Its emergence guaranteed the labor productivity and standardization degree of book printing business. In my own experiments, through the watermark table, I can print 1000 monochrome line versions, or 1000 pages, within six hours, with little difference in paper margin of different printing.

The watermark table in Zizhu (Purple Bamboo) Studio is 1.8 meters long, 1 meters wide, 80 centimeters high, slightly higher than the ordinary desk. My work stool is 65 centimeters high, which is convenient for work at desk. If a large print is printed, it is also convenient to move the body around the table from side to side. When the printer is at work facing the watermarking table, on the right head can be seen a pressing rod protruding from the desktop, through two adjustable screws with a spacing of 80cm connected to the desktop, and if the screws are loosened, the right side of a pile of paper can be clamped under the pressing rod, and then after the screws are tightened, the whole pile of paper is fixed. To the right of the pressure bar is a hole, 15cm wide and 80cm long. When the printing is completed, the paper will be lifted to the right, and the paper will naturally cover over the pressure bar and hang into the hole. I have pondered the choice of fixed point spacing. 80 centimeters happens to be a little more than the width of four feet of full paper (close to 70cm). The ancient measure system is not a metric integer, but the actual length is probably quite close.

There is also a magic moving part of the printing table, which is used as a calibration plate for paper straightening, with two heights used to coordinate different engraving thicknesses, whose formal name of the part is not found in the literature.

The watermark table in Zizhu (Purple Bamboo) Studio, inherited from Rongbao Studio, is the drawing table for my daily work. In other places, from the Guangling Ancient Books Engraving and Printing Co., which still prints ancient books in the traditional way, to the artists' workshops for New Year paintings, I have seen similar printing tables with pressure bars. If there is any difference between the watermarking table in Zizhu (Purple Bamboo) Studio and the one in the 17th century, I think it is in the part that fixes the pressure bar: now it is fixed with two screws, whereas then it was fixed with two ropes. In 2005, the European Woodblock Foundation reproduced a copy of the table, collected now in the London office of the European Woodblock Education Trust.

Working Process

Speaking of watermark woodcut, the steps people often refer to are drawing, engraving, watermarking, and mounting. As for the watermark part, let me introduce the process again.

The first is the preparation of pigments, as detailed above, followed by preparing paper, with a horseshoe knife 5 cm wide to cut the paper. Make the whole stack of paper face down, with the right side pressed under the pressure rod. The Next step is to fix the plate. First of all, pull out the paper at the bottom and determine the position of the printing block according to the format (if you use chromatography, you need to determine the line drawing on the format).

I use Chinese medicine plaster produced by Huqing Yutang in Hangzhou, with plaster lamp heating softening plaster (before the appearance of plaster lamp, probably a piece of plaster is placed in the palm to be softened), and then respectively pile to the place where plate edge and desktop bond. At room temperature, the plaster will return to hardness, which can fully fix the plate. The advantage of using plaster is not hurt the plate, but plaster is more expensive. In the workshops of artists producing New Year pictures, I have seen a lot of practices of fixing printing plates with beeswax. Beeswax is easier to obtain than plaster, and was also a possible choice for the ancients. After the printing plate is fixed, cover the printing plate with a wet cloth, as the saying goes, "to be stuffy", which is removed in half an hour. This step makes the water in the wood fiber fully saturated, to avoid the picture surface is not of the same degree of dryness and wetness before and after the printing.

Next comes the brushing color. Dip a brush in color and apply it to the plate to be printed. Using a round brown brush, holding the brush in your left hand, draw circles in a clockwise direction and sweep the paint evenly. If you need to brush color quickly, use a brush or finger to dot the desired part.

Then the rubbing begins. The rubbing tool, called a rake, is a piece of wood with a palm skin covering the bottom. There are similar tools of the same size made by horsetail in the old stash of Zizhu Studio, but it no longer exists. The fibers of the palm are not arranged in parallel, but superimposed on each other. Therefore, the fibers in the brush line surface both overlap and loosen after pressured, resulting in bumps. When brushing, there is often a granular sense and obvious brush marks. After the rake has been used for a while, the flat overlaps of the palm brush lines will be smoothed, the graininess will replace the smoothness, and the brush marks will disappear. After another period of time, the palm brush line plane appeared a new round of uneven concave and convex, and then brush marks recurrence. Rake made of horsetail, because the fiber is parallel, can effectively avoid brush marks, but with rare application today because of the materials and the production not easy.

The right hand takes the paper from the pressure bar, the front side of the paper is attached to the painted printing plate, and the eye is watching whether the paper surface covering the section of the calibration plate is straight. Then the right hand holds the rake and presses the back of the paper to drag it from bottom to top one time, which step is called "back expansion" or "through printing". If the rake is too new or too old, or too fast and too heavy, it may leave a brush mark on the printing sheet. In Chinese tradition, such a brush mark is not appreciated, regarded as the work of accidental helplessness. In the blackened end page of many ancient books of seventeenth and eighteenth centuries also can be seen similar back extension brush marks, rather than the results because of uneven planing wood.

In order to cope with the change of grain sensation in the life cycle of the rake, today's printers often cover the back of the paper with another lining paper, usually a smoother ripe paper, to weaken the friction effect and avoid the exposure of brushing marks on the front of the paper. Japanese painters of ukiki painting are fascinated by such brushing marks (Japanese: 摺り迹), magnifying this kind of line interest and process interest, deliberately showing, with the influence till today. The Japanese term "Fuji 裏摺", which corresponds to "toku 背拓 and 透印", also puts more emphasis on expressive (not just procedural) brushing marks.[1]。

When printing in brush a single board, it can be directly to the back of the rake. If more than one board is involved, there are multi–board steps to follow, whose order is the line borad first (ink version), and then the color version; with the principle of color version from light to dark. Multicolor printing mapping is different from the common chromatography, which needs to draw line drafts first, clip the line drafts face down into the pressing bar, place them at the bottom

1 Thanks to Mr. Liang Ying from Shanghai Library for presenting the collection above–mentioned, which triggered my thoughts on brushing marks.

of the whole pile of paper, then to follow this line drawing draft step by step to set up the board.

After the whole stack of paper is used up in order to finish printing, then you cut paper with a horseshoe knife, and can get the finished product. As for the difference between different prints of the same image, color is an important perspective. Because of the randomness of color mixing, the improvisation of color brushing and the pigment "abandoned every other day", different printing may take on certain differences in color. But the bigger difference is in the mounting link after the watermark, with different engraver's or collector's preference for different mounting forms—in album, or in butterfly, or in thread, or even in hanging scroll—in the life of the same batch printed for hundreds of years, giving them a variety of appearances.

The examples of chromaticity prints collected in the British Museum from the 17th and 18th centuries

I'll take several examples of chromaticity prints collected in the British Museum now, to talk about the analysis that I have got with its colour.

The multicolor chromatography *Shizhuzhai Shuhua Pu, Calligraphies and Paintings Categories of Ten Bamboo Studio* (Figure 1) printed by Hu Zhengyan (1580–1671)in Chongzhen Period of the Ming Dynasty was a textbook–like album printed from the "Multicolor print", which integrated poetry, calligraphy, paintings and printing art into one, a giant structure in the history of woodblock watermarking. It has the reputation of "white eyebrow of painting garden, red flag of painting forest". There were eight volumes of paintings and calligraphies, bamboo, calligraphies, rocks, feathers, plum, orchid and fruit, with two volumes per type and the whole of sixteen volumes in butterfly form.

There are respectively twenty chromatography paintings and incriptions in Feather type, where Yang Wencong wrote "Little Preface of Feather" Autumn

Beginning Day of Dingmao Year in Tianqi Era", which admiringly reviewed the chromatography method Hu did in: "Hu Yuecong is of his ingenious mind and wonderful hands, going beyond the previous generations, to make a living with the iron pen and to replace silk in pear jujube, and the coloring method, dyeing method, dotting method, as well as the lightness, shallowness, depth, distance, clutch, etc. of the coloring are all in harmony and of beauty, very clever and subtle. That is, it should be viewed as the masterpiece sketching made by hand, thought that the painting is wonderful, and one dare not view it in the view of engraving portrayal." This feather category includes 20 pictures, painted without signatures, which, from the seals, must have been all produced by Ling Yunhan on his own right. Ling Yunhan, with the courtesy name Wuyun "Five clouds", was born in Wanli Years of Chongzhen Era. It is said in *The Record of Ming Paintings* that he was good at painting landscapes, but in fact he was also good at painting flowers and birds of Ling's family, especially painting rocks, which was honored by Hu Zhengyan.

This print is one of the feather category. Light ink plates in the print were first printed to represent the outlines of bamboo stems, rocks and birds, and then colored quickly with water. The second is the thick ink version of the birds' eyes and beaks, moss spots on the rock and sketching bamboo leaves and then colored quickly with water partly. Then two multicolor prints were made, one ochre version to show the head, back and wing tips of birds, and another cyan version to show the birds' tail and wings. Finally, grass green brushed version mixed with bogge and huaqing tone, and then colored quickly with water, partly with very light ochre, completing the coloring of bamboo leaves. The seal red in white on the left side with the seal characters "五云", may be obtained from the seal. The whole painting flexibly uses the brushing color technique, where the color is rich in changes of lightness and darkness, warmness and coldness, vividly reproducing the brushstroke interest of the painting.

The picture depicts two people arguing over a gambling game, with one person acting as a mediator. The print was produced in seven sets of different colors: ink as the main plate. First the outline drawing of the finished picture, the shirt of a character in the back and the shoes of the two characters in the front were printed; the bottom of the gaming table, the round stool, and the fence in the distance are made of pure cyan; the fence made of bamboo and the border of the standing screen are gloomy rattan yellow; the inner frame of the standing screen, the distant mountains inside the landscape of the screen, and the costumes of the two figures on the left are printed with bright cane yellow. The tassels and cheeks of the three figures, and the coat and gown of the figure on the left, are rouge; the top of the stool, the frame of the table and the feet of the standing screen, the coat of the figure on the right are heavier bluish gray; the robes of the first two figures are of a lighter bluish–gray. Finally, with the brush that naturally reduces the moisture after brushing, the blue and gray clothes of the front left figure are dyed with dynamic pleating effect, and the coat outline of the front left figure is dyed with the same method to show the texture of fur.

In the picture, them, the frames of the fence and the screen are rattan yellow with a little ink, made into a slightly green tendency of gray tone; the clothes of the figure on the left were first printed in a lighter blue color, and then red was printed on the plate above, so the overprint produced another purple color; the color of the lower left corner of the stool, table frame, screen foot and the upper shirt of the right figure is in gray blue, harmonic mixed by adding ink to cyan blue.

The color of this painting is stable and clumsy, because the cyan blue, gambogic, rouge and ink are plant pigments, cheaper than mineral pigments, easy to get, which, in the early Chinese folk prints, were used in a large number.

If the previous painting is a demonstration of “brushing color”, this one is special in the overprint and the final dry brush. In the Gaomi New Year paintings in Shandong province of the 20th century, the last step is called “pushing ash”, which means sweeping the toner with a dry brush to wipe out the parts that need to be emphasized and highlighted on the picture. Around 1700 in Suzhou, this similar step is like that I can only use the traditional Chinese painting term "coloring with a dry brushstroke" or "brushing with dry brushstrokes" to express, and what the term is at that time may be the subject worth exploring.

This picture (Figure 3), as well as the previous one, belongs to a set of prints, which should be the New Year paintings at that time. The picture is printed in six sets. Heavy ink as the main plate printed plum branches and swallows; two slightly lighter inks print the wings and the middle part of the trunk; the blossoming plum blossom is rattan yellow; the bud is a stone green; the outline of the grass at the root of the trunk and the blossoming plum blossoms is ochre with a touch of ink, a warm gray. The printing order is generally in the order: ink plate, two light ink plates with one light and and the other dark, gamboge plate, stone green plate, warm gray plate.

The figure in Figure 4 with a red face is popularly known as Guan Yu (ca. 160–220). The long–handled axe in hand was also the symbolic weapon of Cheng Chao–jin (589–665), another historical figure. It may be said that this is a portrait of Guan Yu that appropriates some of the attributes of Cheng.

The printmaking is a combination of overprinting and manual painting. The main lines of the picture are carved from wood blocks, printed in light ink, and then filled in with color. The color used in this painting is also the dyeing pregments used to dye clothes, so it is bright and transparent. These color cannot be called in all the name of traditional Chinese painting pigments, and let's say there are vermilion, rouge, bright yellow, light green, dark blue and thick ink. In particular, the face of the door god was lead white and blackened over time. The color of the whole painting is simple and gorgeous, with strong decorative effects, lines simple and clear, and a strong sense of rhythm. Based on the style characteristics above, it is close to the existing Mianzhu New Year paintings of Sichuan in the 19th century and a rare surviving painting from the 18th century.

The pigment used in this Figure 4 and the preparation method of pigment should be different from that mentioned above. Today, dyestuff is still used as pigments in folk New Year pictures, because it is cheaper.

This picture (Figure 5) takes iris as the main painting object, rocks, primrose in the background, as a fine painting with elegant color. Flowers and rock outlines are printed in ink; leaves in two hues of light grass green as well as dark; flower petals are printed in brushing color printing with cyan green water; stamens and back primrose in rattan yellow; rock background color is printed in bluish gray gained from adding ink to the cyan, by brushing color printing with water. The image is precise and detailed, the color is implicit and evenly meaningful, the tone is elegant and cleanly bright, and the composition is skillful.

This print (Figure 6) is one of a batch of 28 paintings that have been extensively documented in both Japan and China, including Hiroyuki Takimoto, Yoshiro Deli, Bo Songnian and Fan Jingzhong. In the article "The Rise and Fall of Suzhou New Year Pictures and Collection", Bo Songnian wrote about this batch of prints: "The color palette of flower paintings is rich and bright, and the carving and printing techniques are also diverse. Some fruits and melons are not printed in ink lines but are expressed in large color palette, like the boneless method in Traditional Chinese Painting. What's more, some flowers applied arching flower technology, making the flower highlight out of paper surface, showing the three–dimentional effect layer upon layer, very unique... Its printing age is at least before the middle of Kangxi Era, the earlier color woodbprint in Suzhou area." [1] Fan Jingzhong notes that the set of paintings, called "Kämpfer Prints", was named after Engelbert Kämpfer (1651–1716), who purchased them from Nagasaki between 1690 and 1692 and brought them back to Europe in 1693. [2]

This painting was overprinted separately with six color plates in carmine,

---

1 "Cultural Relics World" in *Zhonghua Wenyuan*.www.china—culture.com.

2 Basil Gray, "Sloan and the Kämpfer Collection," in The British Museum Quarterly, London, 1953, p. 18; Joseph Vedlich, The prints of the Ten Bamboo Studio followed by Plates from the Kämpfer Series and Perfect Harmony. Fribourg/Geneve, 1979; Wolfmar Zacken, Die Kämpfer Drucke, Wien, 1995.

cyanine, gamboge, grass green, ochre, and ink. The peony in the middle was first printed with the color plate of the whole flower, and the details in water brushing color; then overprint the colour block in the center of the flower to create levels of depth and shallownes. The magnolia on the right side of the painting is grass green instead of the natural color of white or purple, perhaps in order to avoid printing, or in order to emphasize the contrast between red and green in the whole picture. On the top left of the picture, there is the inscription "Thousand red and ten thousand purple fight spirit, pick flowers with colors new". The signature was "written by Ding Shi from Jinchang", without a seal. The woodblock printing of the whole picture is very beautiful, and chromatography is accurate, which is a rare early woodblock treasure.

Figure 7 is *Baizi Tu, The Picture of 100 Sons*, a printed woodblock print in Suzhou in 1743, collected by British Museum, whose painter is Yun Gu, with are two sayings about Yun Gu, Huang Zeng and Zhang Shuchu.[1] Its printer is Zhang Xingju. On the picture, at the night of Yuanxiao Holiday, plum blossoms and white snow are competing, decorated with lanterns and colorful ornaments, children playing. The picture combines two scenes: below is a beautifully decorated house, children riding ponies, or featuring generals, or pulling rabbit lights, to express the spatial relationship in a traditional way similar to the axis side. A scene of a courtyard facing mountains and rivers is shown above. On the left is a group of children climbing the steps to the pavilion, and on the right is a hall, where another group of children and women are encouraging the children climbing the steps. The pavilion for viewing the scenery takes an upward view, while the hall on the right uses a single focal point (the perspective of the courtyard wall of the rockery on the left is not on a perspective point, slightly expanded, because the painter is doing it at random?). Painting techniques are extremely exquisite, with inscriptions on the painting: "Imitation of Tai Xi brushwork", and it must have been influenced by "perspective" and etchings

1 Clarissa von Spee, *The Printed Images in China,* British Museum Press, 2010, p. 41.

introduced from the West. The most distinctive feature is the depiction of architecture and scenery, which uses fine and orderly parallel lines like etchings, mixed with traditional space expression and western perspective methods to show the integration of courtyards, pavilions, mountains, rivers and the bright moon in a large picture. It can be considered as the unique creation of Gusu prints in the early Qing Dynasty.

This picture is large (98.2 cm × 53.5 cm), or it can be printed in three separate sections made separately. [1] At the top is the character board, followed by the performance of the enjoyment of the middle section, and then by the lower section showing the playing performance in the hall. The middle section and the lower section are respectively offset printing. The outlines of the main building and figures are made of bluish black, which is mixed with ink and indigo. Because it is difficult to cross lines in large area of wood engraving, in each section, the printer used two blue and black lines with different directions of the lines to overlap into a row of lines. The figures' clothing as well as eaves in cinnabar and other figures' clothing in gamboge was respectively overprinted. In this way, the middle section and the lower section were to use four plates, plus the character plate of the upper section, with a total of nine plates. Is there too much work for a New Year painting? If the big version is not easy to get, when printing the upper middle section, the lower section or the upper, middle and lower section spliced fixed, then 9 overprints can be saved for 5 or even 4 times. In addition, I saw a large plate with 180 cm high at the place for carving Sutras in Jinling, which was carved with the statue of Avalokitesvara. Could there have been a plate large enough at that time?

There are variations of color chromaticity in this print, but no brushing color quickly is involved. Because the printing plate is larger, if brushing color quickly, veneer operation time is extended, I am afraid that some pages which have been brushed pregments will lose due moisture.

---

1 id, p. 40.

Word bank

1.watermarking n. 水印

2.woodcarving n. 木雕；木雕品

3.pregment n. 颜料

4.moisture n. 水汽；潮气

5.engraving n. 版画；雕版印刷品；雕刻

6.portrayal n. 画像；描绘

7.inheritance n. 继承物；遗产

8.stack n. 一堆；烟囱；立式烟道

9.horseshoe n. 马蹄铁；马掌

10.randomness n. 无安排；随机性

11.improvisation n. 即兴创作；即席演奏

12.mounting n. 装裱

13.album n. 册页；画册

14.butterfly n. 蝴蝶装

15.thread n. 线装

16.hanging scroll n. 立轴

17.chromaticity n. 色品；色度

18.disassemble v. 拆卸；拆开

19.palette n. 调色板；音色

20.ochre n. 赭石；赭色

21.gamboge n. 藤黄

22.indigo n. 木蓝属植物；靛蓝

23.halo n. 光轮；环

24.multicolor adj. 五彩缤纷的；多色的

25.gradient n. 公路斜面；斜坡；梯度

26.infiltration n. 渗入；渗透

27.dust v. 除去……上的灰尘；把粉等撒在……上

28.polychromatism n. 多色现象

29.exaggerate v. 夸大；夸张

建 筑

The Chinese Architecture

紫禁城与园林

紫禁城，即现在的故宫博物院[1]，曾为明、清两代的皇宫；迄今560多年历史，是中国现存规模宏大、格局完整的古建筑群。故宫分“外朝”和“内庭”两大部分，外朝以三大殿为中心，其中“太和殿”俗称“金銮殿”；内庭是帝后居住、游乐之所，是中国古代建筑艺术的典型代表。其中还含有一个美丽的花园，里面种满来自四海的珍稀植物。无论是紫禁城还是园林对于帝王而言都是一种统治地位的象征。

中国修建园林之风在清朝尤其盛行，甚至影响了西方，譬如英国的丘园。中国园林建筑是园林造景的四大要素之一。园林建筑既满足实际用途，又满足园林绿化的要求。古代造园者文化修养很高，能诗善画，造园时多以画为本，以诗为题，通过凿池堆山、栽花植树，创造出具有诗情画意的景观，被誉为“无声诗，立体画”。

中国园林建筑的突出特点之一就是利用原生态环境，使自然景观与人文情趣融为一体。古典园林建筑常以诗书画作点缀。它们避免沿轴线对称，采用

---

1 此文的编写参考了故宫博物院官网和颐和园官网等资料。故宫博物院官网，访问时间2021年11月3日，https://www.dpm.org.cn/Home.html。

不规则和复杂的布局，构造大量的大、小空间。园林建筑自身的外观应具有美感和表现力，并增强周围环境的美感。在其细节上，运用精美的装饰手段，如漂亮的护栏、花纹窗、格栅等。园林建筑是观赏园内外景色的场所，是园林的重点。所以无论是建筑物的朝向还是门窗的位置，都要考虑视角和路线。

中国园林的基本要素建筑：1. 殿堂、亭台、庙宇、画廊、桥梁、塔楼等。2. 人工山石园：山峰在中国哲学中是美德、稳重、忍耐的象征；3. 荷花池或湖：中国园林中的溪流总是蜿蜒曲折，不时被岩石或植被所掩盖；4. 花草树木以最生动的形式表现自然，与建筑的直线和岩石的恒久、锋利和静态形成鲜明对比。5. “借景”，依时间和季节，如远山的景色或隔壁花园的树木，营造出花园比实际大得多的错觉。6. 隐瞒和惊喜：花园景物并非立刻尽收眼底；它的一系列场景布局逐步呈现。

以北京颐和园[1]为例。颐和园是一座中国清朝皇家园林，占地面积达 293 公顷，以昆明湖和万寿山为基址，以杭州西湖为蓝本，汲取江南园林的设计手法；这样一座大型山水园林，也是保存最完整的一座皇家行宫御苑，被誉为“皇家园林博物馆”，是国家重点旅游景点。

颐和园主要由万寿山和昆明湖两部分组成。各种形式的宫殿园林建筑物 3000 余间，大致可分为行政、生活、游览三个部分。以仁寿殿为中心的行政区，供当年慈禧太后和光绪皇帝坐朝听政和会见外宾。仁寿殿后是三座大型四合院：乐寿堂、玉澜堂和宜芸馆，分别为慈禧、光绪和后妃们的居所。宜芸馆东侧的德和园大戏楼是清代三大戏楼之一。

颐和园自万寿山顶智慧海向下，由佛香阁、德辉殿、排云殿、排云门、云辉玉宇坊，构成了一条层次分明的中轴线。山下是一条长 700 多米的“长廊”，长廊枋梁上绘有彩画 8000 多幅，号称“世界第一廊”，面向昆明湖。昆明湖西堤仿西湖苏堤而建。

万寿山后山和后湖古木成林，有藏式寺庙以及苏州河古买卖街。后湖东端有仿无锡寄畅园而建的小巧玲珑谐趣园。冬天，人们经常在湖中滑冰，因为天寒湖水变成了天然的巨大溜冰场。

1　参考颐和园官网，访问时间2021年10月5日，http://www.summerpalace-china.com/；搜狗百科，访问时间2021年10月5日，https://baike.sogou.com/v8275.htm。

Forbidden City and the Chinese Garden

Forbidden City, called now "The Palace Museum in Beijing", was originally the palace of the emperors in the dynasties of Ming and Qing (1368–1644 and 1644–1911). With a history of over 560 years, it is the largest and most complete ancient architectural complex of China, divided into two parts: the Imperial Court and the Imperia Palace. Three great halls form the center of the court. The Hall of Supreme Harmony is usually called Jinluandian, where the emperor granted audiences. The Imperial Palace was the place where the emperor and the empress resided and entertained themselves. Beijing Palace Museum is a model of China ancient architecture art. It also contains a beautiful garden, which is filled with rare plants from all over the world. For the emperors, both the Forbidden City and the gardens are a symbol of imperial dominance.[1]

The hot trend to build gardens was popular in the Qing Dynasty in China, which even influenced the West, like the Kew Royal Botanic Gardens in Britain. The Chinese garden architecture is one of the four essential factors for garden landscaping. The garden architectures satisfy the requirements both far practical purposes and for landscaping the garden. Ancient Chinese garden builders were all highly educated, and good at verse and painting. Rich in literary allusions and analogous with the freehand brushwork in traditional Chinese painting, the classical gardens of Suzhou are the recreation of nature through the process of the decoration of land by planting trees, shrubs and flowers, and designing and materializing mountains and watercourses. Sometimes they are honored as "a

1 When this part is compiled, the information is reperred to official websites of the Palace Museum and the Summer Palace, https://www.dpm.org.cn/Home.html on Wednesday, accessed on, November 3, 2021.

silent poem and three–dimensional painting".

One of the outstanding characteristics of Chinese garden architectures is taking advantage of the original environment so that the natural scenes and human interest could be merged together. The classic garden architectures are often embellished with calligraphies, poems and paintings. They shun symmetry along an axis and adopt an irregular and complicated layout, with plenty of large and small spaces. The appearance of a garden building itself should be aesthetic and expressive, and enhance the beauty of the surroundings. In its details, exquisite decorative means should be made use of, such as pretty guardrail, patterned windows, grilles, etc. A garden building is a place for viewing the scenery within or beyond the garden and is a key point of the garden. So both the direction of the building and the positions of its doors and windows should take into consideration the viewing angles and the routes.

The essential elements of the Chinese Garden include：

1. Architecture: such as halls, pavilions, temples, galleries, bridges, and towers, etc.

2. Artificial mountains and rock gardens: The mountain peak was a symbol virtue, stability and endurance in the Chinese philosophy.

3. A pond for lotus flowers or a lake: The streams in the Chinese garden always follow a winding course, and are hidden from time to time by rocks or vegetation.

4. Flowers and trees, which represent nature in its most vivid form, and contrast with the straight lines of the architecture and the permanence, sharp edges and immobility of the rocks.

5. "Borrowed scenery", according to time and seasons, such as a view of distant mountains or the trees in the neighboring garden, creates the illusion that the garden was much bigger than it was.

6. Concealment and surprise: Not all the garden was not meant to be seen at the first sight; it is laid out to present a series of scenes step by step.

Taking Summer Palace[1] in Beijing as an example, the Summer Palace is a royal garden during the Qing Dynasty in China, covering an area of 2.93 hectares. The Summer Palace is a large–scale landscape garden built on Kunming Lake and Longevity Mountain, based on West Lake in Hangzhou, drawing on the inspired design techniques of Jiangnan gardens. It is also the most well–preserved imperial court and imperial palace, with the reputation of "the Museum of Imperial Gardens", which is one of the most important national tourist attractions in China.

The Summer Palace is mainly composed of Longevity Mountain and Kunming Lake. There are more than 3000 palace garden buildings of various forms, which can be roughly divided into three parts: administration, life, and sightseeing. The administrative area centered on Renshou Hall was the place where the Empress Dowager Cixi and Emperor Guangxu met with the ministers and foreign guests. Behind the Palace of Renshou are three large courtyards: Leshou Tang, Yulan Tang and Yiyun Pavilion, where Cixi, Guangxu and the concubines lived respectively. The Deheyuan Theater on the east side of Yiyun Pavilion is one of the three major theaters in the Qing Dynasty.

The Summer Palace, along the Wisdom Sea down from the top of Wanshou Mountain, consists of the Buddha Incense Pavilion, Dehui Hall, Paiyun Hall, Paiyun Gate, and Yunhui Yuyu Square, forming a central axis with distinct levels. At the foot of the mountain is a "promenade" with a length of more than 700 meters, on the beams of which there are more than 8,000 colorful paintings, known as the "world's first corridor", which is facing Kunming Lake. The west embankment of Kunming Lake is modeled on the Su embankment of West Lake.

There are thick ancient woods in the back hills of Wanshou Mountain and Houhu Lake, with Tibetan temples and Suzhou Creek Ancient Commercial Street. At the east end of Lake Houhu, there is a humorous garden imitating

1 Referring to the official website of the Summer Palace, http://www.summerpalace–china.com/, accessed on October 5, 2021; Sogou Encyclopedia, https://baike.sogou.com/, accessed on October 5, 2021.

Jichang Garden in Wuxi, small but crafty as well as interesting. In winter, people often skate on the lakes, because they turn into natural huge skating ground when it is very cold.

六和塔

塔是一种东方传统高耸型点式建筑，在亚洲很常见，它有着特定的形式和风格。供奉或收藏佛舍利（佛骨）、佛像、佛经、僧人遗体等，又称“佛塔”、“宝塔”，译成英文是 pagoda。在汉语中，塔也指高耸的塔形建筑，译成英文为 tower，tower 的寓意是高耸、超越或翱翔。

位于浙江省杭州市钱塘江畔的六和塔[1]是一座古佛塔，现为一处旅游名胜，每日游客如织。六和塔始建于宋开宝年间，重建于南宋初年，是中国现存最完好的木结构古塔之一，也是中国古代楼式塔的杰出代表。塔刹为葫芦形，置于八角攒尖顶之上。塔刹为元代元统二年（1334）遗物，由生铁铸成，高达 3.55 米，最大直径约为 3 米。塔刹分为五级，刹座圆形，之上为两层覆盆、宝珠、葫芦、三叉形的宝顶，形制古朴、铸造精细，上有元统二年 (1334) 的小楷铭文。叉戟是佛教界的标志性法器之一，以示具备强大的力量能够祛除种种业障。葫芦谐音“福禄”，含有驱灾辟邪、祈求幸福之涵义。宝珠为中国民间的吉祥八宝之一，被认为是美丽与光明的象征。

六和塔内现有南宋时期砖雕共 174 组，图案题材包括人物、花卉、飞禽、走兽以及回纹、云纹、团花等。雕刻技法采用了中、浅浮雕以及线刻；轮廓清晰，立体感强，造型简洁，古朴洗练，生动活泼，是宋代砖雕的精品，为中国现存最早的建筑专业著作《营造法式》提供了珍贵的物证。

底层北面甬道内壁龛上原有明线刻真武像碑。碑通高 4 米，宽 0.75 米。碑中刻画真武像，笔力遒劲，线条婉转，形象生动，为同类刻像中之精品。真武，又称玄天大帝，即民间和道教遵奉的玄武神。像中真武位于碑之右下方，头秃，手执降魔剑，足踏龟蛇，貌甚威武，气势凌人，其左侧还有一执旗小神，手中之旗迎风招展，周围云彩环绕。

1　编写此文参考了六和塔公园的官方宣传展览介绍。

六和塔
Liuhe Pagoda, the Six Harmonies Pagoda

六和塔是中国四大文学名著之一《水浒传》的故事场所之一，书中“鲁达圆寂”及“武松出家”等典故与六和塔都有直接关联。根据书中描写，鲁智深本名鲁达，与武松一起随宋江南下征讨方腊，武松在此役中痛失左管，功成后两人不愿接受朝廷封官，一起落脚六和寺。鲁智深死后，武松在六和寺出家，后于六和寺圆寂，享年八十高龄。

六和塔是中国古代和合文化的典型建筑，塔内保留了儒、佛及道文化的实物遗存。儒、佛、道不同文化在六和塔内并存，汇聚形成了六和独特的历史、文化和艺术价值。

真武神像

The portrait of God Zhenwu

Liuhe (Six Harmony) Pagoda

Tower 塔 is a kind of Oriental traditional towering point architecture, very common in Asia, bearing a specific form and style. The tower, for the worship or collection of Buddha's relics (Buddha bones), Buddha, Buddhist scriptures, monks' remains, etc., is also known as "Buddha pagoda", or "pagoda", translated into English is Pagoda. In Chinese, 塔 also refers to a tall tower shaped building, translated into English as a tower. Tower has a metaphor meaning to be high, beyond, or soaring.

Liuhe Pagoda[1], the Six Harmonies Pagoda, is an ancient Buddhist pagoda, located on the bank of Qiantang River in Hangzhou, Zhejiang Province, which is now a tourist attraction, with many visitors attracted every day. The Liuhe Pagoda was built during Kaibao Period of the Song Dynasty and rebuilt in the early Southern Song Dynasty. It is one of the most intact, well–preserved old pagodas of brick–timber structure in China, representing the ancient Chinese storey–styled towers. The top of the pagoda, Tasha, is in the shape of a gourd and placed on the octagonal spire, which is a relic from the 2nd year of Yuan Tong (1334) in the Yuan Dynasty. It is cast from pig iron and reaches a height of 3.55 meters with a maximum diameter of about 3 meters. The pagoda is divided into five levels, with the base of the pagoda round, with two layers of cladding, orbs, gourds, and three–pronged roofs, and with the shape simple and finely cast. On it, there are inscriptions in small regular script from the second year of Yuantong (1334). The fork is one of the iconic symbols of Buddhism, showing that it has a powerful force to remove all kinds of obstacles and barriers. The gourd is a

1 Referring to the official introduction of the Six Harmonies Pagoda in the Liuhe Park.

homonym for "Fu and Lu", with Calabash as homophonic blessing, which has the meaning of exorcising disasters and warding off evil spirits and praying for happiness. Baozhu, meaning precious bead, is one of the eight auspicious treasures of the Chinese folk and considered a symbol of beauty and light.

There are a total of 174 groups of brick carvings from the Southern Song Dynasty in Liuhe Pagoda, whose themes of the patterns include figures, flowers, birds, animals, and fret patterns, moire patterns, as well as flower patterns. The carving technique adopts medium relief and bas–relief as well as line carving; it has the characteristics of clear outline, strong three–dimensional impression, simple concise shape, refined in simplicity, vivid and lively, which are the finest piece of brick carvings in the Song Dynasty and the earliest surviving professional architectural work in the Northern Song Dynasty, providing direct and precious material evidence for the earliest existing professional work on architecture in China *Yingzao Fashi, Building Methods*, of the Northern Song Dynasty.

In the inner niche of the tunnel on the north side of the ground floor, there used to be a stele with a statue of Zhenwu carved with lines in the Ming Dynasty. The monument is 4 meters high and 0.75 meters wide, depicting the real military statue, with strong brushstrokes, tactful lines, and vivid images. It is the finest among similar sculptures. Zhenwu, also known as Emperor Xuantian, is Xuanwu God, the god of basaltic martial arts, followed and worshiped by folk and Taoism. The statue of Zhenwu is located at the bottom right of the stele. With his head bald, he is holding a magic sword in his hand, stepping on turtles and snakes, also along with a minor god holding a flag on the left, the flag in his hand waving in the wind, surrounded by clouds.

Liuhe Pagoda is a place included in one of the four great masterpieces, *Water Margin*. The allusions in the book such as "Lu Da Passed Down"and "Wu Song Became a Monk" are both directly related to Liuhe Pagoda. According to the description in the book, Lu Zhishen, whose real name is Lu Da, and Wu

Song went south to conquer Fang La along with Song Jiang. Wu Song lost his left arm in the battle disabled. After winning the battle, the two refused to accept the official titles and ranks given by the imperial court, so they settled in Liuhe Temple together. After Lu Zhishen's death, Wu Song became a monk in Liuhe Temple, and he passed away in Liuhe Temple at his age of eighty with a great longevity.

The Liuhe Pagoda is a typical building of the Chinese ancient harmony culture. The pagoda retains the physical relics of Confucianism, Buddhism and Taoism. The different cultures of Confucianism, Buddhism and Taoism are in harmony in the Liuhe Pagoda, and they converge and merge to form the unique historical, cultural and artistic value of Liuhe.

石窟寺

梁思成[1]

中国现存最早的佛教建筑遗迹是石窟寺。毫无疑问，这个概念是从印度进口的，其原型在卡利、阿旃陀和印度其他地方。虽然石刻墓葬在汉代，可能在公元开始后不久，已经开凿，其中一些进行了建筑处理，但它们是专为死者使用的。虽然像上面提到的那些窑洞，在凿岩墓葬之前无疑已经在使用，但它们并没有自称是纪念性的。直到印度思想传来，洞穴在建筑上才崭露头角。

四世纪中叶，佛教徒开始以凿洞为祭祀场所，并一直延续到明朝（1368—1644）。北魏、北齐、隋唐时期达到高潮，从五世纪中叶到九世纪下半叶，形成了一场广为流行的全国性“运动”，颇具规模。直到早些年，约 7 世纪中叶，洞穴才在建筑上得到处理。在岩壁上雕刻壁龛的想法渐渐地取代了开洞的想法，成为纯粹的雕塑对象。从建筑上而言，最重要的洞穴是甘肃敦煌、山西云冈、麦积山、甘肃天水、山西太原天龙山和河北磁县向塘山。

除了最后一个提到的，在大多数洞穴中，建筑处理手法几乎没有受到印度的影响，而且建筑基本上是中式的。异域影响的唯一明显迹象是洞穴本身的概念和装饰中的希腊式佛教图案，例如莨菪叶、卵锚饰、万字符、花环、珠子等。这些图案丰富了中国装饰图案的词汇，并从此在其中占据了永久的地位。

这些洞窟的建筑可以从两个方面来研究：一是洞穴本身，包括外部和内部的建筑处理；其次，装饰洞窟墙壁的浮雕描绘了当代木材和砖石建筑。后者描绘了众多的殿堂和宝塔，这些建筑的复制品曾经在中国北部和中部的平原和丘陵中大量涌现。

1　梁思成（1901—1972），中国著名建筑史学家、建筑师、城市规划师和教育家，一生致力于保护中国古代建筑和文化遗产。2022年1月9日是梁思成逝世五十周年纪念日。本文节选自梁思成《中国建筑：艺术与工艺品》一书，外语教学与研究出版社，2011年。

克孜尔洞窟外景
Exterior view of Kizil Caves

这些洞穴用石头保存了当时的木结构建筑的忠实复制形象。在显著的特征中，我们注意到，大多数情况下柱子为八角形，柱头为斗形(斗拱中的块)。柱头之上置楣板，而楣板又是用来接收斗拱组的主斗。这种布置在后世得到修改，通过直接将榫眼用榫接合，接在柱子的上端，从而使柱子上的斗与斗拱组合的主斗同时发挥作用。

在这些洞穴的建筑处理中，石雕的木材结构元素对后世最有用。在这里我们注意到斗拱一直是主要的装饰特征。

The Cave Temples

Liang Sicheng[1]

The earliest remains of Buddhist architecture existing in China today are the cave temples. Unquestionably the conception was imported from India, having its prototypes in Karli, Ajanta and elsewhere in India. Although rock–cut tombs were already hewn during the Han Dynasty, possibly shortly after the beginning of the Christian era, and some of them were given architectural treatment, nevertheless they were used exclusively for the dead. Although cave dwellings, like those just mentioned above, undoubtedly were in use even before the hewing of the rock–cut tombs, yet they made no pretension for monumentality. It was not until the arrival of the Indian idea that the cave ascended to architectural prominence.

In the middle of the fourth century, Buddhist believers started hewing caves as places for worship, and the practice was continued till the Ming Dynasty (1368–1644).The high tide was reached during the Northern Wei, Northern Qi, Sui and Tang dynasties, from the middle of the fifth to the later part of the ninth centuries, assuming the scale of a nationwide "movement" of great popularity. It was only during the earlier years, approximately up till the middle of the seventh century, that the caves were treated architecturally. Gradually the idea of opening up a cave was replaced by that of carving niches on the rock cliffs and became

1 Liang Sicheng, famous Chinese architectural historian, architect, urban planner and educator, has devoted his life to protecting ancient Chinese architecture and cultural heritage. January 9, 2022 is the 50th anniversary of Liang Sicheng's death. Liang, Sicheng, *Chinese Architecture: Art and Artfacts*, Foreign Language Teaching and Research Press, 2011.

mere objects of sculpture. Architecturally speaking, the most important caves are those at Dunhuang, Gansu Province, Yungang, Shanxi Province, the Maiji Mountains, Tianshui, Gansu Province, Tianlong Shan, Taiyuan, Shanxi Province and Xiangtang Shan, Cixian, Hebei Province.

In most of these caves, with the exception of the last mentioned, the architectural treatment show surprisingly little influence from India and the architecture is essentially Chinese. The only noticeable indications of foreign influence are the concept of the caves itself and the Greco–Buddhist motifs in the ornaments, such as the acanthus leaf, the egg–and–dart, the swastika, the garland, the bead, etc. These motifs have enriched, and have since taken their permanent positions in the vocabulary of Chinese ornamental motifs.

The architecture of these caves may be studied from two aspects: firstly, the caves themselves, including the architectural treatment of the exterior and interior; and secondly, contemporary timber and masonry architecture depicted in the reliefs decorating the walls of the caves. Among the latter are depicted numerous halls and pagodas, replicas of the structures that once rose in great numbers all over the plains and hills of North and Central China.

These caves have preserved in stone faithful copies of the wooden architecture of their time. Among the salient salient characteristics we notice that the columns in most cases are octagonal, with capitals in the shape of a dou (the block in the dougong). Above the capital is placed the architrave, which, in turn, is to receive the principal dou of the set of dougong. This arrangement was in later ages modified by mortising the architrave directly onto the upper end of the column, thus making the dou on the column to function at the same time as the principal dou of the set of dougong.

In the architectural treatment of these caves, the element most informative to posterity is the presentation of the timber construction in stone carving. Here we notice that the dougong is ever the dominant decorative feature.

Word bank

1.ascend v. 上升

2.prominence n. 声望

3. niche n. 壁龛

4. motif n. 主题

5.ornament n. 装饰

6.acanthus n. 莨菪，叶形装饰

7.swastika n. 万字记号

8.egg–and–dart n. 卵锚饰

9.garland n. 花环

10.timber n. 木材

11.masonry. 砖石建筑

12.relief n. 浮雕

13.replica n. 复制品

14.octagonal adj. 八边形的

15.architrave adj. 框缘

16. mortise v. 用榫接合

17.embellish. 美化，装饰

18.shun v. 躲避

19.guardrail n. 护栏

20.grille n 格子，格栅

21.embankment n. 堤；堤岸

22.concubine n. 妾

23.administrative adj. 企业管理的

24.aesthetic adj. 美感的；美学的；审美的

织　绣

The Chinese Silk Embroideries

官服古制

中国古代“从秦代初次建立统一的封建王朝起，二千年间的设官分职，大体上都是一脉相承的”[1]，中国古代官服定制也严格，中国古代官服定制严格，无论是颜色还是刺绣花纹都依据官级而定。冠服制度是中国古代礼仪制度的重要内容之一，服装的色彩、纹样、款式、质地无不形象地标示着服用者尊卑贵贱的身份和地位起到了“昭名分、辨等威”的作用。[2]《容斋随笔》有“官阶服章”言：

唐宪宗时，因数赦，官多泛阶；又帝亲郊，陪祠者授三品、五品，不计考；府军吏以军功借赐朱紫，率十八；近臣谢、郎官出使，多所赐与。每朝会，朱紫满庭，而少衣绿者，品服太滥，人不以为贵，帝亦恶之，大子少师郑综庆条奏意革。

淳熙十六年，绍熙五年，连有覃霈，转官赐服者众。绍熙元年，予自当涂能稽，过阙，遇起居舍人莫仲于漏舍，仲谦云：“比赴景灵行香，见朝士百数，无一

1　（清）黄本骥：《历代职官表》，上海古籍出版社，2019年，第1页。

2　编写此文参考了中国丝绸博物馆的官方展览介绍，2022年1月13日。

绿袍者。”又朝议、中奉皆直转行，故五品官不胜计，颇类元和也。[1]

另有一记“绯紫假服”曰：

唐宣宗重惜服章，牛丛自司勋员外郎为睦州刺史，上赐之紫，既谢曰：“臣所服绯，刺史所借也。”上遽：“且赐绯。”然则唐制借服色得于君前若之，国朝之制，到阙则不许。

乾道二年，予以起居舍人侍立，见浙西提刑姚中对，紫袍金鱼。既退，一阁门吏蹱其后嗫。后两日，宪辞归平江，乃绯袍。予疑石以焉，以问知阁曾觌曰：“闻临安守与本路监司皆许服所借，而宪昨紫今绯，何也”耳。觌曰：“监司惟置局在辇下则许服，漕臣是也；若外郡则否，前日姚误紫，而谒吏知不告，已申其罚，且备牒使知之，故今日只本色以入。”姚盖失于审也，然考功格未然令既不颁于外，亦自难晓。文惠公知徽州日，借紫，及除江东提举常平，告身不借。予闻尝借者当如旧，与郎官薛良朋言之，于是给公据改借。后于江西见转运院官张坚衣绯，张尝知泉州，紫袍矣，予举前说，张欣然即以申考功，已而部符下不许，扣其故，曰：“唯知州借紫而就除本路，虽运判、提举皆得如初，若他路则不可。”竟不知法如何该说也。若曾因知州府借紫，而后知军州，其服亦借，不以本路他路也。近吴镒以知郴州除提举湖南盐，遂仍借紫，正用前比云。[2]

这种冠服等级制度在明清最高统治者和官员冠服中体现得淋漓尽致，其中以代表王权的龙纹、十二章纹和代表官衔的百官补服最具代表性。[3]

1 （宋）洪迈：《容斋随笔》，北京燕山出版社，2008年，第906—907页。

2 同上，第524—525页。

3 参考了中国丝绸博物馆的官方展览介绍，2022年1月13日。

Ancient Regulations of Chinese Official Uniforms

In ancient China, "since the first unified feudal dynasty was established in the Qin Dynasty, the establishment of officials and the division of positions for two thousand years has generally been in the same line"[1]. Ancient Chinese official uniforms are also strictly regulated and customized, and both colors and embroidery patterns are determined by the official rank. The sumptuary clothing hierarchy system with special strict codes is one of the important contents of the ancient Chinese etiquette system. The color, pattern, style and texture of the clothing all vividly indicate the identity and status of the wearer, and play the clear role of "showing the title and position and distinguishing the status and dignity"[2]. *Rong zhai's Essays* has the item of "Uniforms by official rank":

During the era ruled by Emperor Xianzongshi of the Tang Dynasty, most officials were promoted because of many graces. When the emperor personally went to the southern suburbs to worship the sky every winter solstice, the officials who followed the emperor's sacrifices were awarded the third–rank and the fifth–rank regardless of their merits. Military attachés in the military camp in all likelihood, were rewarded for military merits for the vermilion or purple robes worn by middle and high–ranking officials. If the officials around the emperor were transferred to leave the emperor and the Vice Minister officials were sent outside the court or country, all were promoted by the emperor and given the right to wear vermilion or purple robes. Every day the emperor

1 (Qing) Huang Benji, *List of Officials in Past Dynasties*, Shanghai, Shanghai Ancient Books Publishing House, 2019, p. 1.

2 Referring to the official exhibition introduction of Zhejiang Silk Museum, on January 13, 2022.

met the ministers, the officials in the court were all dressed in vermilion or purple attire, with few wearing low green official uniforms appearing. Because of the excessive rewards of official costumes, people did not honor highly wearing vermilion or purple attire. The emperor also felt that this was too inappropriate, so he ordered the prince's youngest teacher, Zheng Yuqing, to formulate the political reform opinions one by one.

In the 16th year of Chunxi in the Southern Song Dynasty and the 5th year of Shaoxi (1195 AD), many people were promoted and given vermilion or purple official uniforms. In the first year of Shaoxi of the Southern Song Dynasty (1190 AD), I was transferred to Kuaiji (now Shaoxing, Zhejiang) from Dangtu (now southeast of Nanling, Anhui). When passing near the Imperial Palace in the capital, I met Mo Zhongqian, an official in charge of living, in the my humble house. He said to me: "Not long ago did I go to Jingling Temple to worship burning incense, I saw hundreds of officials, but none of them wore the uniform robes of low–level officials in green." In addition, Irregular Founctionary officials and Prestige Title such as the Chaoyi and the Zhongfeng also wore vermilion or purple robes. So it is impossible to calculate how many five–rank officials there are. This phenomenon is very similar to that of Yuanhe Years under Tang Xianzong. [1]

Another note of "Fresh Purple Fake Clothes" says:

Tang Xuanzong paid attention to the system of dressing according to his status. When Niu Cong was transferred to Mu serving as the governor from his rank Sixun Supernumerary Gentleman Cavalier Attendant, the emperor gave him a purple robe. After Niu Cong showed his thanks, he stepped forward and said to the emperor: "The red court uniform on me was borrowed." The emperor hurriedly said, "I will give you this red dress." The clothing system of the Tang Dynasty stipulates that it could be worn in front of the emperor in the color of the robe borrowed. However, it is not allowed to be worn in our court hall.

In the second year of Qiandao (1166 AD) under Xiaozong, I stood serving there as a

1 (Song) Hong Mai, *Rongzhai's Essays*, Beijing Yanshan Publishing House, 2008, pp. 906–907.

living official and saw that when Yao Zhongdui, Judicial Commissioner in West Zhejiang Province, entered the court, he was wearing a purple robe embroidered with goldfish, the court dress. After leaving the court, the officials of the government office followed him in whisper. Two days later, Yao Xian bid farewell to the emperor and returned to Pingjiang, but he was wearing a bright red court dress. I felt very strange, so I asked Zeng Di, who presided over the government office, and said: "I heard that the Lin'an prefect and the Regional Inspectors are allowed to wear the court clothes of the borrowed color. Yao Xian wore a purple robe yesterday but a red robe today. What is the reason?" Zeng Di replied: "the Regional Inspectors are only allowed to wear it in the agency set up in the capital. So it is as a Transport Commissioner; if you are outside in the county, you can't wear it. The day before yesterday, Yao Xian wore a purple robe by mistake, and the clerk did not tell him that he decided to punish him, and he had prepared official documents to let him know, so today Yao Xian only wore the red robe that he should wear to enter the court." Yao Xian is a bit sloppy, but if the criteria for investigating officials' merits and demerits are neither promulgated outside, nor can they know it. When my late brother Duke Wenhui became the prefecture of Jizhou, he borrowed a purple court uniform to wear. When he arrived at Jiangdong to take his office as Supervisor Official in Stabilization Found Bureau for usual routine, he was refused. I heard that the color the person once borrowed for should be the same as that before. I talked about this with Xue Liangpeng, Supernumerary Gentleman Cavalier Attendant, so I gave him the credentials to change the color. Later I saw Zhang Jian the Transport Commissioner Magistrate, wearing a bright red court robe on Jiangxi Road. Zhang Jian used to work as the prefecture of Quanzhou before. At that time, he was wearing a purple court robe. I mentioned to him what the old rules said. Zhang Jian was very in favor of it, and immediately reported his merits. The competent authority issued an order not to approve them. Asked about the reason, they answered: "Except for the prefecture who can borrow the purple, the others, even though they are Transport Commissioner Magistrate and the Supervisor Officials, must be the same as before. If they are appointed as other road officials, it will not work." This way I don't even know what to say about the correct regulations and service system.

If the prefectures and prefects borrow purple clothes, and later they can also borrow their court clothes serving as the outside officials, then you shouldn't separate which part they are from. Recently, Wu Yi was appointed to promote as Tea and Salt Monopoly in Hunan from the prefecture of Chenzhou, and he could still borrow the purple clothes according to the old rules.[1]

This clothing hierarchy is most vividly reflected in the clothing of the highest rulers and officials in the Ming and Qing dynasties, among which the dragon pattern representing the kingship, the twelve seal patterns and the 100 official rank clothing representing the official's are the most representative.[2]

1 (Song) Hong Mai, *Rongzhai's Essays,* Beijing Yanshan Publishing House, 2008, pp. 524–525.

2 Referring to the official exhibition introduction of Zhejiang Silk Museum, on Thursday, January 13, 2022.

龙袍[1]

尽管龙是一种虚拟物种，但是在中国文化中具有重要象征意义。龙不仅为十二属相之一，在中国文化中龙也象征帝王，龙纹样是中华民族最具代表性的装饰纹样之一，数千年经久不衰，在不同的时代呈现出不同的造型，具有非凡的艺术魅力和文化意义。龙纹样是清代帝王服饰中最具特点的装饰纹样，是经由多个朝代更迭而发展来的，它不仅代表着不可侵犯的王权，也反映了清代社会的时代特色和文化审美，在织绣工艺方面的技术发展也更加完善。其着装规定也更加细致。根据清朝（1644—1911）的着装规定，皇帝在农历三月十五或二十五要穿着明黄色的夏袍。

> 凡上供龙袍，我朝局在苏、杭。其花楼高一丈五尺，能手两人扳提花本，织来数寸即换龙形。各房斗合，不出一手。赭黄亦先染丝，工器原无殊异，但人工慎重与资本皆数十倍，以效忠敬之谊。其中节目微细，不可得而详考云。[2]

龙袍，又称龙衮，即皇帝的朝服，皇帝专用，袍上绣着龙形图案。此外，龙袍还泛指古代帝王穿的龙章礼服。公元 581 年隋文帝首次用蚕丝中最好的辑里湖丝，简称辑丝，作为织造龙袍的经纬线。唐高祖武德年间令臣民不得僭服黄色，黄色的袍遂为王室专用之服，自此历代沿袭为制度。960 年，赵匡胤自己“黄袍加身”，兵变称帝，于是龙袍别称黄袍。据《苏州府志》卷 147 记载，在明代万历二十九年（1601）宦官孙隆到苏州充当税监，督造龙袍。1957 年在北京十三陵定陵发掘的出土文物中就有用缂丝制成的龙袍。

龙袍上的各种龙章图案，历代各有所变化。龙袍的空地一般为赭黄色，

1　本文由编者编写而成。

2　（明）宋应星著，潘吉星校注：《天工开物》，上海古籍出版社，2013年。

清朝龙袍，拍摄自中国丝绸博物馆
A Dragon robe of Qing Dynasty, Photographed from China Silk Museum

龙袍上并绣 9 条龙，间以五色云彩。领前后正龙各 1 条，膝部左、右、前、后和交襟处行龙各 1 条，袖端正龙各 1 条。龙袍并不是专供皇帝穿着，郡王及以上身份者都可以穿，只是不能用黄色；其他官员不能穿龙袍，唯有得到皇帝亲赐才能穿着，但穿着的龙袍上龙爪必须“挑去一爪”，以示区别。

在明朝，经改制后的龙袍，称为蟒袍，成为明朝职官常服。龙袍的做工有刺绣和缂丝之分，其中缂丝工艺相对复杂，工艺上称为“连经断纬”。这种缂丝工艺在中国流传已久，宋代时多用于其他装饰之上，到清代多用于服饰，后因缂丝工艺消耗工时过长，所以多用于织造龙袍。

在故宫博物院藏有一件明黄色龙袍，绣有金龙。这件黄色龙袍是乾隆皇帝（1736—1795 年在位）在重大仪式和祭祀仪式上所穿的正式夏袍。[1]

1 参考故宫博物院官网，访问时间2021年11月3日，https://www.dpm.org.cn/Home.html。

Imperial Robes with Embroidered Dragons[1]

Although the dragon is a virtual species, it has important symbolic significance in Chinese culture. Not only is there Dragon in the twelve zodiac signs, but the dragon also symbolizes the emperor in Chinese culture. The dragon pattern is one of the most representative decorative patterns of the Chinese nation. It has been enduring for thousands of years, showing different shapes in different eras, with extraordinary artistic charm and cultural significance. The dragon pattern is the most characteristic decorative pattern among the emperors' costumes in the Qing Dynasty. It was developed through many dynasties, which not only represented the inviolable kingship, but also reflected the characteristics of the times and cultural aesthetics of the Qing society. The technical development of embroidery technology was also nearly perfect. The dress code is also more detailed. For example, according to the Qing–dynasty (1644–1911) regulations for attire, the emperor was to wear a bright yellow summer court robe on the fifteenth or twenty–fifth day of the third lunar month.

The weaving and dyeing bureau of the Ming Dynasty to make the imperial robes with embroidered dragons used by the emperor supplied to the emperor was located in the two places at the junction of Suzhou and Hangzhou, because it produced the best silk Ji Silk in China. The yarn machine used to make the imperial robes with embroidered dragons is as tall as fifteen feet. Two skilled weaving–experts were jacquarding patterns, carrying out by hand. After every few inches were finished, they are transformed into another dragon–shaped pattern. An imperial robe with embroidered dragons should be

1 This is compiled by the complier of this book.

woven in sections by several looms, not by one person. The used silk must be dyed ocher yellow. The tools for weaving are nothing special, but the weavers must be careful, with heavy work, and the labor and cost had to be increased dozens of times to show their loyalty and respect to the court. As for the many details in the weaving process, it is impossible to examine in detail.[1]

The imperial robe with embroidered dragons, also known as Longgun, is the emperor's court attire, dedicated to the emperor, and the robe is embroidered with a dragon–shaped pattern. In addition, the imperial robe with embroidered dragons also refers to the dragon medal gown worn by ancient emperors. In 581, Emperor Wen of the Sui Dynasty first used the finest silk, Jilihu silk, referred to as Jisi, as the warp and weft for weaving the imperial robe with embroidered dragons. During the Wude years under the reign of Emperor Gaozu of the Tang Dynasty, he ordered his subjects were not allowed to be in yellow. The yellow robe was used exclusively by the royal family, which became the system since then. In 960, Zhao Kuangyin dressed himself in "yellow robe" on his own and became emperor in mutiny, so the imperial robe with embroidered dragons was also called the Yellow Robe. According to Volume 147 of *Suzhou Fuzhi,* in the 29th year of Wanli in the Ming Dynasty (1601), Sun Long, the eunuch, went to Suzhou to serve as a tax supervisor and supervise the production of the imperial robes with embroidered dragons. In 1957, the unearthed cultural relics, excavated in the Dingling Tombs of the Ming Tombs in Beijing, contain the imperial robe with embroidered dragons made of tapestry silk.

The various patterns of dragon emblems on the imperial robe with embroidered dragons have changed in different dynasties. The open empty area of the imperial robe with embroidered dragons is generally khaki yellow, and 9 dragons are embroidered on the robe, with five–colored clouds in between.

1 (Ming) Song Yingxing, Pan Jixing proofread, *Tiangong Kaiwu (Heavenly Creations·Naifu·the Imperial Robes with Embroidered Dragons),* Shanghai Ancient Books Publishing House, 2013.

There is one right dragon with the front fasade showing on the front and back of the collar, one dragon on the left, right, front, back and cross of the knees, and one right one with the front fasade showing on either sleeve. The robe with embroidered dragons is not exclusively for the emperor. It can be worn by county princes and above, but the yellow imperial robe with embroidered dragons is not allowed for them. Other officials cannot wear the robe with embroidered dragons. They can only wear the one given by the emperor, with "one claw cut down" to show the difference.

In the Ming Dynasty, the restructured robe with embroidered dragons, called the Mang robe, became the official uniform of the Ming Dynasty. The workmanship of the robe with embroidered dragons is divided into embroidery and tapestry. The tapestry process is relatively complicated, and the process is called "continuous warp and broken weft". This tapestry craft has been sustained in China for a long time. It was mostly used for other decorations in the Song Dynasty, and was mostly for clothing in the Qing Dynasty. Later, because the tapestry craft consumed too much time and too many man–labors, it was mostly used for the imperial robe with embroidered dragons.

In the Palace Museum there is a collection of a bright yellow imperial robe with embroidered gold dragons. This yellow garment was a formal summer robe worn by the Qianlong Emperor (r. 1736–1795) for major ceremonies and sacrificial rituals.[1]

---

1 Referring to the official website of the Palace Museum, accessed on November 3, 2021, https://www.dpm.org.cn/Home.html.

缂丝[1]

中国是丝绸发源地，织绣品历史悠久。织绣是用棉、麻、丝、毛等纺织材料进行织造、编结或绣制的工艺。中国织绣工艺品种繁多．绚丽多彩。主要有刺绣、织锦、缂丝、抽纱、花边、绒绣、机绣、绣衣、绣鞋、珠绣、地毯、手工编结等。

据考古发掘的资料证明，中国的丝织物始于东南地区新石器时代的良渚文化。此后，经过殷商的发展，春秋战国时期的织绣工艺，已具有较高水平。

1982 年，曾在湖北江陵马山发掘了一座楚墓，[2] 出土了大批丝织品、编结和刺绣等。丝织品的品种有绢、罗、纱、锦等。花纹有几何纹、菱形纹、S 形纹等，几何纹中还饰有龙凤、麒麟和人物图案。在大批的刺绣中，有绣衣、绣裤、绣袍等，绣地多用绢，用辫针绣出龙、凤、虎、三头鸟，以及草叶、枝蔓和花朵，线条流畅，技术高超。明清丝绸业在前代生产基础上达到巅峰盛况，江南地区的产量居全国之首。缎、绒、妆花等丝织品种推陈出新，丝绸图案富有吉祥寓意。[3]

宋代的缂丝、元代的棉纺、明代的织锦都有较高成就，清代的刺绣工艺则由于地区的不同与技艺的演变，形成了苏绣、湘绣、粤绣、蜀绣四大名绣，更具民族风格和地方特色。中国织绣工艺品的分布如下：刺绣、织锦、缂丝工艺主要产在江苏、浙江、广东、湖南、四川等地；地毯工艺主要产在新疆、宁夏、青海、西藏、天津、北京等地；抽纱、花边、绒绣工艺主要产在烟台、上海、潮州、汕头、萧山等地。中国织绣工艺在国外享有极高声誉，尤其是手工绣品、手工编结和手工地毯，对中外经济与文化交流起着重要作用。

---

1 本文由编者编写。

2 湖北省荆州地区博物馆：《江陵马山一号楚墓》，文物出版社，1985年。

3 编写此文参考了中国丝绸博物馆的官方展览介绍，2022年1月13日。

缂丝团鹤补，拍摄自中国丝绸博物馆
Kesi tapestry round rank badge with crane motif, Photographed from China Silk Museum.

缂丝，又名刻丝，汉语拼音可为“kesi”或“K’o–ssu”。这种中国传统的丝织工艺品是将绘画移植于丝织品上的特种工艺。织造时，各色纬丝在图案花纹需要处与经丝交织，并不贯穿全幅，即所谓的“通经断纬”。其成品的花纹两面如一。现存最早的缂丝是唐代（618—917）制品。南宋（1127—1279）时，缂丝业兴盛，宋代朱克柔有缂丝《莲塘乳鸭图》。宋代以后的缂丝技法愈趋丰富多变，明、清两代（1368—1911）尤为流行。[1]

现故宫博物院藏元代《缂丝赵佶花鸟方轴》，画幅纵24.5厘米，宽25.3厘米，是以宋徽宗赵佶所绘花鸟册页做蓝本的缂丝杰作。画面上，粉红色牡丹或含苞或怒放；立于牡丹枝头的鸟雀俯视着小瓢虫，曲尽其妙；展翅的蝴蝶风姿绰约。整幅画面洋溢着春天的气息。缂工精致平细，晕色之处以长短戗、木梳戗、掺和戗等技法完成，无着笔。辅以平缂、构缂技法，使画面层次分明，立体感强。鸟羽、蝶翅等细微之处用长短戗技法表现，技艺高超。图中有墨书诗云：“雀踏花枝出素纨，曾闻人说缂丝难。要知应是宣和物，莫作寻

1 此部分引自徐惟诚总编：《不列颠百科全书》，第9卷，中国大百科全书出版社，1999年，第231页。

常莆绣看。”画心有朱缂“御书”印一方。摹缂古人书画作品是元代缂丝作品的特点之一。绘画作品以缂丝技法传承和表现，既可传达出中国画的意境和神韵，又与纯粹用笔墨渲染的绘画相异，别有一番情趣。此缂丝图为这类作品的代表作之一。[1]

近代缂丝工艺逐渐衰落，中华人民共和国建立（1949）后才恢复生产。缂丝题材多仿古代人物、山水、花鸟等绘画，缂丝作品更多以名人书画为稿本，以娴熟、繁复的技法追摹，以求表现原作之神韵。[2]

---

1 殷安妮，故宫博物院官网，访问时间2021年10月23日，https://www.dpm.org.cn/collection/embroider/228791.html。

2 徐惟诚总编：《不列颠百科全书》，第9卷，中国大百科全书出版社，1999年，第231页。

Kesi Art[1]

China is the birthplace of silk and has a long history of weaving and embroidery. Weaving and embroidery is the process of weaving, knitting or embroidering with cotton, linen, silk, wool and other textile materials. There are many varieties of Chinese embroidery crafts, bright and colorful, mainly including embroidery, brocade, tapestry, drawnwork, lace, fleece embroidery, machine embroidery, embroidered clothing, embroidered shoes, bead embroidery, carpets, hand–knitted and so on.

According to data from archaeological excavations, Chinese silk fabrics originated from the Neolithic Liangzhu Culture in the southeast. Since then, after the development of the Yin and Shang dynasties, the weaving and embroidery craftsmanship of the Spring and Autumn Period and Warring States Period has reached a relatively high level.

In 1982, a Chu tomb was excavated in Mashan, Jiangling, Hubei,[2] and a large number of silk fabrics, knitting and embroidery were unearthed. The varieties of silk fabrics include silk, Luo silk, yarn, brocade and so on, whose patterns include geometric patterns, diamond patterns, S–shaped patterns, etc. The geometric patterns are also decorated with dragons, phoenixes, unicorns, and figures. Among a large number of embroidery, there are embroidered clothes, embroidered trousers, embroidered robes, etc. Silk is often used for embroidering, and dragons, phoenixes, tigers, three–headed birds, as well as

---

1 This is compiled by the compiler of this book.

2 Jingzhou Regional Museum, Hubei Province, *Chu Tomb No. 1 Mashan in Jiangling*, Cultural Relics Publishing House, 1985.

grass leaves, branches and flowers are embroidered with braided needles. The lines are smooth and the technique is superb. The silk industry in the Ming and Qing dynasties reached its zenith on the basis of the previous. The silk output of the Jiangnan region ranked first in the country. Such silk products as satin, velvet and brocaded silk with discontinuous supplementary wefts were innovated and broadened the repertory of weave types, with the silk patterns full of auspicious meanings with auspicious motifs auguring good fortune and longevity of life.[1]

Kesi in the Song Dynasty, cotton spinning in the Yuan Dynasty, and the brocades of the Ming Dynasty all had high achievements, and the embroidery craftsmanship of the Qing Dynasty, due to the different regions and the evolution of skills, formed the four famous embroideries of Su embroidery, Hunan embroidery, Yue embroidery, and Shu embroidery, which have more national style and local characteristics. The distribution of Chinese embroidery crafts are like the following: embroidery, brocade and tapestry crafts are mainly produced in Jiangsu, Zhejiang, Guangdong, Hunan, Sichuan and other places; carpet crafts are mainly produced in Xinjiang, Ningxia, Qinghai, Tibet, Tianjin, Beijing and other places; drawnwork, lace and cashmere embroidery are mainly produced in Yantai, Shanghai, Chaozhou, Shantou, Xiaoshan and other places. Chinese embroidery craftsmanship enjoys a high reputation abroad, especially hand–made embroidery, hand–knitted and hand–made carpets, which play an important role in the economic and cultural exchanges between China and foreign countries.

Kesi, also known as 刻丝 , can be “kesi” or “K’o–ssu” in Chinese pinyin spelling. This traditional Chinese silk handicraft is a special craft that transplants paintings into the ones on silk fabrics. When weaving, the weft yarns of each color are interwoven with the warp yarns where the pattern is needed, and do not run through the entire width, which is the so–called “passing warp and breaking weft”. The pattern of the finished product is the same on both sides. The earliest extant Kesi is a product of the Tang Dynasty (618–917). During the Southern

1 Referring to the official exhibition introduction of Zhejiang Silk Museum, on Thursday, January 13, 2022.

Song Dynasty (1127–1279), the Kesi industry flourished. In the Song Dynasty, Zhu Kerou had woven the silk "*Liantan Ruya Tu–Ducklings in Lotus Pond*". After the Song Dynasty, the tapestry technique became more and more varied, especially popular in the Ming and Qing dynasties (1368–1911). [1]

The "*Kesi Zhao Ji's Huaniao Fangzhou–Kesi Square Scroll of Zhao Ji's Flowers and Birds*" produced in the Yuan Dynasty, collected now by the Palace Museum, has a painting size of 24.5 cm in length and 25.3 cm in width. On the painting, pink peonies may be budding or blooming; the bird standing on the branch of the peony looks down on the ladybug, curving to the best of its best; the butterfly with its wings spread out in grace and elegance. The whole picture is permeated with the breath of spring. The craftsmanship is exquisite and thin, and the shading is done with the techniques of length and short, wooden comb, blending and other techniques, without painting. Supplemented by the techniques of flat and structured tassels, the picture has a clear hierarchy and a strong sense of three–dimensionality. Bird feathers, butterfly wings and other subtle points are expressed with long and short techniques, with superb skills. In the picture, there is an ink caligraphy saying: "The bird treads on the flowers and branches out of the plain silk. I once heard people say that the tapestry is difficult. You should know that it should be a Xuanhe object, and don' see it as the ordinary embroidery." In the center of the the painting is a seal with the characters of "Imperial Calligraphy". To produce works of ancient people through kesi is one of the characteristics of the works of Kesi in the Yuan Dynasty. The painting works are inherited and expressed by the Kesi technique, which not only conveys the artistic conception and charm of Chinese painting, but also differs from the paintings rendered purely with brushworks and ink, which has a special taste. This tapestry picture is one of the masterpieces of this type of work.[2]

---

1 Taken from *Encyclopedia Britannica international chinese* Edition, vol. 9, Encyclopedia of China Publishing House, 1999, p. 231.

2 Yin Anni, the official website of the Palace Museum, accessed on October 23th, 2021, https://www.dpm.org.cnlcollectionlembroi–derl 228791.html.

In modern times, the Kesi–making process gradually declined, and production was resumed only after the founding of the People's Republic of China (1949). The Kesi silk subjects are mostly paintings of antique paintings of figures, landscapes, flowers and birds, and more Kesi works are based on celebrity calligraphies and paintings. They are copied with skilled and complicated techniques in order to express the charm of the original art works.[1]

1 Referring to *Encyclopedia Britannica International chinese Edition*, with Xu Weicheng as chiefeditor,Vol. 9, Encyclopedia of China Publishing House, 1999, p. 231.

Word bank

1.symbolize v. 象征；用象征的方法代表

2. inviolable adj. 无法破坏的；不可侵犯的

3. kingship n. 王位；王权

4. embroidery n. 刺绣

5. dress code n. 着装规定

6. attire n. 服装

7. the imperial robes with embroidered dragons n. 龙袍

8. jacquard n. 提花机；提花织物

9.gown n. 长礼服；裙服

10.emblem n. 徽章；纹章

11.restructure v. 改组；重组

12.tapestry n. 挂毯；复杂的一连串的事件

13.warp v. 弯曲；变形 n. 经；经纱

14.weft n. 纬线；一阵微风

15.ceremony n. 宗教庆典；礼仪

16.sacrificial adj. 牺牲的；献祭的

17.ritual adj. 宗教仪式的；惯常的 n. 仪式

陶　瓷

Ceramics

黑陶文化

黑陶文化别称龙山文化[1]，泛指新石器时代晚期的一种文化，时间为公元前2310—公元前1810年左右，在山东省章丘市龙山镇首次发现，分布在黄河中、下游。河南龙山文化，陕西龙山文化和山东龙山文化三类统称为龙山时代。此时，世人以农业为主，畜牧业较发达，出现了磨制石器工具，轮制灰陶。

黑陶最早发现于龙山文化，是其最重要的一个特征。黑陶是指在烧造过程中采用渗碳工艺制成的黑色陶器，在新石器时代晚期的滇藏文化、大汶口文化、龙山文化、屈家岭文化和良渚文化等遗址中都有出土。黑陶采用轮制，器形浑圆工整，造型优美，装饰精巧，具有“黑、薄、光”等艺术特点。黑陶的烧成温度达1000℃左右，黑陶有细泥、泥质和夹砂三种，其中以细泥薄壁黑陶制作水平最高，有“黑如漆、薄如纸”之美誉。制作这种黑陶的陶土经过淘洗、轮制，胎壁厚仅0.5~1毫米，再经打磨，烧成漆黑光亮，有“蛋壳黑陶”之称，表现出惊人的技巧，饮誉中外。这时期的黑陶制品以素面磨光的最多，带纹饰的较少，主要有弦纹、划纹、镂孔等几种图案纹饰。

1　编写此文时参考了徐惟诚总编：《不列颠百科全书》，第10卷，中国大百科全书出版社，1999年，第195页。

Black–pottery Culture

Black–pottery Culture is another name for Longshan Culture[1] referring to a culture of the late Neolithic period, as its most important feature, which was first discovered in Longshan Town, Zhangqiu County, Shandong Province and distributed in the middle and lower reaches of the Yellow River, when agriculture was the mainstay, and animal husbandry was more developed with stone tools for grinding and gray pottery made by wheels.. The Longshan Culture dates from 2310 B.C. to around 1810 B.C., which is divided into Henan Longshan Culture, Shaanxi Longshan Culture and Shandong Longshan Culture, collectively referred to as the Longshan Period.

Black pottery refers to the pottery with black color made by carburizing during the firing process. It was unearthed in the Yunnan–Tibetan culture, Dawenkou Culture, Longshan Culture, Qujialing Culture and Liangzhu Culture in the late Neolithic period. The black pottery is made of wheels, with the round and neat shape, as well as beautiful and exquisite decorations. It has the artistic characteristics of being "black, thin, light, and new". The firing temperature of black pottery is as high as about 1000 degrees. There are three types of black pottery: the type of fine clay, the type of clay and the type of clay with sand, among which the thin–walled black pottery out of fine clay has the highest level of production with the reputation of "as black as lacquer; as thin as paper". This type of black pottery clay has been washed and wheeled, with a wall thickness of only 0.5–1 mm, and then polished and fired into pitch black and bright, called

1 Referring to *Encyclopedia Britannica International Chinese Edition*, vol. 10, "Long shan calture",with Xu Weicheng as chief editor, Encyclopedia of China Publishing House, 1999, p. 195.

“egg–shell black pottery”, exhibiting amazing skills and well–known both at home and abroad. The black pottery of this period was mostly polished with plain surface, and less decorated, with such main patterns as string patterns, scratch patterns, and pierced holes.

龙泉瓷[1]

瓷器是中国文化的瑰宝之一，生活中处处可见瓷器的身影。读《全宋笔记》可见：

今人秘色磁器，世言钱氏有国日，越州烧进为供奉之物，不得臣庶用之，故云"秘色"[2]。尝见《陆龟蒙詩集·越器》云："九秋风露越窑[3]开，夺得千峰翠色来。好向中宵盛沆瀣，共嵇中散斗遗杯。"乃知唐已有秘色矣色。[4]

从上文可知这种"秘色"越窑瓷器早在唐朝就已经发明了。"九秋风露越窑开，夺得千峰翠色来。"这两句属于咏瓷名诗，意思是：九秋时节，窑外一片荒凉，可是开窑一看，窑内青重翠叠，光彩夺目，烧窑工匠的精湛技艺，使得千峰翠色尽在窑中。诗中描绘了陶工巧夺天工的制瓷技艺。不过龙泉也产"秘色"瓷器，"处州龙泉县多佳树，地名豫章，以木而著也。山中尤多古枫木……又出青瓷器，谓之秘色，钱氏所贡，盖取于此。宣和中，禁庭制样须索，益加工巧。"[5]

精品瓷器自古珍之，这诱发了我内心的渴望，一直希望亲手制作一件瓷器。暑假时有机会去了浙江省龙泉的龙泉窑，终于亲自体验了制作龙泉瓷器的快乐。

龙泉瓷为中国名瓷，属中国南方青瓷系统。创烧于北宋早期，盛起于宋

---

1 本文由编者编写。

2 秘色越器指越窑烧制的秘色瓷器。这是为宫廷烧制的一种瓷器，配方、釉色、器形、烧制技术都是保密的。由于没有传到民间，久而久之，技术失传。

3 越窑：唐宋时代著名青瓷窑之一。窑址在今浙江余姚上林湖一带，古属越州，故名越窑。釉色由青中微带黄色，改进到青水般的湖绿色；绘有花鸟、人物或几何图案。所烧瓷器畅销国内，远销海外。

4 《全宋笔记》第四编，第五册，大象出版社，第99页。

5 （南宋）庄绰：《鸡肋编》，《四库全书总目》，子部。

代，南宋中晚期进入鼎盛时期，至明代中叶以后渐趋衰落，元代龙泉瓷器大量远销海外。所产青瓷，色泽光润如玉。龙泉瓷器至今仍驰名国内外。[1]

我前往的龙泉瓷基地是一处幽静的庄园，四周景色宜人。当日下着蒙蒙细雨。制作龙泉瓷器第一步工序是用手揉瓷土，直揉到瓷土均匀为止。我没有体验这一步，土已经被工艺师揉好了。长廊下排列着一排电动拉坯机，坐在机器前面，我直接进入了第二步“拉坯”，拉坯是器件成型的一步，如果成型失败需要重来。我用电动拉坯机，在师傅指导下将揉好的瓷土放在拉坯机上，然后双手沾上些水，轻轻地拍一拍，右脚踩住一个踏板，用踏板控制转盘速度，轻轻往下一踩，转盘便开始旋转起来，双手拢住瓷土，在转盘带动下，按照需要做的器型以手用力，器件成型后松手，拉坯持续了一个小时左右，手随转盘转动的感觉很浪漫，联想到了电影《人鬼情未了》里的经典镜头。经历多次失败之后，我的瓷器成型了。

其余步骤由工艺师完成。据师傅介绍，拉好的坯体，将置于架子上晾干，这就是烘胚。晾干后的坯体还需要修坯，打磨坯体，精细修补晾干后开裂的部位。然后是素烧，将胚体放入窑中烧到近 900 度。待坯体晾干后，至关重要的就是上釉，这关系到最终成品瓷器的釉色质量。上釉有很多方法，可以直接将器件放进釉水里浸泡一下，用手轻轻地将釉水摇匀，也可以用喷枪均匀地喷釉。一般要上 3 次釉。上好釉，放置晾干，待晒干后，用窑炉烧制。窑炉里的温度需要达到 1300 度以上，连续烧 24 个小时，待冷却后，窑里便是晶莹剔透的龙泉青瓷作品了。

据介绍，龙泉青瓷产品有两种：一种是白胎和朱砂胎青瓷，称“弟窑”或“龙泉窑”；另一种是釉面开片的黑胎青瓷，称“哥窑”。“弟窑”青瓷釉层丰润，釉色青碧，光泽柔和，晶莹滋润，胜似翡翠。有梅子青、粉青、月白、豆青、淡蓝、灰黄等不同釉色。“哥窑”青瓷有纹片装饰，如冰裂纹、蟹爪纹、牛毛纹、流水纹、鱼子纹等，釉层饱满、莹洁，素有“紫口铁足”之称，与釉面纹片相映，更显宁静、典雅，堪称瓷中珍品。

现代的龙泉青瓷忠实地继承了中国传统的艺术风格，在继承和仿古的基础上，更有新的突破，研究成功紫铜色釉、高温黑色釉、虎斑色釉、赫色釉、

---

1 参见徐惟诚总编：《不列颠百科全书》，第10卷，中国大百科全书出版社，1999年，第195页。

龙泉瓷　私人收藏

An Article of Longquan porcelain, Private collection

茶叶末色釉、乌金釉和天青釉等。在工艺美术设计装饰上，有“青瓷薄胎”、“青瓷玲珑”、“青瓷釉下彩”、“象形开片”、“文武开片”、“青白结合”、“哥弟窑结合”等。

两个月后我满心欢喜地收到了我的作品，这件龙泉瓷器特色鲜明，釉色如玉，明净如镜，声震如磬，观感极佳，面对着静雅的龙泉瓷器，内心滋生出一种宁静超然的情愫。

Longquan Porcelain[1]

Porcelain is one of the treasures of Chinese culture, which can be seen everywhere in life. Reading *Quansong Biji, Complete Diaries of the Song Dynasty*, I have found:

It is said that today's secret color porcelain, when the Qian family owned his state, was an imperial offering baked by the Kiln of Yuezhou, and it was not allowed to be used by officials and ordinary people, so it is called "secret color". [2] I have seen in *Lu Guimeng's Poetry Collection · Yue Qi*: "Open the Yue Kiln [3]in the wind and dew of the nine month of autumn, win the green color of thousands of peaks. The mouths are upright to the sky for the dew in the midnight, like the remains of the wine left by Ji Zhongsan." So it is known that in the Tang Dynasty there was secret color porcelain. [4]

It can be seen from above that this "secret color" porcelain by Yue Kiln was invented as early as in the Tang Dynasty. "Open the Yue Kiln in the wind and dew of the nine month of autumn, win the green color of thousands of peaks." These two lines belong to the famous porcelain poem, meaning in the nine

---

1 This essay in compiled by the compiler.

2 Secret color Yueware refers to the secret color porcelain fired in Yue kiln. This is a kind of porcelain for the court. The recipe, glaze color, shape and firing technique are all kept secret. Since it was not spread to the ordinary people, the technology was lost over time.

3 Yue Kiln is one of the famous celadon kilns in the Tang and Song Dynasties. The kiln site is located in the area of Shanglin Lake in Yuyao, Zhejiang. It belonged to Yuezhou in ancient times, hence the name Yue Kiln. The glaze is slightly yellowish from blue to greenish lake green, painted with flowers, birds, figures or geometric patterns. The porcelains fired are sold well both domestically and overseas.

4 *Quansong Biji, Complete Diaries of the Song Dynasty*, Part Four, Book Five, Elephant Publishing House. p. 99.

month of autumn, the outside of the kiln is desolate, but when the kiln is opened, the inside of the kiln is full of blue and green porcelain wares. The brilliance is dazzling, and the exquisite skills of the kiln–fired craftsmen make the green color of a thousand peaks collected in the kiln. The poem depicts the potter's ingenious porcelain making skills. However, Longquan also produces "secret color" porcelain, "There are many good trees in Longquan County, Chuzhou, named Yuzhang, famous for wood. There are many ancient maple woods in the mountains there... and celadon wares are produced, called the secret color, and the tribute porcelain dedicated to the imperial court by the Qian family may come from here. During the Xuanhe Era, the sample preparation must be requested from the court because of the prohibition, and it will be more skillful in processing." [1]

Fine porcelain has been cherished since ancient times, which has inspired my inner desire, and I have always desired to make a piece of porcelain by myself. During the summer vacation, I had the opportunity to go to Longquan Kiln in Longquan County, Zhejiang Province, and finally experienced the delight making personally Longquan Porcelain by myself.

Longquan porcelain is a type of famous Chinese porcelain, belonging to the celadon system of southern China. It was created in the early Northern Song Dynasty, flourishing in the Song Dynasty, entered its heyday in the middle and late Southern Song Dynasty, and gradually declined after the middle of the Ming Dynasty. Large quantities of Longquan porcelain in the Yuan Dynasty were sold overseas. The celadon wares produced have a luster as bright as jade in color. Longquan porcelain enjoys a widespread fame still at home and abroad. [2]

The Longquan Porcelain Base where I paid a visit is a secluded manor, surrounded by pleasant scenery and it was drizzling raining that day. The first

---

1 (Southern Song Dynasty) Zhuang Chuo, *Jilei Bian, Collections of Chicken Ribs*, Siku Quanshu General Catalogue, subsection.

2 See *Encyclopedia Britannica International Chinese Edition*, Xu Weicheng as chief–editor,Vol. 10, Encyclo‑pedia of China Publishing Houses, 1999, p. 195.

step in making Longquan porcelain is to knead the porcelain clay by hand until the clay is even. I did not experience this step, the soil has been kneaded by the craftsman. There was a row of electric blank drawing machines lined up under the corridor. Sitting in front of the machine, I went directly to the second step of "drawing blank". The blank drawing is the step of forming the device. If the forming fails, it needs to be restarted. I use an electric drawing machine, under the guidance of the master, put the kneaded porcelain clay on the drawing machine, then dip my hands in some water, pat lightly, step on a pedal with my right foot, and use the pedal to control the speed of the turntable. Step down lightly, and the turntable will start to rotate. With both hands holding the porcelain clay, the turntable is driven to make the shape of the instrument according to the needs. After the device is formed, let go. The drawing lasts for about an hour, and the hand rotates with the turntable. It feels very romantic and reminds me of the classic scenes in the movie "*Human Ghosts Are Coming*". My porcelain has taken shape after several failures.

The remaining steps are completed by the technologist. According to the master, the drawn body will be placed on a shelf to dry, which is the baked embryo. The dried body also needs to be repaired, polished, and finely repaired cracked parts after drying. Then there is biscuits, the embryo is put into a kiln and burned to nearly 900 degrees. After the green body is dried, the most important thing is to glaze, which is related to the glaze quality of the finished porcelain. There are many ways to glaze. You can directly put the device in the glaze water and soak it, gently shake the glaze water with your hands, or spray the glaze evenly with a spray gun. Generally, the glaze is applied 3 times. Put the glaze on, let it dry, and then fire it in a kiln. The temperature in the kiln needs to reach more than 1300 degrees, and it will be burned continuously for 24 hours. After cooling down, the kiln will be full of crystal clear Longquan celadon works.

According to the introduction, there are two types of Longquan celadon:

one is white and cinnabar celadon, called “Di kiln” or “Longquan kiln”; the other is glazed black celadon, called “Ge kiln”. The glaze layer of “Di kiln” celadon is rich, with the glaze blue, the luster soft, and the crystal moisturizing, better than jade. There are different glaze colors such as plum green, pink green, moon white, bean green, light blue, gray yellow and so on. “Ge Kiln” celadon is decorated with patterns, such as ice cracks, crab claw patterns, cow hair patterns, flowing water patterns, caviar patterns, etc., with the glaze layer full and shiny, known as the “purple iron foot”, and the glazed surface patterns contrast with each other, which is more tranquil and elegant, called the treasure of porcelain.

Modern Longquan celadon faithfully inherits the traditional Chinese artistic style. On the basis of inheritance and antiques, it has made new breakthroughs. It has successfully studied copper–colored glaze, high–temperature black glaze, tiger–colored glaze, he–colored glaze, and uncolored tea glaze, Ujin glaze and Sky Celadon glaze, etc. In the design and decoration of arts and crafts, there are “Celadon Thin Tire”,“Celadon Linglong”, “Celadon Underglaze Color”, “Pictogram Opening”, “Central and Martial Art Opening”, “Blue and White Combination”, “Brothers Kiln Combination”, etc..

Two months later, I received my work with great joy. This Longquan porcelain has distinctive characteristics, with glaze like jade, clear and clean like a mirror, and the sound like a chime. It has an excellent look and feel. Facing the quiet and elegant Longquan porcelain, a feeling grows out of my heart, a kind of quiet and transcendent affection.

Word bank

1.porcelain n. 瓷器

2.bake v. 烘；焙；烤

3.kiln n. 窑

4.dew n. 露水

5.upright adj./adv. 垂直的（地）；笔直的（地）

6. brilliance n. 光辉；光彩；才华

7.dazzling adj. 耀眼的；眼花缭乱的

8.craftsmen n. 工匠（craftsman 的复数）

9. ingenious adj. 机灵的；有独创性的

10. maple n. 槭树；枫树

11.tribute n. 表示感激的行动；礼物；贡税

12. dedicate v. 把（时间；精力）献于；谨以（书或其他艺术品）献给

13. prohibition n. 禁止；禁酒令；禁令

14.cherish v. 爱护；珍爱

15.spray v. 喷；喷洒 n. 小枝

16.glaze n. 浇涂物；釉面 v. 装玻璃于；给……上釉

17.crystal n. 晶体；水晶玻璃

18.celadon n. 灰绿色；青瓷

19.crack n. 裂缝；裂口

20.crab claw patterns n. 蟹爪纹

21. caviar pattern n. 鱼子酱纹

22.layer n. 层次

23.tranquil adj. 平静的；镇静的

24.breakthrough n. 突破；重要发现

25.chime n. 钟；铃；编铃 v. 发出和谐响声

26.transcendent adj. 超越的；超常的；超验的

27.moisturize v. 使……湿润；给……增加水分

哲　学

The Chinese Philosophy

三孔

孔子为中国古圣人，享誉中外。在国内外多地都建有孔庙，譬如杭州孔庙。但是“三孔”却只有孔子的故乡山东省曲阜才有。“三孔”包括孔府、孔庙和孔林。[1]

孔府又称“圣公府”。孔子嫡传后裔住地，位于曲阜市内，始建于公元968年。现存府第九进，占地240余亩，为明清两代所建，是一座典型的封建贵族庄园。孔子嫡系长支世代居住的府第，是中国现存历史最久、规模最大、保存最完整的衙宅合一的古建筑群，有“天下第一家”之称。孔子去世以后至宋代以前，长子长孙依庙居于阙里故宅，守护孔子遗物，奉祀孔子，称“袭封宅”。历代帝王在尊崇孔子推行儒家文化的同时，对其子孙一再加官封爵，赐地建府。宋宝元年间，首封孔子四十六代孙孔宗愿为“衍圣公”，兼曲阜县令，并新建府第，改称衍圣公府。衍圣公世代恪守“诗礼传家”的祖训，着意收集历代礼器法物，藏品达10万余件，尤以孔子画像、元明衣冠、衍圣公及夫人肖像著称于世。孔府最著名的珍藏还有明清文书档案，它是孔府400多年各种

1　本文由编者编写，编写此文时参考了曲阜市官网资料，部分节录自官网。http://www.qufu.gov.cn/，访问时间2021年10月10日；以及https://baike.sogou.com/v110419.html，访问时间2021年10月10日。

曲阜孔庙（卢卫中教授拍摄于曲阜）
Confucian Temple in Qufu, photographed by Professor Lu Weizhong in Qufu

活动的实录，共有 30 多万件，是中国数量最多、时代最久的私家档案。

孔庙是中国三大宫殿建筑之一，也是中国最大的祭孔要地。孔庙毗邻孔府，始建于公元前 478 年。孔庙是祭祀孔子和表彰儒学的庙宇。孔庙始建于周，自汉代起，不断扩建重修，规模宏大，完成于明清时期，是世界上两千余座孔庙中最大的一座。孔庙现占地 14 万平方米，三路布局，九进庭院，贯穿在一条中轴线上，左右作对称排列。整个建筑群包括五殿、一阁、一坛、两堂、17 座碑亭，共 466 间，分别建于金、元、明、清和民国时期。主体建筑大成殿，四周有巨型石柱 28 根，为全国独有，重檐九脊，黄瓦飞甍，周绕回廊。汉以来的历代碑刻 1040 多块，连同大量书、画、牌、匾等珍贵文化遗存，是中国重要的文物宝库。

孔林亦称“至圣林”，位于曲阜城北，是孔子及其家族的墓地，占地三千余亩。围墙高一丈。林内有古树十万余株，树种繁多，是中国最古老的人造园林。

“三孔”是国际著名的旅游胜地。

Three Kongs

Confucius is an ancient sage in China and well–known both at home and abroad. Confucian temples have been built in many places in China, such as Confucian Temple in Hangzhou. But the "Three Kongs" is only available in Qufu, the hometown of Confucius, Shandong Province. "Three Kongs" includes Confucian Mansion, Confucian Temple and Confucian Forest. [1]

Kongfu, Confucian Mansion, is the mansion house of Confucius, where his lineal descendants in different dynasties lived, located in the city of Qufu. It was first built in 968 and now there are 9 layers of houses covering an area of 16 hectares. They were built in the dynasties of the Ming and Qing (1368–1911). Confucian Mansion is a typical manor of the feudal nobles. Confucius's family is the mansion where the Changzhi has lived for generations. It is the oldest, largest and most well–preserved ancient building complex in China, which is known as the "The first family in the world". After the death of Confucius and before the Song Dynasty, the eldest son, as well as the eldest grandson, lived in the old residence of Queli, took care of Confucius' relics, and enshrined Confucius, called "Xifeng House". While admiring Confucius and promoting Confucian culture, the emperors of the past dynasties repeatedly added official ranks and noble titles to their descendants and gave them land for building mansions. During the Baoyuan Period of the Song Dynasty, the forty–sixth–generation descendant of Confucius Kong Zong was granted "Yanshenggong" by the emperor for the first time, who served as the magistrate of Qufu County,

---

1 This is compiled by the compiler of this book, referring to Qufu's official website, http://www.qufu.gov.cn/, accessed on October 10, 2021; and https://baike.sogou.com/v110419.html, accessed on October 10, 2021.

and built a new mansion, renamed Yanshenggong Residence. YanShenggong has abided by the ancestral motto of "poetry and ritual heirs" for generations, and collected more than 100,000 pieces of ritual objects from the past dynasties. His collection is especially famous for Confucius' portraits, the robes from Yuan and Ming dynasties, and Yanshenggong's and his wife's portraits. The most famous collection of Confucius Mansion is also the document archives of the Ming and Qing dynasties. It is a record of various activities of the Confucian Mansion for more than 400 years, with a total of more than 300,000 pieces. It is the largest number of private archives and the oldest in China.

Kongmiao, Confucian Temple, is one of the three major palace buildings in China, and also the largest place for worshipping Confucius in China, adjacent to the Confucian Mansion. Its construction was started since 478 B.C., a temple dedicated to Confucius and commending Confucianism. It was built in Zhou; since the Han Dynasty, it had been continuously expanding and rebuilding, with a grand scale; and was completed in the Ming and Qing dynasties. It is the largest of more than 2,000 Confucian temples in the world. The Confucian Temple currently covers an area of 140,000 square meters, with a three–way layout, nine courtyards, running through a central axis, and symmetrically arranged on the left and right. The entire building complex includes five halls, one pavilion, one altar, two halls, and 17 stele pavilions, a total of 466 rooms, which were built during the Jin, Yuan, Ming, Qing dynasties and the Republic of China. The main building, Dacheng Hall, is surrounded by 28 giant stone pillars, unique to the country, with double eaves and nine ridges, yellow tiles flying around, and surrounding corridors. There are more than 1,040 inscribed steles in the past since the Han Dynasty, together with a large number of precious cultural relics such as books, paintings, plaques and tablets, which is an important treasure–house of cultural and historical relics in China.

Konglin, Confucian Forest, is the burial site of Confucius and his families, lying north of Qufu. With a 3–meter–high enclosing wall, the ground covers an area of 200 hectares. There are over 20000 trees of various kinds in the graveyard. It is the most ancient artificial woods in China.

"Three Kongs" is an internationally famous tourist attraction.

《论语》[1]

亚瑟·韦利[2]

《论语》成书于30到50年间。尽管第一部完整的《论语》的确切出版日期无法确定，这部著作开始于春秋时期，可能成于战国时期。《理想国》虽然声称是苏格拉底文集，实际上却包含了其弟子柏拉图的原创思想，同样，尽管《论语》主要关于孔子本人及其思想，但几乎肯定的是它由孔子弟子和次代弟子撰写和编纂的。

《论语》按个别主题划分章节。然而，并未以任何特殊方式进行章节安排，思想或理念的连续性并未保持。事实上，章节顺序可以说是完全随机的，相邻章节的主题毫不相关。

此外，中心主题在不同的章节中反复出现，有时措辞完全相同，有时略有变化。这使得一些人认为，这本书并非出自一人之手，而是许多人共同努力的结果。然而，《论语》的最终编者很可能是曾子的弟子，曾子是孔子最著名的学生之一。

《论语》的一个版本，写在公元前55年以前的竹简上，1973年在河北省定州或定县的一座墓中发现，并于1997年出版。尽管这个版本颇为零碎，但它的解读如果被充分利用在一个评注版本中，可以对《论语》的文本传统产生相当大的影响。

西汉末年，成帝的老师张豫将《论语》合并为鲁、齐两本，但保留了《论

1　作为中国儒家经典的《论语》不仅在国内影响深远，也被外译成多种语言。亚瑟·韦利这篇文章对《论语》这部儒家经典进行概述，描述了它的起源、中心主题、不同版本和注解以及它对世界各个领域产生的影响。

2　亚瑟·韦利（1889—1966）是著名英国汉学家和翻译家，他精通多种语言。他一生撰著和译著共200余种，其中大部分都与中国文化有关，其坚持不懈地研究东方学与中国学，并致力于把中国古典名著翻译成英文。

语》的章节数。张氏版本后世称为《张侯论》，这是我们今天所知的大部分版本。

E.B. 布鲁克斯和 A.T. 布鲁克斯在他们的著作《论语辨》中，提出了一种基于文本内语言使用模式的章节和架构的替代解释。这表明，我们得到的《论语》文本是大量累积的，由许多代各流派领袖作了补充。由于政治、社会和文化环境的变化，不同的儒家学派领袖对前人褒贬不一，甚至对社会习俗和仪式环境的描述也迥然不同。两位布鲁克斯认为《论语》的一个子集代表原始孔子思想，他们生活在这样一个亲和时代，当时武士基础的传统背景中，人格本位社会正在分解，变化为由源自古旧军事精英的更广泛贵族主导的、更加调解的社会，更少与君王直接接触：这些早期的章节代表了对上级的极度忠诚和对下属亲人般关爱，几乎不强调礼仪，就像后面的章节所暗示的那样。

自孔子时代以来，《论语》对中国乃至后来的其他东亚国家的哲学和道德价值观都产生了深远的影响。与四书的其他三卷一起，它教导基本的儒家价值观，包括礼、义、忠、孝，所有这些都围绕孔子的中心思想——人性。

近两千年来，《论语》一直是中国学者学习的基础必修课，因为一个人如果不学习孔子的著作，就不会被认为是正直的或开明的。科举考试始于晋朝，最终在清朝末年废除，它强调儒学，并希望考生在文章中引用和应用孔子的言论。

《论语》也被译成多种语言，其中最著名的是詹姆斯·莱格、亚瑟·韦利、查尔斯·穆勒和威廉·爱德华·苏希尔的英译本。16 世纪末，《论语》的部分内容被西方基督教传教士译成拉丁文。

特别有趣的是该书的第十章，其中详细描述了孔子在各种日常活动中的行为。伏尔泰和庞德曾指出这一点，以表明孔子在极大程度上只是一个凡人。最近将《论语》翻译成英法两种语言的西蒙·莱伊说，这本书很可能是人类历史上第一本描述个人、历史人物生活的著作。类似地，伊莱亚斯·卡内蒂写道：“孔子的《论语》是人类最古老的完整的智力和精神写照。这是一本现代著作；它所包含和所缺乏的一切都是重要的。”

The Analects of Confucius[1]

Arthur Waley[2]

The *Analects* were written over a period of 30 to 50 years. Begun some time during the Spring and Autumn Period, the work was probably finished during the Warring States Period, though the exact publication date of the first complete *Analects* cannot be pinpointed. Much as the *Republic* purports to be a collection of Socrates' discussions but actually contains original material from his disciple Plato, the *Analects* were almost certainly penned and compiled by disciples and second–generation disciples of Confucius, albeit being mostly about Confucius himself and his thought.

Chapters in the *Analects* are grouped by individual themes. However, the chapters are not arranged in any sort of way so as to carry a continuous stream of thought or idea. In fact, the sequence of the chapters could be said to be completely random, with the themes of adjacent chapters completely unrelated to each other.

Moreover, central themes recur repeatedly in different chapters, sometimes in exactly the same wording and sometimes with small variations. This has led some to believe that the book was not written by a single individual, but was the

1 *The Analects of Confucius*, as the Chinese Confucian classic, not only has a far–reaching influence in China, but it has also been translated into many languages. Arthur Willy's passage provides an overview of the Confucian classic, depicting its origin, central themes, different versions and interpretations as well as its impacts on various fields all over the world.

2 Arthur Willy (1889–1966) is a famous British Sinologist and translator. He is proficient in multiple languages. He has written and translated more than 200 books in his lifetime, most of which are related to Chinese culture. He persevers in the study of Orientalism and China Studies, and is committed to translating Chinese classics into English.

collective effort of many. However, the final editors of the *Analects* were likely disciples of Zengzi, who was one of the most established students of Confucius.

A version of the *Analects*, written on bamboo strips from before 55 BC, was discovered in a tomb at Dingzhou/Dingxian in Hebei province in 1973 and published in 1997. Although fragmentary, the version could shed considerable light on the textual tradition of the *Analects* if its readings were ever fully employed in a critical edition.

Towards the late Western Han Dynasty, Zhang Yu, who was a teacher of Emperor Cheng, combined the Lu and Qi versions of *Analects* but kept to the number of chapters in the *Lu Analects*. Zhang's version then came to be known as the *Marquis Zhang Analects*, which is largely the version we know today.

E. B. Brooks and A. T. Brooks, in their work *The Original Analects*, suggest an alternative interpretation of the chapters, organization, based on language usage patterns within the text. This work suggests that the text of the *Analects* as we have received them is heavily accreted, and represents the additions of many generations of school heads. Due to the changing political, social, and cultural environments, different heads of the Confucian school chose to praise or denigrate different of their predecessors, and even described very different social practices and ritual environments.

Brooks and Brooks view a subset of *Analects* as representing the ideas of the original Confucius, who lived during a time when the traditional bonds of a warrior–based, personality–based society were breaking down to change to a more mediated society with a broader nobility from the old military elite and with less direct access to the king: these early chapters represent the old military ethic of extreme faithfulness to superiors and paternal care for inferiors, with almost no emphasis on mannered ritual, as chronologically later chapters might suggest.

Since Confucius' time, the *Analects* has heavily influenced the philosophy and moral values of China and later other East Asian countries as well. Together with the other three volumes of the *Four Books*, it teaches the basic Confucian values including propriety, righteousness, loyalty, and filial piety, all centered about the central thought of Confucius—humanity.

For almost two thousand years, the *Analects* had also been the fundamental course of study for any Chinese scholar, for a man was not considered morally upright or enlightened if he did not study Confucius' works. The imperial examination, started in the Jin Dynasty and eventually abolished in the dying years of the Qing Dynasty, emphasized Confucian studies and expected candidates to quote and apply the words of Confucius in their essays.

The Analects of Confucius has also been translated into many languages, most notably into English by James Legge, Arthur Waley, Charles Muller, and William Edward Soothill. Portions were translated into Latin by western Christian missionaries in the late 16th century.

A particular point of interest lies in Chapter 10 of the book, which contains detailed descriptions of Confucius' behaviors in various daily activities. This has been pointed at by Voltaire and Ezra Pound to show how much Confucius was a mere human. Simon Leys, who recently translated the *Analects* into English and French, said that the book may well have been the first in human history to describe the life of an individual, historic personage. Similarly, Elias Canetti writes: "*The Analects of Confucius* are the oldest complete intellectual and spiritual portrait of a man. It strikes one as a modern book; everything it contains and indeed everything it lacks is important."

《论语》节选[1]

10.1 孔子于乡党，恂[2]恂如也，似不能言者。其在宗庙朝廷，便[3]便言，唯谨尔。

10.2 朝，与下大夫言，侃侃如也；与上大夫言，訚[4]訚如也。君在，踧踖[5]如也，与与如也。

10.3 君召使摈，色勃如也，足躩[6]如也。揖所与立，左右手，衣前后，襜[7]如也。趋进，翼如也。宾退，必复命曰："宾不顾矣。"

10.4 入公门，鞠躬如也，如不容。立不中门，行不履阈[8]。过位，色勃如也，足躩如也，其言似不足者。摄齐[9]升堂，鞠躬如也，屏气似不息者。出，降一等，逞颜色，怡怡如也。没阶，趋进，翼如也。复其位，踧踖如也。

10.5 执圭，鞠躬如也，如不胜。上如揖，下如授，勃如战色，足蹜[10]蹜如有循。享礼，有容色。私觌[11]，愉愉如也。

10.6 君子不以绀緅[12]饰，红紫不以为亵[13]服。当暑，袗絺綌[14]，必表而出之。缁[15]衣，羔裘；素衣，麑裘；黄衣，狐裘。亵裘长，短右袂。必有寝衣，长一身

---

1 《论语·乡党篇》第10章，参见杨伯峻译注：《论语译注》，中华书局，2007年，第138–148页。
2 恂读作xún。
3 便读作pián。
4 訚读作yín。
5 踧踖读作cù jí。
6 躩读作jué。
7 襜读作chān。
8 阈读作yù。
9 齐读作zī。
10 蹜读作sù。
11 觌读作dí。
12 绀緅读作gàn zōu。
13 亵读作xiè。
14 絺綌读作chīxì。
15 缁读作zī。

有半。狐貉之厚以居。去丧，无所不佩。非帷裳，必杀[1]之。羔裘玄冠不以吊。吉月，必朝服而朝。

10.7　齐，必有明衣，布。齐必变食，居必迁坐。

10.8　食不厌精，脍不厌细。食饐[2]而餲[3]，鱼馁而肉败，不食。色恶，不食。臭恶，不食。失饪，不食。不时，不食。割不正，不食。不得其酱，不食。肉虽多，不使胜食气。唯酒无量，不及乱。沽酒市脯，不食。不撤姜食，不多食。

10.9　祭于公，不宿肉。祭肉不出三日，出三日，不食之矣。

10.10　食不语，寝不言。

10.11　虽疏食菜羹，瓜祭，必齐如也。

10.12　席不正，不坐。

10.13　乡人饮酒，杖者出，斯出矣。

10.14　乡人傩，朝服而立于阼阶。

10.15　问人于他邦，再拜而送之。

10.16　康子馈药，拜而受之，曰："丘未达，不敢尝。"

10.17　厩焚。子退朝，曰："伤人乎？"不问马。

1　杀读作 shài。
2　饐读作 yì。
3　餲读作 ài。

Excerpts from *The Analects of Confucius*[1]

In his village, Confucius was sincerely quiet, as if he could not speak. In the ancestral temple or the court, he was eloquent, but extremely cautious. Speaking to the junior grandmasters in court, he was candid and at ease; speaking to the senior grandmasters, he was straightforward but formal. At the presence of the ruler, he straightened up ceremoniously, but with a calm demeanor.

He took on a serious expression on his face, and walked briskly when summoned to take care of important guests by the ruler. He bowed to them as greeting, with his left and right hands holding his garment in front and back, keeping it properly adjusted. He moved forward quickly with his arms swaying like wings. When the guest was leaving, he would watch seeing them off certainly, and return to report, "the guest has stopped looking back."

When coming through the court door, he shrunk down deferentially with caution, as if there was not enough space. Once inside, never did he stand in the middle, nor would he step on the threshold. When passing in front of the ruler's position, his expression became serious, and he stepped carefully in small steps; he talked cautiously, and it seemed difficult for him to speak. He lifted up the hems of his skirt when entering the hall nodding deeply in respect. He held his breath as if he could not breathe. Upon leaving, once he had gone down one step, his countenance became relaxed, and he appeared to be contented. Reaching the bottom of the stairs he began to move briskly, his arms swaying like wings.

---

1 The passage is based on an excerpt from Chapter 10 of the *Analects of Confucius* (《论语·乡党篇》), Annotation of the Analects of Confucius by Yang Bojun, Zhonghua Book Company, 2007, pp. 138–148, translated by Charles Muller. It gives a detailed account of Confucius' behaviors in various daily activities.

Returning to his original position, he was deferential.

He was bent over with deference, when holding the jade scepter, as if he could not support such a heavy thing. He held it from above in a folding way, and from below in an offering way. He showed a serious and anxious expression, walking in a straight line with shuffling steps. In the presentation ceremony, he showed a genial expression. In private meetings, he seemed relaxed without concerns.

The noble man did not wear decorative cuffs colored violet and puce; for his house clothes, he would not wear the red and maroon. During hot weather, he would wear thin, unlined garments made of fine and coarse vine–fiber when he went out. With a black robe he wore a black sheepskin mantle: with an uncolored robe he wore a fawnskin mantle; with a yellow robe he wore a foxskin mantle. His house robe was long, with a short right sleeve. He always slept in sleeping garments, which were half as long as his body. At home, he was seated on thick fox and badger rugs.

When not in a mourning period, there was nothing he would not wear on his decorative belt sash. If clothes were not ceremonial, he would definitely adjust their length. He would not wear a black sheepskin mantle or a black hat when paying visits of condolence. He always showed up in court on the first of the month properly attired in court garb. When fasting, he always wore clean white clothes of linen. During the fast he would always change his diet, as well as his seat.

When he ate, never was he averse to refined rice, nor to finely minced meat. He would not eat rice that was rancid or had gone rotten, nor fish and meat that had spoiled. He would not eat food that had a bad color or smell; he would not eat food that was not cooked to the proper level, or which was out of season; nor would he eat food that was not properly sliced, or did not come with the appropriate condiments. Even if there was a lot of meat, he would not eat it greater quantity than rice. It was only wine with which he did not limit himself, but at the same time, he never lost control of himself.

He would not drink wine or eat dried meat that came from the marketplace. He would not refrain from eating food with ginger, but he would not overdo it. When there was a sacrifice for the ruler, he would not keep the meat overnight. As for sacrificial meats in general, he would not keep them more than three days, and if they were more than three days old, he would not eat them. He did not chat while eating, and did not talk after retiring. No matter what kind of simple fare it might be, such as coarse rice or broth, he would always make an offering, doing so with due solemnity.

Word bank

1.analects n. 文选

2.publication n. 出版物

3.disciple n. 弟子

4.compile v. 汇编；编辑

5.albeit conj. 虽然

6.bamboo strip n. 竹片

7.fragmentary adj. 支离破碎的；由碎片组成的

8.predecessor n. 前任；前辈

9.subset n. 一部分；一小套；子集

10.bond n. 结合；债券

11.warrior–based adj. 武士本位的

12.personality–based adj. 人格本位的

13.mediated adj. 间接的；要靠媒介的

14.nobility n. 高贵；高尚；贵族

15.elite n. 精英；杰出人物

16.ethic adj. 道德规范的；伦理的

17.faithfulness n. 诚实；忠诚

18.paternal adj. 父亲的；父亲般的

19.inferior n. 下级

20.chronologically adv. 按年代地；按时间前后排列地

21.propriety n. 正当；得体

22.filial piety n. 孝；孝道

23.humanity n. 人类；人道

24. enlighten v. 启发；启迪

文　学

The Chinese Literature

《山海经》节选

《山海经》是先秦古籍，许多中国古代神话盛宴于此，是研究历史、民俗、古代地理和科学技术的重要资源；也是世界上最早的矿物记录文献。由于年代久远，这本书的作者、编者和写作日期难以确定。

这本书篇幅长度为 31000 字，全书共分十八部，其中有山经 5 部、海经 8 部、大荒经 4 部以及海域经。记载了 100 多个小邦的山水、神话故事、特产、巫术、宗教信仰、民间医药和风俗等，涵盖南到广东南海、北到内蒙古、东至山东、西至新疆等广大地区。

《山海经》记载了许多中国古代神话故事，包括第一生物、万物创造者巨人盘古、用泥土创造人类的创世女神女娲、夸父——追逐太阳渴死的神等等。这些故事在中国代代相传。《山海经》对中国文学影响很大。《诗经》和后世许多优秀的诗歌、传奇和小说，都是根据《山海经》中的神话故事改编和创作的。其中影响最大、流传最广的作品有《封神演义》《明西游记》和《花清镜》，尤其是《楚辞》。记录了大量古代神话故事。此外，《老子》《庄子》《淮南子》等道教典籍，在很大程度上也借鉴了古代神话，并对其进行了哲理化。

在中国考古美术中处处可以见到来自《山海经》的艺术母题。下面为《山海经》节选《南山经》。[1]

南山经之首，曰䧿山。其首曰招摇之山，临于西海之上，多桂，多金玉。有草焉，其状如韭而青华，其名曰祝余，食之不饥。有木焉，其状如榖而黑理，其华四照，其名曰迷榖，佩之不迷。有兽焉，其状如禺而白耳，伏行人走，其名曰狌狌，食之善走。丽麂之水出焉，而西流注于海，其中多育沛，佩之无瘕疾。

又东三百里，曰堂庭之山，多棪木，多白猿，多水玉，多黄金。

又东三百八十里，曰猨翼之山，其中多怪兽，水多怪鱼，多白玉，多蝮虫，多怪蛇，多怪木，不可以上。

又东三百七十里，曰杻阳之山，其阳多赤金，其阴多白金。有兽焉，其状如马而白首，其文如虎而赤尾，其音如谣，其名曰鹿蜀，佩之宜子孙。怪水出焉，而东流注于宪翼之水。其中多玄龟，其状如龟而鸟首虺尾，其名曰旋龟，其音如判木，佩之不聋，可以为底。

又东三百里，曰柢山，多水，无草木。有鱼焉，其状如牛，陵居，蛇尾，有翼，其羽在下，其音如留牛，其名曰鯥，冬死而夏生，食之无肿疾。

又东四百里，曰亶爰之山，多水，无草木，不可以上。有兽焉，其状如狸而有髦，其名曰类，自为牝牡，食者不妒。

又东三百里，曰基山，其阳多玉，其阴多怪木。有兽焉，其状如羊，九尾四耳，其目在背，其名曰猼訑，佩之不畏。有鸟焉，其状如鸡而三首、六目、六足、三翼，其名曰䳜䳏，食之无卧。

又东三百里，曰青丘之山，其阳多玉，其阴多青雘。有兽焉，其状如狐而九尾，其音如婴儿，能食人，食者不蛊。有鸟焉，其状如鸠，其音若呵，名曰灌灌，佩之不惑。英水出焉，南流注于即翼之泽。其中多赤鱬，其状如鱼而人面，其音如鸳鸯，食之不疥。

又东三百五十里，曰箕尾之山，其尾踆于东海，多沙石。汸水出焉，而南流注于淯，其中多白玉。

凡䧿山之首，自招摇之山以至箕尾之山，凡十山，二千九百五十里。其神状皆鸟身而龙首。其祠之礼：毛用一璋玉瘗，糈用稌米，白菅为席。

---

1 高山编：《山海经·南山经》第一册，光明日报出版社，2015年，第3—27页。

南次二经之首，曰柜山，西临流黄，北望诸毗，东望长右。英水出焉，西南流注于赤水，其中多白玉，多丹粟。有兽焉，其状如豚，有距，其音如狗吠，其名曰狸力，见则其县多土功。有鸟焉，其状如鸱而人手，其音如痺，其名曰鴸，其鸣自号也，见则其县多放士。

东南四百五十里，曰长右之山，无草木，多水。有兽焉，其状如禺而四耳，其名长右，其音如吟，见则郡县大水。

又东三百四十里，曰尧光之山，其阳多玉，其阴多金。有兽焉，其状如人而彘鬣，穴居而冬蛰，其名曰猾褢，其音如斲木，见则县有大繇

又东三百五十里，曰羽山，其下多水，其上多雨，无草木，多蝮虫。

又东三百七十里，曰瞿父之山，无草木，多金玉。

又东四百里，曰句余之山，无草木，多金玉。

又东五百里，曰浮玉之山，北望具区，东望诸毗。有兽焉，其状如虎而牛尾，其音如吠犬，其名曰彘，是食人。苕水出于其阴，北流注于具区，其中多鮆鱼。

又东五百里，曰成山，四方而三坛，其上多金玉，其下多青雘。阕水出焉，而南流注于虖勺，其中多黄金。

又东五百里，曰会稽之山，四方，其上多金、玉，其下多砆石。勺水出焉，而南流注于湨。

又东五百里，曰夷山，无草木，多沙石，湨水出焉，而南流注于列涂。

又东五百里，曰仆勾之山，其上多金玉，其下多草木，无鸟兽，无水。

又东四百里，曰洵山，其阳多金，其阴多玉。有兽焉，其状如羊而无口，不可杀也，其名曰䍺。洵水出焉，而南流注于阏之泽，其中多茈蠃。

又东四百里，曰虖勺之山，其上多梓柟，其下多荆杞。滂水出焉，而东流注于海。

又东五百里，曰区吴之山，无草木，多沙石。鹿水出焉，而南流注于滂水。

又东五百里，曰鹿吴之山，上无草木，多金石。泽更之水出焉，而南流注于滂水。水有兽焉，名曰蛊雕，其状如雕而有角，其音如婴儿之音，是食人。

东五百里，曰漆吴之山，无草木，多博石，无玉。处于东海，望丘山，其光载出载入，是惟日次。

凡南次二经之首，自柜山至于漆吴之山，凡十七山，七千二百里。其神状皆

龙身而鸟首。其祠：毛用一璧瘗，糈用稌。

南次三经之首，曰天虞之山，其下多水，不可以上。

东五百里，曰祷过之山，其上多金玉，其下多犀、兕，多象。有鸟焉，其状如䴔而白首、三足、人面，其名曰瞿如，其鸣自号也。泿水出焉，而南流注于海。其中有虎蛟，其状鱼身而蛇尾，其音如鸳鸯，食者不肿，可以已痔。

又东五百里，曰丹穴之山，其上多金玉。丹水出焉，而南流注于渤海。有鸟焉，其状如鸡，五采而文，名曰凤皇，首文曰德，翼文曰义，背文曰礼，膺文曰仁，腹文曰信。是鸟也，饮食自然，自歌自舞，见则天下安宁。

又东五百里，曰发爽之山，无草木，多水，多白猿。泛水出焉，而南流注于渤海。

又东四百里，至于旄山之尾，其南有谷，曰育遗，多怪鸟，凯风自是出。

又东四百里，至于非山之首，其上多金玉，无水，其下多蝮虫。

又东五百里，曰阳夹之山，无草木，多水。

又东五百里，曰灌湘之山，上多木，无草；多怪鸟，无兽。

又东五百里，曰鸡山，其上多金，其下多丹雘。黑水出焉，而南流注于海。其中有鱄鱼，其状如鲋而彘毛，其音如豚，见则天下大旱。

又东四百里，曰令丘之山，无草木，多火。其南有谷焉，曰中谷，条风自是出。有鸟焉，其状如枭，人面四目而有耳，其名曰颙，其鸣自号也，见则天下大旱。

又东三百七十里，曰仑者之山，其上多金玉，其下多青雘。有木焉，其状如穀而赤理，其汗如漆，其味如饴，食者不饥，可以释劳，其名曰白䓘，可以血玉。

又东五百八十里，曰禺稾之山，多怪兽，多大蛇。

又东五百八十里，曰南禺之山，其上多金玉，其下多水。有穴焉，水出辄入，夏乃出，冬则闭。佐水出焉，而东南流注于海，有凤皇、鹓雏。

凡南次三经之首，自天虞之山以至南禺之山，凡一十四山，六千五百三十里。其神皆龙身而人面。其祠皆一白狗祈，糈用稌。

右南经之山志，大小凡四十山，万六千三百八十里。

如此富于想象力且妙趣横生的文本，读来收获颇多。

Excerpts from *The Classic of Mountains and Seas*

The Classic of Mountains and Seas, as an ancient book of pre–Qin dynasties, features lots of ancient Chinese mythologies, which is an essential source for research into history, folk customs, ancient geography and science and technologies. Due to its old age, its author, editor and composing date are hard to establish.

The book is in 31,000 characters in length, divided into 18 sections, including 5 sections of *Mountain Classics*, 8 sections of *Sea Classics*, 4 sections of *Classics of the Great Wilderness* and the section of *Classics of Regions within the Seas*. It recored landscapes, mythological stories, special products, witchcraft, religious beliefs, folk medicine and customs, etc in more than 100 small states, covering a wide range of areas from Nanhai of Guangdong in the south to Inner Mongolia in the north, from Shandong in the east to Xinjiang in the west.

There are numerous ancient Chinese mythological stories recorded in *The Classic of Mountains and Seas*, including Giant Pangu, the first living being and the creator of all, Nüwa, the creator goddess who created human beings with mud, and Kuafu, the sun–capturing god who died of thirst, and so on. These stories are widely spread in China from one generation to another.

The Classic of Mountains and Seas had a great impact on Chinese literature. Both *Shi Jing* (*The Book of Songs*) and lots of outstanding poems, legends and novels of later ages were all based on myths in *The Classic of Mountains and Seas*, with some adaptation and creation. Among them, the most influential and widely spread works include *Fengshen Yanyi* (*The Creation of the Gods*) and *Journey to the West* of the Ming Dynasty and *Flowers in the Mirror* of the Qing

Dynasty, and especially *Chu Ci* (*The Songs of Chu*), which recorded a large number of ancient mythological stories. In addition, Taoist classics like *Laozi, Zhuangzi* and *Huainanzi* in large part drew on ancient myths and philosophize them. The artistic motifs from *The Classic of Mountains and Seas* can be seen everywhere in Chinese archaeological art. The following is an excerpt from *the Classic of Nanshan* in *The Classic of Mountains and Seas*.

The first series of mountains in *the Classic of Nanshan* is named Queshan. The first mountain of Queshan is called Mount Zhaoyao, close to the West Sea, and there are many laurel trees growing on the mountain, as well as many gold and jade. There is a kind of grass with the name as Zhuyu in the mountains, shaped like leeks, with blue flowers. People will not feel hungry if they eat it. There is also a kind of tree growing in the mountains, with the shape like broussonetia papyrifera, a paper mulberry tree, on which there are black textures. Its blooming flowers can glow and illuminate the surroundings and its name is Mishou, so you won't get lost if you wear it on your body. There is a beast in the mountains, which looks like a macaque but with white ears. It walks on its stomach and can walk upright like a human, whose name is Shengsheng 狌狌. If people eat its meat, they can run faster. Liji River originates from Mount Zhaoyao and flows westward into the sea, with a lot of Yupei in the water. Wearing it on your body will prevent you from suffering from diseases caused by parasites.

Three hundred li further to the east, there stands a mountain called Tangting Mountain, where there are many Diospyros lotus trees Yan tree, white apes, as well as crystals and gold.

Three hundred and eighty li further to the east is a mountain called Yuanyi Mountain. There are many monsters in the mountain, and there are many strange fishes in the water. There are many white jades, vipers, and strange snakes on the mountain. There are also many weird trees. As a result, people cannot climb it up.

Three hundred and seventy li further to the east, there is a mountain named Mount Niuyang. There is a lot of red gold on the south side of the mountain, and a lot of platinum on the north side. There is a kind of beast in the mountain, shaped like a horse, with a white head, a tiger–like pattern on its body, and a red tail, whose voice is like singing. Its name is Lushu. Wearing its fur can benefit the descendants. There is a strange river coming from Luyang Mountain and flowing eastward into Xianyi River. There are many black turtles living in the water, shaped like a tortoise, with a head like a bird, and a tail similar to that of a snake. This animal is called a Xuan tortoise, whose voice is like the sound of cutting wood. Wearing it can prevent deafness and also heal calluses on hands and feet.

Three hundred li further to the east, there is a mountain called Mount Di, where there is a lot of water, but no vegetation. There is a kind of fish in the mountains, whose shape is like an ox, living on the hills. It has a snake–like tail and wings growing under the flanks. It calls like a wild yak. Its name is bluefish 鯥. It hibernates in winter and wakes up in summer. Whoever eats its meat will no longer have poisonous cankers.

Four hundred li further to the east, there is a mountain called Mount Qiyan. The mountains are so full of water without vegetation that people cannot climb them. There is a kind of beast in the mountains that looks like a lynx and has hair on its head. This beast is called Lei. It has both sexes in hermaphroditism. Whoever eats its meat will no longer be jealous.

Three hundred li further eastward, there is a mountain called Mount Ji. There are many jades on the south side of the mountain, and many strange trees on the north side. There is a kind of beast in the mountains, shaped like a sheep, with nine tails, four ears, and eyes on the back. Its name is Pò 猼. Wearing its fur makes people fearless. There is a bird in the mountains that looks like a chicken, but has three heads, six eyes, six legs, and three wings. Its name is Xiangfu 鹇鸺. Whoever eats its meat will no longer be sleepy.

Three hundred li further eastward, there is a mountain called Mount Qingqiu. There are many jades on the south side of the mountain, and many minerals that can be used as cyan pigments on the north side of the mountain. There is a beast in the mountains, shaped like a fox, with nine tails, and its sound is like the cry of a baby. It can eat humans. Whoever eats its meat will no longer be attacked by poisonous gas. There is a kind of bird in the mountains that looks like a dove and screams like people's scolding voice. The name of this bird is Guanguan灌灌 . Whoever wears its feathers on the body will no longer be confused. Yingshui River originates from Qingqiu Mountain and flows southwards to Yize River, where there are many red horns in the water, similar in shape to fish, with a human–like face, and the sound like the singing of a mandarin duck. Whoever eats its meat will no longer get scabies.

Three hundred and fifty li further eastward is Mount Jiwei, whose tail is located on the coast of the East Sea of China, full of sand and rocks on the mountain. Fangshui River originates from this mountain and flows into Yushui River to the south. There are a lot of white jades in Fangshui River.

In total, the Queshan mountain system includes, counting from the first mountain, Shaoyao Mountain, to Mount Jiwei, a total of ten mountains with a length of 2,950 li. Of all these ten mountains, the shape of the mountain god of each mountain is the one of dragon head with a bird body. The ritual to worship the mountain god is: bury the furry animals and a piece of jade in the ground, use glutinous rice as polished rice for sacrifice to the gods, and use white grass as a straw mat to spread under the mountain gods' seats.

The first mountain in the Southern Second system is named Mount Gui, close to Liuhuang on the west, seeing Zhupi 岻 on the north and Changyou Mountain on the east. Yingshui River originates from Mount Gui and flows into Chishui River to the southwest, with many white jades and cinnabar in the water. There is a kind of beast in the mountains, shaped like a piggy, with claws like chicken's, and it makes a sound like a dog barking. Its name is Lili. In whichever county it appears, it will be greatly under construction. There is a kind of bird, its shape like a harrier, with human hands, and its voice is like a Bi singing. Its name is Zhu 鴸 , and it screams as if it is calling its own name. In whichever county it appears, many people will be exiled.

Four hundred and fifty li further southeast, there is a mountain called Changyou Mountain. There is no vegetation but a lot of water in the mountain. There is a kind of beast in the mountain that looks like a macaque with four ears. Its name is Changyou. It gives out voices like a human being groaning. A large flood occurs in whichever county it appears.

Three hundred and forty li further to the east, there stands a mountain named Mount Yaoguang, with a lot of jades on its south side and a lot of gold on its north side. There is a kind of beast in the mountain, shaped like a man, with a mane like a pig. It lives in a cave and hibernates in winter. Its name is Huahuai, and its cry is like the sound made when cutting wood. In whichever county it appears, there will be labor disasters.

Three hundred and fifty li further east is a mountain called Mount Yu. There is a lot of water at the foot of the mountain, and there is plenty of rain on the mountain. There is no vegetation but many snakes.

Three hundred and seventy li further east, there lies Mount Qufu. There is no vegetation on the mountain, but a lot of gold and jade.

Four hundred li further east, there is Mount Juyu, with no vegetation on the mountain, but a lot of gold and jade.

Five hundred li further east, there is a Fuyu Mountain, from where Taihu Lake can be seen to the north, and Zhupi can be seen to the east. There are beasts in the mountain, shaped like tigers, tails like oxen, and sounds like dog barking. It is named Zhi 彘 and can eat humans. Shaoshui River originates from the north of this mountain and flows northward into Taihu Lake. There are many fish Coilia macrognathos Bleeker in the water.

Five hundred li further east, there is a square mountain, like three overlapping altars. This mountain is rich in gold and jade, and there are many minerals that can be used as blue pigments. 阏 River originates from here, flowing southward into Biaoshao River, with much gold in the water.

Five hundred li further to the east, there is a mountain called Kuaiji Mountain, square in shape. The mountain is rich in gold and jade, and there are many jade–like stones at the foot of the mountain. Shao River originates from the Kuaiji Mountain and flows southward into Huang River.

Five hundred li further east, there is a Yi Mountain, with no vegetation on the mountain, but a lot of sand and rocks. Huang River originated from here and flows southward into Lietu River.

Five hundred li further east, there stands Pugou Mountain. There are a lot of gold and jade on the mountain, and there are a lot of vegetation at the foot of the mountain. There are no birds and beasts in the mountain, nor is there water either.

Four hundred li further to the east, there is a mountain called Mount Xun, with a lot of gold on the south side of the mountain and a lot of jade on the north side. There is a kind of beast in the mountain, shaped like a sheep and with no mouth, but it will not starve to death. Its name is Huan 䍺 . Xun River originates from this mountain and flows southward into Eze Loch, with many purple snails in the water.

Four hundred li further east lies Mount Hushao. The mountain is full of catalpa trees and phoebe trees, with many wattles and wolfberries growing under it. Pang River originates from this mountain and then flows eastward into the sea.

Five hundred li further east, there lies a Mount Quwu with no vegetation but a lot of sand and rocks. Lu River originates here and flows southward into Pang River.

Five hundred li further east is a mountain named Luwu Mountain, with no vegetation on it but a lot of gold and stones. Zegeng River originates here and flows into Pang River to the south. There is a kind of beast in the water, named Gu Eagle, with its shape like an eagle with horns on its head. It sounds like a baby crying and can eat human beings

Five hundred li further east stands a mountain named Qiwu Mountain, with no vegetation on it. There are stones that can be used for gambling everywhere but no jade. This mountain is in the East Sea of China, and another mountain can be seen from on the top of the mountain. The light and shadow of the mountain are flickering, the place where the sun lies.

In the second series, from Mount Gui to Qiwu Mountain, there are a total of 17 mountains with a distance of 7,200 li. All mountain gods are with a dragon body and a bird head. The ritual to worship the mountain gods is: bury the furry animals and a piece of Jade Bi together in the ground, and use glutinous rice as the polished rice to worship the mountain gods.

The first mountain in the third Southern Classics is Tianyu Mountain. There is so much water under the mountain that people cannot climb it.

Five hundred li further to the east is a mountain called Qiguo Mountain. There are many gold and jade on the mountain, and many rhinos and scorpions as well as many elephants under the mountain. There is a kind of bird in the mountain, shaped like a the fishing cormorant, with a white head, three legs, and a human face. Its name is Quru, and it makes a sound like calling its own name. Yin River originates from this mountain and flows south to the sea. There is a tiger–fish in the water, which is shaped like a fish–body and snake–tail, making a sound like a mandarin duck screaming. Eating its meat will not cause venomous cankers, but can also treat hemorrhoids.

Five hundred li further east, there stands a Danxue Mountain with a lot of gold and jade, where Dan River originates flowing south to the South Sea of China. There is a bird in the mountain, shaped like a chicken, with colorful feathers on its body and a pattern in the form of characters. Its name is phoenix. The pattern on its head is like the character De 德 and the ones on its wings is like the character Yi 义 ; the one on the upper part resembles li 礼 ; the one on the chest Ren 仁 , and the one on the abdomen Xin 信 . This kind of bird eats calmly, and sings and dances freely. When it appears, it means that the world will be in great peace.

Five hundred li further to the east lies a mountain called Fashuang Mountain. There is no vegetation in the mountain, but a lot of water as well as many white apes. Fan River originates from Fashuang Mountain and flows south to the South Sea of China.

Four hundred li further east, the end of Yanshan Mountain can be seen. To the south is a valley called Yuyi. There are many strange birds in the valley, and the south wind blows out of this valley.

Four hundred li further east can be found the front end of the mountain, where there are a lot of gold and jade, but no water, and many vipers are under the mountain.

Five hundred li further to the east can be seen a mountain called Yangjia Mountain, without any vegetation on it but a lot of water.

Five hundred li further east, there stands Guanxiang Mountain, covered by many trees but no grass. There are many strange birds but no wild animals in the mountain.

Five hundred li further to the east lies a mountain called Mount Ji, where there are a lot of gold on it, and there are many red minerals that can be used as pigments at its foot. Black River originates from here and poured into the sea to the south. There is a kind of fish in the water, like a crucian with pig–like hairs, making a sound like a piglet. Whenever it appears, a severe drought will occur.

Four hundred li further east is a Lingqiu Mountain, in which there is no vegetation, with fire burning everywhere. There is a valley to its south, called Zhong Valley, out of which the northeast wind blows. There is a bird in the mountain, shaped like an owl with a human face, four eyes and ears, and its name is Yong 颙 . It makes a sound like calling its own name. Whenever it appears, the world will severely suffer a drought.

Three hundred and seventy li further to the east stands Lunzhe Mountain, full of gold and jade, and many blue minerals that can be used as pigments under it. There is a kind of tree growing in it, shaped like a paper mulberry tree, with a red texture on the body. The sap out of the branches is like lacquer, with the taste as sweet as sugar. Whoever eats it doesn't feel hungry with the fatigue relieved. This tree is called White Gao, which can be used to dye jade.

Five hundred and eighty li further to the east, there lies a mountain called Mount Yuli, in which there are many monsters as well as many big snakes.

Five hundred and eighty li further to the east is a mountain named Nanyu Mountain. There is a lot of gold and jade on the mountain, and a lot of water under the mountain. There is a cave in the mountain, water flowing into it in spring, and water flowing out of it in summer, but with no water in the cave in winter. Zuo Water originates from this mountain and flows into the sea to the southeast. There are phoenixes and young birds 鹓雏 alike by the water.

There stand 14 mountains in total in the third southern meridian, from Tianyu Mountain to Nanyu Mountain, with a distance of 6,530 li. The god of each mountain is with a dragon body and a human face. When offering sacrifices to mountain gods, one must kill a white dog to pray, and use glutinous rice as polished rice for sacrifice.

The above mentioned are the mountains recorded in the Nanshan Classic, totally forty large and small mountains with a distance of 16,380 li.

Such an imaginative and witty text is it that much is gained after reading.

《诗经》节选

《诗经》是中国第一部诗歌总集，它被翻译成各种英文译名，譬如 *The Book of Poetry, the Classic of Poetry, the Book of Songs, Book of Odes*, 或者简单的 *the Odes* 和 *Poetry*。子曰："不学诗，无以言。"《诗经》共收录自西周初年至春秋中叶大约五百多年的诗歌 311 篇，在中国乃至世界文化史上都占有重要地位，是中国现实主义文学的第一座里程碑，因为《诗经》关注现实、抒发现实生活触发的真情实感，这种创作态度，使其具有强烈深厚的艺术魅力。"《诗经》是迄今为止战国与汉初最重要、引用频率最高的文本。它不仅仅是儒家传统所使用的一个特殊文本，事实上还是儒家传统以此为中心而自我安排的文本。"[1]

《诗经》为"五经"之一，据说由孔子编成，在内容上共分《风》《雅》《颂》三大部分，《风》包括了十五个地方的民歌，《雅》是周王朝国都附近的乐歌，《颂》就是赞美盛德的音乐和舞曲。该诗集是当时中国社会生活面貌的形象反映，其中有先祖创业的颂歌，祭祀神鬼的乐章；也有贵族之间的宴饮交往，劳逸不均的怨愤；也有反映劳动、打猎以及大量恋爱、婚姻、社会习俗方面的篇章。它描写现实、反映现实的写作手法，开创了诗歌创作的现实主义优良传统，历代诗人的诗歌创作不同程度地受到《诗经》的影响。宋代不仅有《诗集传》刻本，在南宋时期宫廷画家马和之绘制《毛诗图》、皇帝宋高宗题书，合作阐释《诗经》。[2]

《诗经》两千年以来为中国及周边国家学者研读和传诵。清代以后，在古汉语音韵研究中，也对它的韵律进行了分析。下面是《诗经》节选。

1　孙康宜、宇文所安主编，刘倩等译：《剑桥中国文学史》，生活·读书·新知三联书店，2013年，第46页。

2　请参阅毕夏的硕士论文《南宋太学石经与〈毛诗图〉》，中国美术学院，2017年。

七月流火，九月授衣。
一之日觱发，二之日栗烈。
无衣无褐，何以卒岁。
三之日于耜，四之日举趾。
同我妇子，馌彼南亩，田畯至喜。

七月流火，九月授衣。
春日载阳，有鸣仓庚。
女执懿筐，遵彼微行，
爰求柔桑。春日迟迟，
采蘩祁祁。女心伤悲，殆及公子同归。

七月流火，八月萑苇。
蚕月条桑，取彼斧斨，
以伐远扬，猗彼女桑。
七月鸣鵙，八月载绩。
载玄载黄，我朱孔阳，为公子裳。

四月秀葽，五月鸣蜩。
八月其获，十月陨箨。
一之日于貉，取彼狐狸，
为公子裘。二之日其同，
载缵武功，言私其豵，献豜于公。

五月斯螽动股，六月莎鸡振羽，
七月在野，八月在宇，
九月在户，十月蟋蟀入我床下。
穹窒熏鼠，塞向墐户。
嗟我妇子，曰为改岁，入此室处。

六月食郁及薁，七月亨葵及菽，
八月剥枣，十月获稻，
为此春酒，以介眉寿。
七月食瓜，八月断壶，
九月叔苴，采荼薪樗，食我农夫。

九月筑场圃，十月纳禾稼。
黍稷重穋，禾麻菽麦。
嗟我农夫，我稼既同，
上入执宫功。昼尔于茅，
宵尔索綯。亟其乘屋，其始播百谷。

二之日凿冰冲冲，三之日纳于凌阴。
四之日其蚤，献羔祭韭。
九月肃霜，十月涤场。
朋酒斯飨，曰杀羔羊。
跻彼公堂，称彼兕觥，万寿无疆。

此诗共88行，8个诗节，每一小节11行。诗中描写了四季劳作的辛苦场景和劳动者的情感，既具叙事性又充满诗情画意。

Excerpts from *The Book of Poetry*

Shijing is China's first collection of poems. It is translated variously as English translations including *The Book of Poetry, the Classic of Poetry, the Book of Songs, Book of Odes,* or simply known as *the Odes or Poetry.* As Confucius says: "If you don't study *The Book of Poetry*, you can't speak well at all." As the oldest existing collection of Chinese poetry, comprising more than 300 poems dating from the 11th to 7th century BC from the early Western Zhou Dynasty to the middle of the Spring and Autumn Period over 500 years, it occupies an important position in the history of Chinese and even the world's culture. It is the first milestone of Chinese realist literature, because *The Book of Poetry* pays great attention to reality and expresses the true feelings triggered by real life, whose creative attitude gives it a strong and profound artistic charm. "The Poetry was by far the most prominent and most quoted text in Warring States and the early Han Dynasty. It was not merely a particular text used by the Confucian classicist tradition, it was the text around which this tradition arranged itself."[1]

It is one of the "Five Classics" and said to have been compiled by Confucius, whose content is divided into three parts: *Feng—Wind*, including fifteen local folk songs; *Ya—Elegance*, musics and songs near the capital of the Zhou Dynasty, and *Song—Ode,* music and dance music that praises righteous morality. This collection of poems is an image reflection of the social life in China at that time. It includes odes to ancestors' entrepreneurship and music to sacrifice to gods and ghosts; there are also banquets and exchanges between

1 Kang Sun Chang and Stephen Owen ed., *Cambridge History of Chinese Literature*, Cambridge, Cambridge University Press, 2010, p.19.

nobles, and the resentment of uneven work and rest; there are also reflections of labor, hunting, and a large number of loves, marriage, and social customs. It describes and reflects reality in writing techniques, and created a fine tradition of realism in poetry creation. The poetry creation of poets in the past dynasties has been influenced by *the Book of Songs* to varying extents. In the Song Dynasty, there was not only a block–printed version of *Shijing Zhuan*, but in the Southern Song Dynasty, Ma Hezhi as a court painter drew paintings *Maoshi Tu*, where Emperor Gaozong of the Song Dynasty wrote inscriptions, to co–interprete *The Book of Songs*.[1]

The Book of Poetry has been studied and memorized by scholars in China and neighboring countries over two millennia. Since the Qing Dynasty, its rhyme patterns have also been analyzed in the study of old Chinese phonology. The following is an excerpt *Month Seven* from *The Book of Poetry*.

Month Seven hardly spots Fire Star westward;
Month Nine sees the warm clothes for winter allotted.
Month Eleven feels the north wind blow strongly cold;
Month Twelve suffers severe weather with the breath held.
Without a cloth coat whether it is coarse or fine,
How can we survive going through the winter time!
In Month One we repair the plough;
In Month Two we begin to mow.
Women and children leave the house,
Carrying food to the field down south;
The surveyor puts the food to his mouth.

Month Seven hardly spots Fire Star westward;

1 See Bi Xia's master's thesis " The Stele Scriptures of the National Academy of the Southern Song Dynasty and the Illustrations of *the Book of Odes*," China Academy of Art, 2017.

Month Nine sees the warm clothes for winter allotted..
When the sun shines warm in spring,
The orioles wake to start singing.
Carrying deep baskets in hand,
The maidens walk to the farmland
To gather mulberries along the strand.
As the spring sun goes its course,
They pick baskets of wormwood outdoors.
Yet they are worried when they are alone,
For fear the dandies will take them home to marry.

Month Seven hardly detects Fire Star;
Month Eight sees reeds collected.
When we trim mulberries in Month Three,
We use both axes and hatchets
To cut the long boughs and branches,
And pick the leaves from soft branches.
In Month Seven the shrikes shriek overhead;
In Month Eight we twist the hempen thread
And dye it black, or yellow instead.
We may dye it red, which is so bright,
To make skirts for the young knight.

Month Four has the milkworts in seeds;
Month Five sees the cicadas chirp in the trees.
In Month Eight we gather in the crops;
In Month Ten leaves from the trees drop.
In Month Eleven we hunt the raccoon–dogs
And go on to skin the fox

To make fur coats and frocks.
In Month Twelve we have a grand chase,
To complete the hunt with good grace.
We keep the yearlings for our hoard;
We present the old boars to the lord.

Month Five sees the grasshoppers hop about;
Month Six finds the crickets starting to skip out.
In Month Seven they live in the fields;
In Month Eight they stay under the eaves;
In Month Nine in the room they keep;
In Month Ten under the bed they sleep.
We smoke the mice and stop the holes;
We seal the doors and the windows.
Wretched are our children and spouses;
Not until the new year comes around
Can they move into those small houses.

Month Six sees plums and wild grapes eaten;
Month Seven finds mallows and beans cooked.
Month Eight sees the dates knocked down;
Month Ten has the grains taken in.
With the grains we make rice wine;
Drinking the wine grants us a great longevity
In Month Seven we eat the melons;
In Month Eight we cut the gourds;
In Month Nine we collect the hemps.
We pick wild herbs and cut firewood;
These things make our livelihood.

In Month Nine we prepare the threshing floor;
In Month Ten we put the crops in store
There's rice, sorghum and glutinous millet,
Also sesame, beans, wheat and millet.
We farmers have much to deplore;
As soon as we put the crops in store,
We must build houses for the lord.
We gather thatch grass in the morning
And twist ropes in the evening.
When we are finished with houses,
We are busy again at the ploughs.

Month Twelve sees the ice chopped with hammers;
Month One has it moved to the cellars.
In Month Two we use it in sacrifice,
To preserve the lamb and the chive.
In Month Nine it is cold with frost;
In Month Ten we clean the threshing floor.
With two pitchers of wine in our hands,
We then begin to kill the lambs.
Together we go to the lord's hall,
Raise the horn cups above us all,
And wish our lord a great longevity.[1]

There are 88 lines in this poem, 8 stanzas with 11 lines in each stanza. The poem describes the hard work through the four seasons and the emotions of the laborers, which is both narrative and full of poetic images.

---

1 See Wang Gepei and Pan Zhidan (Translated), *The English Translation of the Book of Songs·National Style,* Shanghai Foreign Language Education Press, 2008.

Word Bank

1.allot v. 分配，拨给，分派

2.coarse adj. 粗糙的

3.plough n. 犁

4.mow v. 收割

5.mulberry n. 桑树；桑葚

6.wormwood n. 艾叶

7.dandy n. 花花公子

8.reed n. 芦苇

9.trim v. 修剪

10.hatchet n 短柄小斧

11.shrike r. 伯劳鸟（喙弯而坚，常将捕捉的小鸟和昆虫穿挂在荆棘上）

12.hempen adj. 麻制的

13.milkwort n. 远志（植物名，可作药用）

14.cicada n. 蝉

15.raccoon–dog n. 貉

16.frock n. 长袍

17.yearling n. 一岁至两岁 的动物

18.hoard n. 囤积

19.eaves n.(pl.) 屋檐

20.wretched adj. 可怜的

21.plum n. 李子

22.mallow n. 葵

23.date n. 枣

24.gourd n. 葫芦

25.hemp n 大麻

26.thresh. 打谷

27.threshing floor: 打谷场

28.glutinous millet 黄米

29.millet n. 黍，小米

30.sesame n. 芝麻

31.thatch n. 茅草屋顶

32.cellar n. 地窖

33.chive n. 韭菜

34.pitcher n. 大罐

饮 食

The Chinese Culinary

东坡肉

东坡肉是盛行于江浙一带的一道中国名菜。它之所以被称为“东坡肉”，是因为据说它是由宋朝伟大的诗人、政治家苏东坡创作的。苏东坡可以被称为美食家，特别注重养生，曾写了许多关于美食的诗篇，譬如《记三养》:“东坡居士自今日以往，不过一爵一肉。有尊客，盛馔则三之，可损不可增。有召我者，预以此先之，主人不从而过是者，乃止。一曰安分以养福，二曰宽胃以养气，三曰省费以养财。”[1]

东坡肉是一种炖肉，用猪肉做成。制作方法比较简单，将五花猪肉切成大块，一般是一块约二寸许的方正形猪肉，一半为肥肉，一半为瘦肉，用葱姜垫锅底，加上水、酒、糖、酱油，用文火慢焖。慢火，少水，多酒，是制作这道菜的诀窍。做好的肉肥而不腻，带有酒香，色泽红亮，味醇汁浓，酥烂而形不碎，其色、香、味俱佳，十分美味，深受人们喜爱。

关于东坡肉的来历，有许多不同的版本。有故事说，这道猪肉菜是苏东坡在黄州被流放时发明的。有一天，他正在炖猪肉，这时他的一位朋友来访。这位朋友向苏东坡挑战下了一盘围棋，而且比赛十分激烈。苏东坡因此完全忘

---

1 《全宋笔记》，第1编，第9册，大象出版社，第23页。

记了炉子上炖的猪肉。直到比赛结束厨房里传来了香味，他才想起了炖肉。他和朋友们一起品尝了猪肉，惊讶地发现肉的味道美妙极了。一道美味佳肴就此诞生，饱了世人口福。

Dongpo Pork

Dongpo Pork is a famous Chinese dish that prevails in Jiangsu and Zhejiang provinces. It is called "Dongpo Pork" because it is said to be created by Su Dongpo, a great poet and statesman in the Song Dynasty. Su Dongpo can be titled as a gourmet, and once wrote many poems about delicious food, paying special attention to health preservation, so he has written many poems about food, such as "Records of the Three Health Preservation": "Since today, the lay Buddhist of Dongpo has only had one title and one meat. There are respected guests, and delicious food is three of them, which can be reduced but not increased. If you call me, you should put it first, and if the master doesn't follow going beyond this, he will be stopped. One saying is to keep your balance in order to nourish your fortune, the second is to widen your stomach to nourish your qi energy, and the third is to save money to nourish your wealth."[1]

Dongpo Pork is a kind of stewing dish, made of pork. The production method is relatively simple. The belly pork is cut into large pieces, usually a square of about 2 inches of pork, half of which is fat meat and the other half is lean meat. The pot is padded with scallion and ginger, filled with water, wine, sugar and soy sauce. The pork is put into the pot and then stewed with a slow fire. Slow fire, less water and more wine are the keys to making this dish. The meat tastes fat but not greasy, with wine fragrance, red and bright color, mellow juice thick, soft, and its shape not broken. Besides its nice color and fragrance, it is very delicious, loved by people.

There are many different versions of stories about the origin of Dongpo

---

1 *Notes of the Song Dynasty*, Vol. 1, Vol. 9, Elephant Publishing House, p. 23.

Pork. One story goes that this pork dish was created when Su Dongpo was in Huang Zhou as a banished official. One day he was stewing pork when one of his friends paid a visit to him. The friend challenged Su Dongpo to a game of Chinese chess and in the heat of the game, Su Dongpo totally forgot about the pork being stewed on the stove. It was not until the end of the game that the amazing aroma from his kitchen reminded him of it. He tasted the pork with his friends and was shocked to find how wonderful the taste was. A delicious dish was born, therefore, with the world tasting it happily.

月饼[1]

民以食为天，每一个民族都有自己独特的饮食文化。中国美食艺术属于中国传统文化的一个重要组成部分，往往与四季节日相关。月饼是久负盛名的中国传统糕点之一，食月饼为中秋节节日食俗。在位于乌鲁木齐的新疆维吾尔自治区博物馆可以看到出土的唐代遗物：月饼。据博物馆展介可知，此月饼为唐代产物，直径 6.5 厘米，图案为“宝相花纹”，1972 年出土于吐鲁番阿斯塔那 230 号墓。月饼外皮材质为小麦粉，“模压成型，烘烤制成。呈圆形，为黄色，表面花纹轮廓清。中心为圆圈，由两组联纹组成，还绕有一周连；外装饰似松针。月饼制作精致，花纹图案搭配的错落有致，造型新颖别致，充分体现了当时人们高超的面点制作技艺。”[2] 在此介绍中提及的时代为唐朝，可见早在唐代时西域就有了月饼，只是未提及是否与中秋节有关，那么古时月饼应该已经出现了。“月饼的前身是汉代以来的胡饼”[3] 一说却无从考证，但这一考古发现可以证明月饼自古就是南北共享的美食。

月饼英语为“moon cake”，此短语见于《新英汉词典》的“moon”词条，未见于《牛津英汉高级双解词典》，可见这个词语并非英语语境中的原生词汇。《汉英大辞典》中释义为“a pastry with mostly sweet fillings made for the Moon Festival, hence loosely translated as a moon cake”，可见“a moon cake”为翻译的表达。而且正确的拼写形式是 moon cake，而不是 mooncake，此处 moon 用来表现月饼的形状类似月亮，因为月饼大多是圆的，具有象征意义。

据说中秋节吃月饼的习俗始于唐朝，关于月饼的现存文字记载，最早见于唐代《洛中见闻》，其中载有：中秋节新科进士曲江宴[4]时，唐僖宗李儇

---

1 本文由编者编写。

2 《新疆维吾尔自治区博物馆画册》，香港金版文化出版社，2006年，第115页。

3 黄涛、王心愿：《中秋月饼考》，《温州大学学报（社会科学版）》，2014年第2期，第33—41页。

4 曲江宴是唐时考中的进士，放榜后大宴于曲江亭，又名曲江会。

（862—888）命御膳房用绫包裹月饼赏赐进士。

中秋汉族传统节日，农历八月十五日。这晚月亮又圆又亮，全家人团聚在一起，一边赏月，一边吃月饼。此俗延续至今。[1]

八月十五中秋节，此日三秋恰半，故谓之“中秋”。此夜月色倍明于常时，又谓之“月夕”。“此际金风荐爽，玉露生凉，丹桂香飘，银蟾光满，王孙公子，富家巨室，莫不登危楼，临轩玩月，或开广榭，玳筵罗列，琴瑟铿锵，酌酒高歌，以竟之欢。至如铺席之家，亦登小小月台。安排家宴，团子女，以酬佳节。虽陋巷贫之人，解衣市酒勉强迎欢，不肯虚度。此夜天街买卖，直至五鼓，玩月游。”[2]

藏故宫博物院的宋画《瑶台步月图》，绢本设色，纵 25.6 厘米，横 26.7 厘米。此图无款印。对开清乾隆皇帝题七言绝句一首。钤乾隆内府诸收藏印。图写中秋纤秀仕女立于楼阁台子赏月情景。[3] 此图证明了中秋赏月的习俗自古有之。

瑶台步月图　故宫博物院藏

Enjoying the Moon Walking on the Platform, The Collection of Palace Museum

古代中秋节需要祭拜月神，古代月饼被作为祭品在中秋节供奉祭品。“月神天体崇拜的一种形态。月亮对人类没有太阳那样强大的影响，地位低于日

1　沈善洪：《中国语言文化背景汉英双解词典》，商务印书馆，1998年，第515页。

2　（宋）吴自牧：《梦粱录》，浙江人民出版社，1984年，第26页。

3　故宫博物院藏品，访问时间2021年11月4日，https://www.dpm.org.cn/collection/paint/228755.html。

神。传说月宫仙子名叫嫦娥，月中有一只白兔，捣不死之药。现在民间每逢农历八月十五，仍有祭拜月亮的风俗。”[1]

每逢中秋夜祭月仪式上，设大香案，摆上月饼、水果等祭品。无论是否晴夜月朗，人们都将拜祭月亮分食月饼。记得幼时长者就带领我行过祭礼。月饼作为拜祭月神的供品，历史应悠久。根据现存文献，“月饼”一词曾收录于南宋吴自牧的《梦粱录》：“市食点心，四时皆有，任便索唤，不误主顾。且如蒸作面行卖……菊花饼、月饼、梅花饼、开炉饼……”[2]可见当时月饼已位列常供点心。宋代周密在记叙南宋都城临安见闻的《武林旧事》中也提到“月饼”之名称。月饼在宋代苏东坡的《留别廉守》诗文里又称“小饼”：“小饼如嚼月，中有酥与饴”[3]，可知当时月饼已夹内馅，酥油拌糖。明代的《西湖游览志会》才有明确记载：“八月十五日谓之中秋，民间以月饼相遗，取团圆之义”。明代沈榜《苑署杂记》录：“士庶家俱以是月造面饼相遗，大小不等，呼为月饼。”[4]明代刘若愚在《酌中志》录：“八月，宫中赏秋海棠、玉簪花。自初一日起，即有卖月饼者，至十五日，家家供奉月饼、瓜果。如有剩月饼，乃整收于干燥风凉之处，至岁暮分用之，曰团圆饼也。”[5]此文点明了月饼的特殊寓意。《明实录·神宗实录》[6]里就记载了皇帝多次赐给大臣月饼。《帝京景物略》曰：“八月十五祭月，其祭果饼必圆。”“家设月光位于月所出方，向月而拜，则焚月光纸，撤所供，散之家人必遍。月饼月果，戚属馈相报，饼有径二尺者。”[7]可见到了明代，中秋节吃月饼和以月饼祭拜的习俗更加普遍，且有具体的形态规定。

清人袁枚《随园食单》“点心菜”中介绍道：刘方伯月饼“用山东飞面，作酥为皮，中用松仁、核桃仁、瓜子仁为细末，微加冰糖和猪油作馅，食之不觉

1　沈善洪：《中国语言文化背景汉英双解词典》，商务印书馆，1998年，第493—494页。

2　（宋）吴自牧：《梦粱录》，浙江人民出版社，1984年，第147页。

3　（宋）苏轼：《留别廉守》，《苏轼诗集》卷二十五，见古诗词网 https://so.gushiwen.cn/shiwenv_e22676b5c859.aspx，访问时间2022年1月13日。

4　（明）沈榜：《苑署杂记》，北京古籍出版社，1983年。

5　（明）刘若愚：《酌中志》，北京古籍出版社，1994年。

6　（明）明代官修《明实录·神宗实录》，访问时间2022年1月13日，国学大师网http://www.guoxuedashi.net/a/5682wpxo/88218w.html。

7　（明）刘侗：《帝京景物略》，北京古籍出版社，1963年；（明）刘侗、于弈正著，孙小力注：《帝京景物略》，上海古籍出版社，2001年。

甚甜，而香松柔腻，迥异寻常。”[1]还有花边月饼“明府家制花边月饼，不在山东刘方伯之下。余常以轿迎其女厨来园制造，看用飞面拌生猪油子团百搦，才用枣肉嵌入为馅，裁如碗大，以手搦其四边菱花样。用火盆两个，上下覆而炙之。枣不去皮，取其鲜也；油不先熬，取其生也。含之上口而化，甘而不腻，松而不滞，其工夫全在搦中，愈多愈妙。”[2]

随着社会的发展，中国月饼文化更加多元化，月饼品种多样，甚至出现了非圆形的月饼，但中秋佳节之际总是选用圆圆的月饼，寓意家人团团圆圆。

---

1 （清）袁枚：《随园食单》，三秦出版社，2005年；访问时间2022年1月13日，https://www.zggdwx.com/suiyuan/13.html。

2 同上。

Moon Cakes[1]

Food is what matters to the people, and every nation has its own cuisine culture. Chinese food art belongs to an important part of Chinese traditional culture, which is often related to the festivals of the four seasons. The moon cake is one of the most famous traditional Chinese cakes. The moon cakes, relics of the Tang Dynasty, can be seen unearthed in the Xinjiang Uygur Autonomous Region Museum located in Urumqi. According to the exhibition, the moon cake, a product of the Tang Dynasty, has a diameter of 6.5 centimeters and a pattern of "Baoxiang design (rosette design)". It was unearthed in 1972 from Tomb 230 in Astana, Turfan. The moon cake is made of wheat flour, "molded and baked. It is round, yellow, and the surface pattern is clear, whose center is a circle, composed of two lines of pearl groups, around which is a circle of linked–petal patterns. The exterior decoration is like pine needles. The moon cakes are exquisitely made, with well–arranged patterns and novel shapes, which fully reflect the superb pastry making skills of the people at that time."[2] In this introduction, it is mentioned that the time is the Tang Dynasty, so it can be seen that there were moon cakes in the western regions of China at the time as early as the Tang Dynasty, but it is not mentioned whether it is related to the Mid–Autumn Festival, so the moon cakes should have appeared in ancient times. It is impossible to prove that the moon cake originated from Hu Cake since the Han Dynasty,[3] but this archaeological discovery can prove that the moon cake has

1 This is compiled by the compiler of this book.

2 *Xinjiang Uygur Autonomous Region Museum Album*, Hong Kong Gold Edition Culture Press, 2006, p. 115.

3 Huang Tao, Wang Xinyuan, Research on Mid–Autumn Moon Cake, *Journal of Wenzhou University* (Social Science Edition), 2014, (02):33–41.

been a common delicacy in the north and south since ancient times

The English word for 月饼 is "moon cake". This phrase appears in the entry of "moon" in *The New English–Chinese Dictionary*, but not in *the Oxford Advanced English–Chinese Dictionary*, indicating that this word is not a native word in the English context. In the Chinese–English Dictionary its meaning is "a pastry with mostly sweet fillings made for the Moon Festival, resulting in only translated as a Moon cake", therefore "A moon cake" is a translated expression. And the correct spelling is "moon cake", not "mooncake", which is used to indicate that moon cakes are shaped like the moon because they are mostly round with symbolic significance.

It is said that the custom of eating moon cakes at the Mid–Autumn Festival began in the Tang Dynasty. The earliest written records about moon cakes can be found in *Luozong Xizhou* of the Tang Dynasty. It said: Li Dong (June 8, 862 – April 20, 888) Emperor Xizong of the Tang Dynasty, ordered the official of the imperial kitchen to award the new Jinshi (a successful candidate in the highest imperial examinations)[1] with moon cakes wrapped in a silk dish while the new loyal scholars were feasting on the Qujiang feast at the Mid–Autumn Festival.

"Mid–autumn Festival: on the 15th day of the 8th lunar month, a traditional festival of the Han nationality. That night the moon is at its brightest and fullest phase and people get together to enjoy looking at the moon in a family reunion while eating moon cakes. This custom has continued to the present day."[2]

Mid–Autumn Festival is on August 15, the day just at the half of the autumn, and therefore it is called "Mid–Autumn Festival" or "Moon Festival". This night moonlight is times brighter than the usual, also known as the "moon night", when the autumn wind is blowing, with cool dews, the osmanthus sweet scent floating, and shining silver cups full. All the princes, and the rich families, go up the high buildings to enjoy watching the moon. Some gather in a wide

1 Qujiang Banquet was also known as Qujianghui, that is, after the announcement of the name list, a banquet was held in Qujiang Pavilion for those Jinshis who passed the examination in the Tang Dynasty.

2 Shen Shanhong, *A Chinese–English Dictionary with Cultural Background Information*, The Commercial Press, Beijing, 2010, p. 515.

open pavilion, with delicious dishes, listening to sonorous music from harps and other musical instruments, drinking wine and singing, in order to experience unexpectedly enjoyment. As to such as the small families of the mat, they also get together to have a small moon get–together, arranging family banquets, and getting children together, in order to celebrate the festival. Although the people of the alley are poor, they trade the clothes for some wine, to reluctantly celebrate the festival, refusing to idle away. This night the business on the street goes on until the five watches of the night, with moon tours.[1]

The painting of the Song Dynasty *Enjoying the Moon at Yaotai Platform*, collected by the Palace Museum, is painted on silk, 25.6 cm in length and 26.7 cm in breadth, without seals and signature on this painting. On the other side, Qianlong, the Emperor of the Qing Dynasty, wrote a seven–character poem, with several collection seals of Qianlong's imperial court storehouse. The painting depicts the scene where five delicate ladies standing in the pavilion are enjoying the moon on the Mid–Autumn Festival, which proves that the custom of appreciating the moon on Mid–Autumn Festival has been around since ancient times. [2]

The ancient Mid–Autumn Festival requires the worship to the Moon God, and the ancient moon cakes are as sacrifices. It is a form of celestial worship. The moon has no more powerful influence on human beings than the sun. It is inferior to the legend that the moon fairy is named Chang'e and there is a white rabbit smashing medicine for longevity of non–death in the moon. Now every lunar calendar August 15, there is still in the prevalence of the custom worshiping the moon in the folk.[3]

During the Mid–Autumn Festival, a large incense table was set up to offer

---

1 (Song Dynasty) Wu Zimu, *Mengliang Lu, Records of Dreaming Liang*, Zhejiang People's Publishing House, 1984, p. 26.

2 The Palace Museum, accessed on November 4, 2021, https://www.dpm.org.cn/collection/paint/228755.html.

3 Shen Shanhong, *A Chinese–English Dictionary with Cultural Background Information*, The Commercial Press, Beijing, 2010, pp. 493–494.

sacrifices such as moon cakes and fruits. Whether it's with moonlight or cloudy, people always worship the moon and eat mooncakes. I remember when I was a child the elders led me through the rites. Mooncakes as a sacrifice to the Moon God should have a long history. According to existing literature, the word "moon cake" was once included in *Meng Liang Lu* written by Wu Zimu in the Southern Song Dynasty: "All kinds of dessert and pastry are available in the market all the time through four seasons, and customers can call upon convently as they like without and mistakes or delay. … chrysanthemum bread, moon cake, …"[1]So mooncakes were often served as dessert even then. In the Song Dynasty, the name of "moon cake" was also mentioned by Zhou Mi in *Old Stories of Wulin*, a narrative of Lin'an, the capital of the Southern Song Dynasty. Mooncakes in Su Dongpo's poem *Liubie Lianshou* of the Song Dynasty are also called as "small cakes": "small cakes such as chewing the month, they are crisp with candy inside",[2] known at that time the moon cake was clamped inside the filling, butter and sugar. *West Lake Tour Records*[3] of the Ming Dynasty recorded: "August 15 is called the Mid–Autumn Festival, when people in the folk send moon cakes to each other as presents, taking the meaning of reunion." Shen Bang of the Ming Dynasty in *Yuanshu Records* said: "In this month, whether they are officials or ordinary ones, all families make cakes to send to each other as presents, with different sizes, called the moon cake." [4] Liu Ruoyu of the Ming Dynasty in *Zhuozhong Zhi* wrote down: "In August, people in the palace appreciate the apple and hosta. From the first day, there are people selling moon cakes; on the 15th, every family sacrifices moon cakes, fruits and melons. If there are moon cakes left, they will be put away closed in a dry and cool place; to the end of

1 (Song Dynasty) Wu Zimu, *Mengliang Lu,* Zhejiang People's Publishing House, 1984, p.147.

2 (Song Dynasty) Su Shi, *"Liubie Lianshou",* Ancient Poetry Website, https://so.gushiwen.cn/shiwenv_e22676b5c859.aspx, accessed on January 13, 2022.

3 (Ming Dynasty) Shen Bang, *Miscellaneous Notes of the Court Administration*, Beijing, Beijing Ancient Books Publishing House, 1983.

4 (Ming Dynasty) Shen Bang, *Miscellaneous Notes of the Court Administration*, Beijing, Beijing Ancient Books Publishing House, 1983.

the year they will be eaten distributed, called Reunion Cakes." [1]This article points out the special meaning of moon cakes. *The Ming Shilu · Shenzong Shilu* [2]recorded that the emperor gave moon cakes to his ministers many times. The *Dijing Jingwu Lue* said: "On the festival of August 15 to sacrifice the moon, its fruits and cakes should be round." "At home moonlight position set is located in the direction from which the moon comes out; people pray to the moon worshipping, then burn moonlight paper, remove them to scatter among the family all over. Mooncakes and fruits are presents among the relatives, even with the cake diameter two feet."[3] It can be seen that in the Ming Dynasty the custom of eating and worshipping moon cakes on Mid–Autumn Festival became more common, with specific form codes.

Yuan Mei, a scholar of the Qing Dynasty, introduced in "Desserts and Dishes" of *Suiyuan Food List* that to make Liu Fangbo moon cakes, "Shandong flying doughs are used to make the crispy skin; pine nuts, walnut kernels, and melon seeds as fine powder, and rock sugar and lard slightly added. When you eat them, you will not feel the stuffing sweet and fragrant, but soft and greasy, which is quite unusual."[4] There are also lace mooncakes, "Home–made lace mooncakes by Ming Family are as good as those Liu Fangbo of Shandong. I often invite his female chef in a sedan chair to my garden to make them. Mix the raw lard balls with flying doughs by scratching it hundreds of times, then embed the jujube meat into the stuffing, cut it into pieces as big as a bowl, and rub the four sides of the diamond pattern with hands. Use two braziers to cover the top and bottom and fry them. The jujube is not peeled, just for taking it as fresh; the

---

1 (Ming Dynasty) Liu Ruoyu, *Zhuozhong Zhi*, Beijing, Beijing Ancient Books Publishing House, 1994.

2 (Ming Dynasty) Official Edition in Ming Dynasty, *The Ming shilu·shenzong shilu*, accessed on, January 13, 2022, Sinology Master Website http://www.guoxuedashi.net/a/5682wpxo/88218w.html.

3 (Ming Dynasty) Liu Tong, *Dijing Jingwu Lue, A Brief History of the Imperial Capital,* Beijing, Beijing Ancient Books Publishing House, 1963; (Ming Dynasty) Liu Tong and Yu Yizheng; annotated by Sun Xiaoli, *Dijing Jingwu Lue, A Brief History of the Imperial Capital*, Shanhai Ancient Books Publishing House, 2001.

4 (Qing Dynasty) Yuan Mei, *Suiyuan Food List*, Sanqin Publishing House, 2005; accessed on January 13, 2022, https://www.zggdwx.com/suiyuan/13.html.

oil is not boiled first, for keeping it as raw. The moon cake melts on being put into the mouth, sweet but not greasy, loose but not stagnant; the effort is all in the scratching; the more the better. [1]

With the development of the society, the culture of moon cakes has become more diversified. There are various kinds of moon cakes, and even non–round moon cakes appear. However, on the occasion of the Mid–Autumn Festival, the moon cakes are always round, implying that the family is reunited.

---

1 (Qing Dynasty) Yuan Mei, *Suiyuan Food List*, Sanqin Publishing House, 2005; accessed on January 13, 2022, https://www.zggdwx.com/suiyuan/13.html.

《茶经》节选

陆羽

日常生活中，茶为必需且高雅之饮品。中国茶文化历史悠久，宋人苏轼有诗《论茶》曰："除烦去腻，不可缺茶。"[1] 中国美术史上有许多画家都描绘了品茗图或煮茶图，譬如明代文徵明。早在公元 758 年左右，中国唐代茶学家陆羽[2] 撰写了《茶经》，这是中国乃至世界最早、最完整、最全面介绍茶的专著，被誉为茶叶百科全书。这属于一部综合性论著，是重要的茶学专著，书中涉及了茶叶生产的历史、源流、现状、生产技术以及饮茶技艺、茶道原理等。它将普通日常饮茶升格为美妙的文化艺术，推动了中国乃至世界茶文化的发展。譬如日本文化的茶道，"茶道是发源于中国、开花结果于日本的高层次的生活文化。'茶道'一词初见于唐代。在唐代，茶道已脱离日常啜饮范围而成为一种优雅的精神文化。陆羽的《茶经》就是其光辉的足迹。其后不久，茶道传到了日本，与日本的传统文化相结合，获得了新的发展，成为具有深远哲理和丰富艺术表现的综合文化体系。"[3] 可见在茶文化中《茶经》十分重要。下面是《茶经》选段。

之源

茶者，南方之嘉木也，一尺二尺，乃至数十尺。其巴山峡川有两人合抱者，伐而掇之，其树如瓜芦，叶如栀子，花如白蔷薇，实如栟榈，蒂如丁香，根如胡

1　（宋）苏轼：《论茶》，《全宋笔记》，第1编，第九册，大象出版社，第210页。

2　陆羽（733—804），字鸿渐、季疵，号竟陵子、桑苎翁、东岗子，唐朝复州竟陵（今湖北天门市）人，被誉为"茶仙"，尊为"茶圣"，祀为"茶神"，有"茶山御史"之称。陆羽一生嗜茶，精于茶道，对茶叶长期实施调查研究，熟悉茶树栽培、育种和加工技术，并擅长品茗。他著成《茶经》，使茶叶成为一门独立的学问，对世界茶文化产生深刻影响。

3　滕军：《日本茶道文化概论》，［日］裹千家家元哲学博士千宗室审订，东方出版社，1992年，第Ⅳ页。

桃。其字或从草，或从木，或草木并。其名一曰茶，二曰槚，三曰蔎，四曰茗，五曰荈。其地：上者生烂石，中者生栎壤，下者生黄土。凡艺而不实，植而罕茂，法如种瓜，三岁可采。野者上，园者次；阳崖阴林紫者上，绿者次；笋者上，牙者次；叶卷上，叶舒次。阴山坡谷者不堪采掇，性凝滞，结瘕疾。茶之为用，味至寒，为饮最宜。精行俭德之人，若热渴、凝闷、脑疼、目涩、四支烦、百节不舒，聊四五啜，与醍醐、甘露抗衡也。采不时，造不精，杂以卉，莽饮之成疾，茶为累也。亦犹人参，上者生上党，中者生百济、新罗，下者生高丽。有生泽州、幽州、檀州者，为药无效，况非此者！设服荠苨，使六疾不瘳。知人参为累，则茶累尽矣。

之造

凡采茶，在二月三月四月之间。茶之笋者生烂石沃土，长四五寸，若薇蕨始抽，凌露采焉。茶之牙者，发于丛薄之上，有三枝四枝五枝者，选其中枝颖拔者采焉，其日有雨不采，晴有云不采。晴采之，蒸之，捣之，拍之，焙之，穿之，封之，茶之干矣。茶有千万状，卤莽而言，如胡 人靴者蹙缩然，犎牛臆者廉檐然，浮云出山者轮菌然，轻飚拂水者涵淡然。有如陶家之子罗，膏土以水澄泚之。又如新治地者，遇暴雨流潦之所经，此皆茶之精腴。有如竹箨者，枝干坚实，艰于蒸捣，故其形篵然；有如霜荷者，至叶凋，沮易其状貌，故厥状委萃然，此皆茶之瘠老者也。自采至于封七经目，自胡靴至于霜荷八等，或以光黑平正，言嘉者，斯鉴之下也；以皱黄坳垤言佳者；鉴之次也。若皆言嘉及皆言不嘉者，鉴之上也。何者？出膏者光，含膏者皱，宿制者则黑，日成者则黄，蒸压则平正，纵之则坳垤，此茶与草木叶一也，茶之否臧，存于口诀。

之饮

翼而飞，毛而走，去而言，此三者俱生于天地间。饮啄以活，饮之时，义远矣哉。至若救渴，饮之以浆；蠲忧忿，饮之以酒；荡昏寐，饮之以茶。茶之为饮，发乎神农氏，闻于鲁周公，齐有晏婴，汉有扬雄、司马相如，吴有韦曜，晋有刘琨、张载远、祖纳、谢安、左思之徒，皆饮焉。滂时浸俗，盛于国朝，两都并荆俞间，以为比屋之饮。饮有粗茶、散茶、末茶、饼茶者，乃斫，乃熬，乃炀，乃

杭州茶园
A Tea Garden in Hangzhou

春，贮于瓶缶之中，以汤沃焉，谓之茶。或用葱、姜、枣、橘皮、茱萸、薄荷之等，煮之百沸，或扬令滑，或煮去沫，斯沟渠间弃水耳，而习俗不已。于戏！天育万物皆有至妙，人之所工，但猎浅易。所庇者屋屋精极，所着者衣衣精极，所饱者饮食，食与酒皆精极之。茶有九难：一曰造，二曰别，三曰器，四曰火，五曰水，六曰炙，七曰末，八曰煮，九曰饮。阴采夜焙非造也，嚼味嗅香非别也，膻鼎腥瓯非器也，膏薪庖炭非火也，飞湍壅潦非水也，外熟内生非炙也，碧粉缥尘非末也，操艰搅遽非煮也，夏兴冬废非饮也。夫珍鲜馥烈者，其碗数三；次之者，碗数五。若坐客数至，五行三碗，至七行五碗。若六人已下，不约碗数，但阙一人而已，其隽永补所阙人。

明　文徵明《煮茶图》
Making Tea, Wen Zhengming, in the Ming Dynasty

Excerpts from *The Classic of Tea*

Lu Yu

In daily life, tea is a necessary and elegant thing, and Chinese tea culture enjoys a long history. Su Shi from the Song Dynasty wrote in his poem *On Tea*: "To get rid of boredom, tea is indispensable."[1] There are many painters in the history of Chinese art who have depicted pictures of drinking tea or making tea, such as Wen Zhengming in the Ming Dynasty. As early as around AD 758, Lu Yu, the Chinese tea expert[2] of the Tang Dynasty, wrote *The Classic of Tea*, which is the earliest, most complete and comprehensive introduction to tea in China and the planet, known as the tea encyclopedia. The book, a comprehensive treatise and an important tea monograph, involves such things of tea production as the history, origin, current situation, production technology, tea drinking techniques, and principles of tea ceremony, and so forth. Upgrading ordinary daily tea drinking into a wonderful culture and art, it has promoted the development of Chinese tea culture and even that of the world. Take the tea ceremony of Japanese culture for example. "Tea ceremony is a high–level life culture that originated in China and blossomed and bore fruit in Japan. The term 'tea ceremony' first appeared in the Tang Dynasty, when tea ceremony has become

1 (Song Dynasty) Su Shi, *On Tea, Quansong Biji, Notes of the Entire Song Dynasty*, 9in the 1st edition, Elephant Publishing House, p. 210.

2 Lu Yu, (733–804), with the courtesy name Hongjian, Jibian, named Jinglingzi, Sangjuweng, Donggangzi, was born in Jingling (now Tianmen City, Hubei) in the Tang Dynasty and was known as Tea Immortal, revered as "Tea Sage", worshiped as "Tea God", known as "Tea Mountain Imperial History". Lu Yu, addicted to tea all his life and proficient in tea ceremony, had conducted long–term investigation and research on tea, familiar with tea plant cultivation, breeding and processing technology, and was good at tasting tea. He took time to write *The Classic of Tea,* which made tea an independent subject and had a profound impact on the world's tea culture.

a whole developing into an elegant spiritual culture beyond the scope of daily sipping and drinking. Lu Yu's *The Classic of Tea* is its glorious footprint. Soon afterwards, the tea ceremony spread to Japan, combined with traditional Japanese culture, obtained new development, and became a profound philosophical and rich artistic expression of a comprehensive cultural system." [1]It can be seen that *The Classic of Tea* is very important in the tea culture. The following is some excerpts from *The Classic of Tea*.

The Origin of Tea

Tea is a type of fine tree in southern China, one foot or two feet tall and some even as high as tens of feet. In the areas of Bashan and Xiachuan, there are tea trees whose stems are thick enough for two people to hug. The branches must be cut down before the buds and leaves can be picked. The shape of the tea tree is like a melon. The leaves are shaped like gardenias. The flowers are like white roses, and the seeds are like palms. The stalk resembles a clove, and the root resembles a walnut.

The structure of the character 茶 , some are from the "grass" 艹 radical (written as " 茶 "), some from the "wood" 木 radical (written as " 木茶 "), and some from the "grass" 艹 radical and the "wood" 木 radical (written as " 茶 "). There are five names for tea: one is 茶 , the second is 檟 , the third is 蔎 , the fourth is 茗 , and the fifth is 荈 . The best soil for growing tea is the soil with fully weathered rocks, with gravel soil with gravel as the second, and yellow clay the worst.

Generally speaking, if the technique of transplanting tea seedlings is not properly mastered, tea trees rarely grow lush after transplanting. The method of planting is like growing melons. Tea can be picked three years after planting. The tea of the best quality is grown naturally in the mountains and wildness, and the ones cultivated in plantations are inferior in quality.

On the sunny hillside, the purple buds and leaves of the tea trees growing under

---

1 Teng Jun, *Introduction to Japanese Tea Ceremony Culture,* Japan Tuoqianjia Moto Doctor of Philosophy Chisong Room Review, Oriental Publishing House, 1992, p. IV.

the shade of woods are better than the green ones. The long buds and leaves with the shape slender like a bamboo shoot in internodes are better than the weaker thin ones. The recurring green leaves are better than the leaves with the surface flat. The leaves growing on shady hillsides or valleys are not of good quality and not worth picking. Because of its stagnant nature, drinking it will cause abdominal distension.

The tea has a function of, because of its cold nature, reducing fire, and is most suitable as a beverage. People with good behavior and thrifty virtues drink four or five sips, if they have a fever, thirst, chest tightness, headache, astringent eyes, weak limbs and joints, and the effect is comparable to the best beverages such as glutinous rice and nectar. However, if it is picked untimely, with the production not fine, mixed with weeds and fallen leaves, it will make the people sick to drink it.

Tea, like ginseng, has different origins and different quality, which may even bring adverse effects. The top–grade ginseng is produced in Shangdang, the middle–grade ginseng in Baekje and Silla, and the lower–grade ginseng in Goryeo. If the ginseng produced in Zezhou, Yizhou, Youzhou, and Tanzhou (of the worst quality) is used for medicinal purposes, there is no curative effect, not to mention they are inferior to them! If you mistakenly take the marmoset as ginseng, the disease will not be cured. If you understand the analogy of ginseng, you can understand the bad effects of tea.

Tea Harvesting

Tea is picked in February, March, and April of lunar calendar. The buds and leaves, which are as fat as bamboo shoots, grow on the soil with weathered stone fragments, up to four to five inches long, just like the young stems of viburnum and fern that just come out of the soil. They are picked with dew in the morning. The second–class buds and leaves (short and thin) occur on the tea branches mixed with vegetation. Pick the straight ones out of three, four, and five shoots from an old branch. On a rainy day, there is no picking and neither is there on sunny days with clouds, and there can be picking only on sunny days without clouds. With the buds and sprouts picked, they are steamed in a retort, pounded with a mortar, put in a model and patted into a certain shape, and then roasted and dried, and finally pieced through into a string, packaged, and then the tea can be kept dry.

The shape of the tea varies greatly. Roughly speaking, some resemble the boots of a Human (Tang Dynasty), with the leather crumpled; some resemble the chest of a fat cow, with subtle creases; some resemble floating clouds rising out of the mountains, twisting round and round; Some are like breeze blowing on the water rippling; some are as smooth and moist as the fine clay that a potter sifts out and then precipitated with water; some is like newly formed land, washed up and down by heavy rain and rapids. These are exquisite and high–quality teas. Some leaves resemble bamboo shoot shells, with hard stems and difficult to steam, so the made tea leaves are shaped like sieve; some are like frosted lotus leaves, with the stems and leaves withered and changed, so the appearance of the made tea withered, which are bad teas and old teas.

From picking to packaging, there are seven processes; from the shrunken shape resembling a boot to the decayed one resembling a frosted lotus leaf, there are totally eight grades. (For finished tea) Some people regard light, black, and flatness as the signs of good tea, which is the inferior identification method. Taking shrinkage, yellowness, and unevenness as the characteristics of good tea is a less inferior identification method. If you can not only point out the good points of tea, but also tell the bad, you will be the best at distinguishing tea. Why? Because the tea juice is pressed out, it will be bright, and shrunk with the tea juice; the color that is made after the night is black, and the color that is made on the same day is yellow; if after steamed it is pressed tightly, it will be smooth, and it will be convex and concave if it is natural. This is the common feature of tea and plant leaves. There is a set of methods orally taught to identify the quality of tea.

Tea Drinking

Birds can fly with wings, beasts run with abundant hair, people can speak; and all the three are born in the world between heaven and earth, relying on drinking and eating to maintain life activities. It can be seen that drinking has a great effect and far–reaching significance. To quench thirst, you must drink water; for excitement and sorrow and boredom, you must drink wine; for refreshment and relieving drowsiness, you must drink tea.

Tea, as a beverage, began from Shennong, and was known to all written as a record by Zhou Gongdan. In the Spring and Autumn Period, Yan Ying from the Qi State, Yang Xiong and Sima Xiangru in the Han Dynasty, Wei Yao from the Wu State in the Three Kingdoms, and Liu Kun, Zhang Zai, Lu Na, Xie An, and Zuo Si in the Jin Dynasty all loved tea. Later, it spread day by day and gradually became a trend. In our Tang Dynasty, it reached its peak. In the two capitals of Xi'an and Luoyang, as well as Jiangling and Chongqing, there is tea drinking at every household.

The types of tea include crude tea, loose tea, powdered tea, and cake tea. (When you want to drink the cake tea) Use a knife to chop it open, fry it, dry it, mash it, put it in a bottle, and flush it with boiling water. This is called "jamming tea". Or add green onions, ginger, dates, orange peel, cornel, mint, etc., and boil it for a long time to raise the tea soup to clear it, or remove the "foam" on the tea after boiling. This tea is tantamount to pouring waste water in the ditch, but people are generally used to doing this!

Ah, everything born in the world has its most subtle features, and what people are good at are only those simple and easy to do. What people live in is a house, and the structure of the house is exquisite; what people wear are the clothes, and they are exquisitely made; what makes people's stomachs full is the food and wine, and they are wonderful. (And is tea drinking so? But people are not good at it.) In summary, tea has nine difficulties: the first is manufacturing; the second is identification; third is utensils; fourth is firepower; fifth is water quality; sixth is roasting; and seventh is mashing; eighth is roasting; ninth is tasting. Picking tea on a cloudy day and roasting it at night will result in improper manufacture; chewing in mouth and smelling the fragrance in nose will result in improper identification; using pots that are contaminated with mutton gas and fishy smells will result in improper appliances; oily wood and the charcoal roasting the meat is improper fuel; the water that is flowing very fast or stagnant is improper to use; if it is cooked with outer mature and inner rawness, it is improperly broiled; if it is mashed greatly into a green powder, it is improperly mashed ; if the operation is unskilled and the stirring is too fast, the cooking is improper; if it is only drunk in summer but not in winter, it is improper drinking.

There are only three bowls (one furnace) of precious, delicious and fragrant tea, followed by five bowls. If the number of guests to drink tea reaches five, then scoop out three bowls and drink them by passing on one by one; if the number reached seven, scoop out five bowls and drink them by passing on one by one; if there are six people, don't worry about the number of bowls (meaning that they will scoop three bowls like five people), there's just a lack for one person, with eternality to supplement it.

Word bank

1.encyclopedia n. 百科全书；专科全书

2.comprehensive adj. 全面的；无所不包的；综合性的

3.treatise n. 论文；专著

4.monograph n. 专著；专论

5.tea ceremony n. 茶道

6.spiritual adj. 精神上的；心灵的

7.sip v. 小口地喝；啜饮

8.footprint n. 脚印；足迹

9.gardenia n. 栀子属植物

10.stalk n. 茎；秆

11.clove n. 丁香干花；丁香树

12.walnut n. 胡桃；胡桃树

13. transplant v. 使迁移；转移

14. plantation n. 种植园；种植场

15.inferior adj. 低等的；下级的

16.stagnant adj. 停滞的；不流动的

17.abdominal adj. 与腹部有关的

18.distension n. 扩张；膨胀

19.thrifty adj. 节约的；节俭的

20.astringent adj. 收缩的；严厉的

21.limb n. 肢；肢体

22.beverage n. 饮料

23.glutinous adj. 胶质的；黏的

24.nectar n. 花蜜；众神饮用的酒

25.fragment n. 碎片；碎块；片段

26.viburnum n. 荚蒾

27.crumple v. 把……弄皱；崩溃；起皱

28.shrinkage n. 收缩；皱缩

29.drowsiness n. 睡意；困倦；假寐

30.crude adj. 天然的；未加工的

31.foam n. 泡沫；唾沫

32.tantamount adj. 相当于的

33.contaminate v. 使不纯；污染

34. broiled adj. 烤过的

35. mash v. 将……捣成糊状；将……调成麦芽浆；〈英；非正式〉泡（茶）

36. scoop n. 长柄勺；球形勺

37.eternality n. 外部性；外部效应

中　医

The Chinese Medicine

《梦溪笔谈》节选

沈括[1]

旧说用药有“一君、二臣、三佐、五使”之说。其意以为药虽众，主病者专在一物，其他则节级相为用，大略相统制，如此为宜。不必尽然也。所谓君者，主此一方者，固无定物也。《药性论》[2]乃以众药之和厚者定以为君，其次为臣、为佐，有毒者多为使。此谬说也。设若欲攻坚积，如巴豆辈岂得不为君哉。

汤、散、丸各有所宜。古方用汤最多，用丸、散者殊少。煮散古方无用者，唯近世人为之。大体欲达五脏四肢者莫如汤，欲留膈中者莫如散，久而后散者莫如丸。又无毒者宜汤，小毒者宜散，大毒者须用丸。又欲速者用汤，稍者用散，甚者用丸。此其大概也。近世用汤者全少，应汤者皆用煮散。大率汤

1　沈括（1031—1095），浙江杭州人，北宋政治家、科学家。此部分除了参考2015年中华书局版《梦溪笔谈》，还参照了《大中华文库汉英对照梦溪笔谈》，第820—827页。中医在中国文化中是最关乎民生的又一项国粹，在国际上也声誉日隆。此文选自宋代沈括的《梦溪笔谈》，从中可以窥见古人的博学多识。《梦溪笔谈》是一部百科全书，由609条笔记组成，并进一步分为17个部分，覆盖面很广。本文摘录的是与医学相关的部分。这本书不仅因其学术和历史价值而闻名，而且因其科学和技术价值而闻名。（宋）沈括：《梦溪笔谈》，中华书局，2015年。

2　甄权，隋唐年间著名针灸医家，医学著述颇多，包括《药性论》。

剂气势完壮，力与丸、散倍蓰。煮散者不过五钱极矣，比功较力，岂敌汤势？然汤既力大，则不宜有失消息。用之全在良工，难可以定论拘也。

古法采草药多用二月、八月，殊未当。但二月草已芽，八月苗未枯，采掇者易识耳，在药则未为良时。大率用根者，若有宿根，须取无茎叶时采，则津泽皆归其根，欲验之，但取芦菔、地黄辈观，无苗时则实而沈；有苗时采，则虚而浮；其无宿根者，即候苗成而未有花时采，则根生已足而又未衰。如今之紫草，未花时采，则根色鲜泽；过而采，则根黯恶，此其效也。用叶者，取叶初长足时；用芽者自从本说；用花者，取花初敷时；用实者，成实时采：皆不可限以时月。缘土气有早晚，天时有愆伏。如平地三月花者，深山中则四月花。白乐天大林寺诗云“人间四月芳菲尽，山寺桃花始盛开”，盖常理也。此地势高下不同也；如筀竹笋有二月生者，有三四月生者，有五月方生者谓之“晚筀”；稻有七月熟者，有八九月熟者，有十月熟者谓之“晚稻”。一物同一畦之间，自有早晚，此性之不同也。岭峤微草，凌冬不凋，并、汾乔木，望秋先陨；诸越则桃李冬实，朔漠则桃李夏荣，此地气之不同也，一亩之稼，则粪溉者先芽，一丘之禾则后种者晚实，则道者先芽川一之则后种者实，此人力之不同也，岂可一切拘以定月哉？

Excerpts from *Brush Talks from Dream Brook*

Shen Kuo[1]

Traditional Chinese Medicine was a prescription in the past. Herbal medicines have been said to be composed of four categories: primary, secondary, tertiary and auxiliary (i.e efficacy–enhancer added to herbal medicines). This means that, only the primary plays the decisive role in curing the disease while others function in accordance with their order of place although there are several herbal medicines in a prescription. Generally they are related to each other and each has its own role to play in the prescription. Such a job of division is reasonable, but not every prescription should conform to this rule. The so–called primary herbal medicine is the one that takes the dominating position in the prescription. Originally it can refer to, any herbal medicine. However, in the book entitled *On the Property of Herbal Medicine*[2], the tender, cool and mild herbal medicines are taken as primary; on the country, the less tender, cool and mild ones are listed to be secondary or tertiary while the poisonous ones are

---

1 Shen Kuo (1031–1095), a native of Qiantang County, Hangzhou, Zhejiang, a statesman and scientist in the Northern Song Dynasty. In addition to referring to the 2016 Zhonghua Book Company Edition *Mengxi Bi Tan, Brush Talks from Dream Brook*, this part also refers to *the Great China Library Chinese–English Comparison of Brush Talks from Dream Brook*, pages 820–8272. Traditional Chinese medicine is another national quintessence that is most related to people's livelihood in Chinese culture, and its reputation is also growing internationally. This article is selected from *Mengxi Bitan, Brush Talks from Dream Brook*, written by Shen Kuo in the Song Dynasty, from which we can glimpse the erudition and knowledge of the ancients. *Brush Talks from Dream Brook* is a collection of works. This encyclopedic book is composed of 609 jottings and is further classified into 17 parts covering a wide area. The excerpts selected in this unit are from the section related to medicine. This book is famous not only for its academic and historical value, but also for its scientific and technological value. *Brush Talks from Dream Brook* Beijing, Zhonghua Book Company, 2015.

2 (The Tang Dynasty) Zhen Quan, famous acupuncturists in the Sui and Tang dynasties, who wrote many medical books, including *On the Property of Herbal Medicine.*

mostly designated to be the efficacy–enhancers. This is indeed an erroneous statement. If a doctor wants to cure the stubborn disease such as indigestion and constipation, can't he use poisonous defatted croton seed powder as primary herbal medicine?

Traditional Chinese Medicine is often made into a decoction, powder or pellet. And each has its own functions. In ancient times, traditional Chinese medicine was often prescribed in the form of a decoction rather than in the form of a powder or pellet. The medicine in the form of a powder boiled in water was rare. Only recently have doctors begun to write out prescriptions of this kind. Generally, if we are to make the efficacy of the medicine reach the entire body of the patient, the decoction of Chinese medicinal herbs is most effective. If we are to make the potency of the medicine stay in the stomach, the powdered one is the best. And if we are to sustain the efficacy of the medicine before it shows its effect, the pellet is the best. What is more, the poisonless medicine should be made in the form of a decoction. The medicine containing a few poisonous elements should be made in the form of a powder. And the extremely poisonous medicine should be made in the form of a pellet. The medicine in the form of a powder goes into effect a bit slower while the medicine in the form of a pellet is the slowest to go into effect. These are general cases in which the traditional Chinese medicine is used. Recently few doctors prescribe medicine in the form of decoctions. And the medicine in the form of powder boiled in water has almost replaced the one in the form of a decoction. Normally the medicine in the form of a decoction is potent enough to produce tremendous effect, and its efficacy is several times stronger than that of the medicine in the form of a powder or pellet. In contrast if the medicine made into the form of a powder is boiled in water, the patient can only take three to five qian at a time. So in terms of medical efficacy, it can never match the medicine in the form of a decoction. Now that the efficacy of the medicine in the form of a decoction is potent enough, the total amount that a patient should take should not go wrong. To sum up, it all depends on a doctor's medical knowledge to choose the form of the medicine to be used for the patient. The stipulation of a/fixed rule is not feasible.

In ancient times medicinal herbs were usually plucked in February and August, which is indeed inappropriate. Though in February plants have already sprouted and in August vegetation has not withered, which will be easy for people to identify the herbs, these two months are not the best months for plucking them. Normally if the old roots of medicinal herbs are to be used as the medicine, it is best to dig them out when the herbs are still stemless or leafless, because at this time the roots are the essence. To verify this, all you need to do is take a look at radishes and glutinous rehmannia. If they are pulled up when they are still stemless or leafless, their roots will be heavy and plump. If they are pulled when they already have leaves and stems, their roots will be light and hollow. For those herbs which do not have old roots, the best time to pull them up is when their stems and leaves are already in good shape and are yet to bloom, because it is in this period that their roots are fully grown without showing any signs of becoming old. For example, if Chinese gromwell is pulled up before it blooms, its roots will be fresh and moist. If it is pulled up after it has already bloomed, its roots will be dark and dry. If the leaves are to be used as medicine, they should be plucked when they have just grown up. If the sprouts are to be used as medicine, they should be plucked in February as mentioned above. Similarly, if the flowers are to be used as medicine, they should be plucked when they should be plucked when they have just ripened into maturity. We cannot set the time limit for plucking these herbs, as the temperature and humidity of the soil vary in different places with the change of weather. For instance, a plant may put forth flowers in March in a flat country, but in remote mountains its flower may come out in April. In the poem "*Visiting the Temple in the Forest*", the poet Bai Juyi wrote: "All flowers in late spring have fallen far and wide, /But peach blossoms are, full–blown on the mountainside." This is due to topographical difference. The bamboo shoots of guizhu may geminate in February, March or geminate in February, March or April. Those germinate in May are called "late bamboo shoot". Rice also may ripen in July, August or September. And the one that ripens in October is called "late rice". Sometimes the maturation period of the same plant that grows in the same field may vary from each other owing to the differences in properties. The grass in Lingqiao [1]will not wither in winter while the leaves of trees in Bingzhou and Fenzhou will fall in the early autumn. Peaches and plums in Liangguang region will bear fruit in winter while those in the north will blossom in summer. All these are due to the different temperature and humidity of the soil in different laces. Sometimes on the same piece of farmland, the crops that have been adequately fertilized and irrigated will grow faster. Similarly the seedlings, that are planted late may bear fruit late. All these are due to different human factors. Therefore, how can we set time limit for plucking medicinal herbs?

---

1 Lingqiao, another name for Wuling, refers to the five ridges of Yuecheng, Dupang, Mengqing, Qitian, Dageng, etc.

Word bank

1.auxiliary adj. 辅助的

2.prescription n. 药方

3.decisive adj. 决定性的

4.conform to 符合

5.dominating adj. 支配的

6.designate v. 指明

7.erroneous adj. 错误的

8.indigestion n. 消化不良

9.constipation n. 便秘

10.croton n. 巴豆

11.decoction n. 煎汁

12.pellet n. 药丸

13.potency n. 效力

14.potent adj. 强有力的

15.tremendous adj. 极大的

16.stipulation n. 规定

17.feasible adj. 可行的

18.pluck v. 采摘

19.inappropriate adj. 不恰当的

20.wither v. 枯萎

21.essence n. 精华

22.rehmannia n. 地黄

23.plump adj. 丰满的

24.gromwell n. 紫草

25.sprout n. 幼芽

26.ripen v. 成熟

27.humidity n. 湿度

28.full–blown adj. 盛开的

29.topographical adj. 地形上的

30.guizhu n. 笙竹

31.germinate v. 发芽

32.property n. 特征

33.fertilize v. 施肥

34.irrigate v. 灌溉

中医与现代西医

丹尼尔·雷德[1]

传统中医是世界上最古老、最全面，也可以说是最安全、最有效的人类卫生保健体系。它保持了世界上持续时间最长的文明的健康和长寿逾5000年，在此期间，在横跨3000多年的有文字记载的中世纪档案中，它的从业者仔细记录了他们细致的研究结果和临床经验。由于中国书面语言的表意文字性质，它永远不会像字母语言那样随着变幻莫测的白话文而改变，这些古老的中国文献，对于今天的当代实践者来说，仍然清晰易懂，就像它们对于那些世世代代抄写它们的人一样。

中医是一棵知识古树，历经历史的风雨洗礼，在今天继续生长、硕果累累。它根植于阴阳、五行等“道”的基本原理，在人类医疗保健的广阔领域中，广泛传播其治疗分支，覆盖“天下万物”。在这棵脆弱的老树的许多分枝中，中药是最大的也是最重要的一个分枝。它也是最古老的：中国人认为，5000多年前，传说中的神农皇帝发现了草药。两千年前，伟大的汉代史学家司马迁写道：“神农尝百草”。“医学的艺术就此诞生了。”

中草药最初是在中国古代云雾缭绕的高山上进化而来的，是道教隐士们不断寻求难以捉摸的长生不老药的副产品，据说长生不老药能使人类长生不老。经过数千年的反复试验，用几乎所有的植物、动物和大自然的矿物质进行试验，老道圣贤终于得知：唯一真正的“灵丹妙药”是一种无形之力，深藏在人类系统内，任何人类可以实现的唯一“不朽”是纯粹的精神，而不是肉身。但在探索的过程中，深山隐士发现，他们一直长久摆弄的植物，确实具有各种实际物理疗效，不过凡人和人体，若正确组合且处理得当时，它们可以带给人

1　D. 雷德：《中草药手册》，新加坡：Periplus，2001年，第3—6页。

类健康和长寿。

现代西方医学认同疾病的“单媒”理论，即每一种疾病都由特定的外部病原体从外界侵入人体而造成。因此，用刀、辐射和旨在“杀死”所谓入侵者的强效化学制剂攻击病原体，在此过程中，这些武器往往破坏内脏器官，削弱人体免疫反应，消耗生命能量，从而为以后患上更严重的疾病埋下病根。

传统中医采取了不同的方法。它将所有疾病的根源追溯至控制和调节整个身体的各种内部能量之间的严重失衡和不足。当这种失衡或缺乏的状态长期不受控制时，它们最终会导致身体、生物化学和内部器官系统的严重故障，进而损害免疫力，降低抵抗力，并造成脆弱的条件，允许细菌、毒素、寄生虫和其他病原体在体内立足。当现代医学公认的明显症状出现时，疾病已经到了关键阶段，很难治愈。此外，疾病的症状往往表现在远离根本原因的身体部位，这是传统治疗师所熟知的现象，但受过只治疗人体某一部分训练的现代“专家”却往往忽略了这一现象。

现代西方医学将疾病视为必须消灭的敌人的外来恶意入侵，而传统中医则将其视为“放松警惕”，让致病的恶媒和能量进入体内。中医不是像现代医学那样治疗疾病，而是通过纠正病人能量系统的严重失衡来治疗，而正是这种失衡首先为疾病敞开了大门。有两千年历史的中国医学文献这样写道：“当能量过剩或不足时，恢复平衡是医生努力的主要目标。”这就是所谓的“治标不治本”。通过它们对医生所瞄准的特定器官和能量的“归经”，中药重新建立了最佳的能量平衡，恢复了整个人体系统的有机和谐，从而关闭了脆弱的窗口（通常是由于我们自己的疏忽而打开的）。让疾病进入体内并在体内发展。《黄帝内经》有两千年的历史，至今仍是中医培训的标准读物。《黄帝内经》中写道：“热则降温；如果太冷，就给它加热；如果太满了，就倒空它；如果太空了，就填满它。”它指的是特定的人类能量系统的不平衡造成的问题。

现代西方医疗实践的一个典型例子是它对获得性免疫缺陷综合征（艾滋病）的反应。西医声称，这种疾病是由最近发现的人类免疫缺陷病毒（HIV）引起的，针对这一挑战，西医采取了全面的“细菌战”，使用类似 AZT 的毒性药物杀死入侵者，甚至对没有明显艾滋病症状的人，制药业争相开发疫苗，据称可以保护未感染者不感染艾滋病毒，从而战胜艾滋病。相比之下，传统中医认为，艾滋病是由于长期暴露于严重的内外环境污染而造成的极端脆弱状况，是不良饮食和其他个人习惯才导致疾病而非健康而进一步恶化。在这种情况下，这只是与免疫系统缺陷相关的许多症状之一，而不是它的原因。中国治疗艾滋病的传统方法是先对人体系统的主要器官解毒，特别是肝脏和血液，然后消除个人习惯，如摒弃损害人体免疫反应的“垃圾食品”，通过适当的营养、锻炼以及专门为增强人体免疫反应而设计的补充中药和配方。

“一针救九”一直是传统医学的一个基本原则，认为任何疾病的发作都是预防保健的前线失败，将健康和疾病的主要责任放在病人自己的个人生活方式上。如今，人们倾向于吃、喝、做自己喜欢的任何事情，然后一旦出了问题就跑去看医生“快速解决”，就好像他们的身体是机器，而不是活的有机体。这种对生活基本事实的大规模忽视的最终结果是出现了一场正在迅速失控的全球健康危机，而现代医学显然未能应对这场灾难。

Traditional Chinese Medicine and Modern Western Medicine[1]

Daniel Reid

Traditional Chinese Medicine (TCM) is the oldest and most comprehensive– and arguably the safest and most effective—system of human health care in the world. It has sustained the health and longevity of the world's longest ongoing civilization for over five thousand years, during which time its practitioners have carefully recorded the results of their meticulous research and clinical experience in medieval archives that span, more than three thousand years of written history. Due to the ideogramic nature of the Chinese written language, which never changes with the vagaries of vernacular speak as alphabetic languages do, these ancient Chinese texts remain as clear and intelligible to contemporary practitioners today as they were to those who transcribed them through the ages.

Traditional Chinese Medicine is like an ancient tree of knowledge that has survived the storms of history and continucs to grow and bear fruit today. Deeply rooted in the Great Principle of Yin and Yang, the Five Elemental Energies, and other primordial principals of the Tao, it spreads its healing branches far and wide to cover "everything under heaven" in the broad field of human health care. Among the many branches that have sprouted from the vulnerable old tree, herbal medicine constitutes the biggest and most important one. It's also the most ancient: the Chinese Credit the legendary emperor Shen Nung with discovering herbal medicine over five millennia ago. "Shen Nung tasted the myriad herbs,

1 D. Reid, *A Handbook of Chinese Healing Herbs*, Singapore: Periplus, 2001, pp. 3–6.

wrote the great Han Dynasty historian Ssu–ma Chien two thousand years ago. “and so the art of medicine was born.”

Chinese herbal medicine first evolved high up in the misty mountains of ancient China, as a by–product of Taoist hermits’ perpetual search for the elusive Elixir of Life purported to Elixir of Life confer physical immortality to humans. After thousands of years of trial–and–error experimentation with virtually every plant, animal, and mineral in nature’s domain, the old Taoist sages finally learned that the only true “elixir” is an invisible force that lies hidden deep within the human system and that the only “immortality” any human can achieve is purely spiritual, not physical. But in the course of their search, the mountain hermits discovered that the plants they’d been fiddling with for so long did in fact have all sorts of practical therapeutic benefits for the physical, albeit mortal, human body, and that when correctly combined and properly prepared, they could confer health and long life to all human beings.

Modern Western medicine subscribes to the “single agent” theory of disease, whereby every disease is blamed on a specific external pathogen that invades the body from outside. Disease pathogen is thus attacked with knives, radiation, and powerful chemical agents designed to “kill” the allege invader, and in the process these weapons often lay waste to the internal organs, impair immune response, and deplete vital energies, thereby sowing the seeds of even more severe ailments later.

Traditional Chinese Medicine takes a different approach, which traces the root cause of all diseases to critical imbalances and deficiencies among the various internal energies that govern and regulate the whole body. Whenever such states of imbalance or deficiency are left unchecked for too long, they, eventually give rise to serious malfunctions in the body’s, biochemistry and internal organ systems, and that in turn impairs immunity, lowers resistance, and, creates the conditions of vulnerability which permit germs, toxins, parasites, and other pathogens to gain a foothold in the body. By the time the obvious symptom recognized by modern medicine appear, the disease has already reached a critical stage and is very difficult to cure. Moreover, symptoms of disease often manifest themselves in parts of the body far removed from the root cause, a phenomenon well known to traditional healers but usually lost on modern "specialists" trained to deal with only one part of the human body.

While modern Western medicine views disease as a malevolent external invasion by an enemy that must be killed, traditional Chinese medicine sees it more as a matter of "letting down your guard" and give entry to the malevolent agents and energies that cause disease. Rather than treating the disease, as modern medicine does, the traditional Chinese physician treats the patient by correcting the critical imbalances in his or her energy system that opened the door to disease in the first place. "To restore equilibrium when energies are in excess or deficiency is the main object of the physician's endeavors," states a two–thousand–year–old Chinese medical text. This is known as "curing the root cause rather than treating the superficial symptoms". By virtue of their "natural affinity" (guijing) for the specific organs and energies targeted by the physician, medicinal herbs reestablish optimum energy balance and restore organic harmony within the whole human system, thereby closing the windows of vulnerability (usually flung open by our own negligence), which allow ailments to enter and develop inside. States *The Yellow Emperor's Classic of Internal Medicine*, a two thousand–year–old text that remains standard reading in TCM training today, "If it's too hot, cool it down; if it's too cold, warm it up; if it's too full, empty it; if it's too empty, fill it." It refers to the particular human energy system whose imbalance is responsible for the problem.

A typical example of modern Western medical practice is its response to acquired immune deficiency syndrome (AIDS). Western medicine claims that this disease is caused by the recently discovered human immunodeficiency virus (HIV), and it has responded to this challenge with total "germ warfare," using toxic drugs such as AZT, to kill the invader, even in people who show no overt symptoms of AIDS, which the pharmaceutical industry rushes to develop vaccines that will supposedly protect the uninfected from ever contracting HIV, thereby conquering AIDS. By contrast, traditional Chinese Medicine views AIDS as condition of extreme vulnerability acquired by chronic term exposure to acute environmental pollution, both internal and external, further aggravated by poor diets and other personal habits that promote illness rather than health. In this scenario, is just another one of many symptoms associated with immune system deficiency, not the cause of it. The traditional Chinese solutions to AIDS is first to detoxify the major organs of the human system, particularly the liver and bloodstream, then to eliminate the personal habits, such as "junk food diets", that impair human, immune response and gradually rebuild immunity and vitality with proper nutrition, exercise, and supplemental herbs and formulas specifically designed to enhance human immune response.

"A stich in time saves nine" has always been a fundamental tenet of traditional medicine, which regards the onset of any disease as a front–line failure in preventive health care, a view which places primary responsibility for health and disease on the patient's own personal lifestyle. Today, people tend to eat, drink, and behave in whatever manner pleases them, then run to the doctor for a "quick fix" whenever something goes wrong, as though their bodies were machines rather than living organisms. The net result of such mass negligence toward the basic facts of life is a global health crisis that is rapidly spinning out of control, and modern medicine has clearly failed to cope with this catastrophe.

Word bank

1.longevity n. 寿命

2.meticulous adj. 细微的

3.ideogramic adj. 表意的

4.vagary n. 多变

5.vernacular adj./n. 地方话（的），行话

6.intelligible adj. 可理解的

7.primordial adj. 本初的，原始的

8.millennia n. 千年

9.Elixir of Life 长生不老药

10.immortality n. 永生

11.fiddle with 鼓，摆弄

12.ailment n. 小疾病

13.germ n. 细菌

14.parasite n. 寄生虫

15.malevolent adj. 小恶性的

16.optimum adj. 最佳的

17.fling flung v. 掷投，使陷入

18.aggravate n. 加重，恶化

19.catastrophe n. 大灾难

影 视

The Chinese Movies

小蝌蚪找妈妈[1]

1960 年，盛特伟和钱家俊执导的世界首部水墨动画电影《小蝌蚪找妈妈》[2]摄制完成。该动画片根据方惠珍和盛璐德创作的同名童话改编，讲述了青蛙妈妈产卵后离开了，蝌蚪们慢慢发育长大，生出尾巴，随后它们决定去寻找自己的妈妈。一路它们错把金鱼、螃蟹、乌龟、鲇鱼当做了自己的母亲。最后，小蝌蚪们终于成功地找到了自己的妈妈。

此水墨动画电影取材于画家齐白石创作的鱼、虾等形象。影片开头，银幕上出现了一本素雅的中国画画册，它的封面徐徐展开，呈现出一幅幽然的荷塘静景，镜头渐渐推向画面，随古琴和琵琶乐曲悠扬流淌着，观众置身于优美抒情的水墨动画世界。春天的池塘里，一群小蝌蚪慢慢游动起来，它们看到岸边的小鸡与妈妈十分亲热，十分羡慕，于是决定去寻找自己的妈妈。它们不

---

1 上海美术电影制片厂官网，访问时间2021年11月4日，https://www.ani-sh.com/；参照搜狗百科，https://baike.sogou.com/v64820143.htm;jsessionid=1A87056C931700178D11E0A79876D03A，访问时间2021年10月4日。

2 其英译名称有多种，*Baby Tadpoles Look for Their Mother, Little Tadpole Looks for Mommy, Tadpoles Looking for Their Mother,* 参照百度百科https://baike.baidu.com/item/%E5%B0%8F%E8%9D%8C%E8%9A%AA%E6%89%BE%E5%A6%88%E5%A6%88/4820144?fr=aladdin，https://baike.sogou.com/v64820143.htm;jsessionid=1A87056C931700178D11E0A79876D03A，访问时间2021年10月4日。

知妈妈是何模样，就向虾公公请教，虾公公描述了它们母亲的特征："你们的妈妈有两只大眼睛。"它们于是开始寻母之旅。它们历经波折，先后误认金鱼、螃蟹、乌龟、鲇鱼为妈妈，最后成功找到了自己的妈妈。小蝌蚪们遇见长着两只大眼睛的金鱼，高兴得忙叫"妈妈"。金鱼说："你们的妈妈有个白肚皮。"小蝌蚪们看到螃蟹是白肚皮，又高兴地叫"妈妈"。螃蟹说："你们的妈妈只有四条腿。"小蝌蚪们见乌龟有四条腿，又围上去叫"妈妈"。旁边的小乌龟着急地说："她是我的妈妈，妈妈和孩子长得一样嘛！"小蝌蚪们只好继续往前游，鲇鱼张开大口吓唬它们。正在这时，青蛙妈妈赶来了，小蝌蚪终于找到了自己的妈妈。影片里小蝌蚪活泼可爱，犹如天真烂漫的童子。

这部水墨动画代表作短片时长仅 14 分钟，却享誉天下。这部动画片第一次使用中国特有的水墨画效果。漫画家方成说："这部片子具有独特的艺术风格。可以说每个镜头都是一幅动人的画面，使观众感到像是走进了艺术之宫。"法国《世界报》评论这部影片时赞扬说："中国水墨画，画的景色柔和，笔调细致，以及表示忧虑、犹豫和快乐的动作，使这部影片产生了魅力和诗意。"1962 年，茅盾看了这部影片，写下诗一首："白石世所珍，俊逸复清新。荣宝擅复制，往往可乱真。何期影坛彦，创造惊鬼神。名画真能动，潜翔栩如生。柳叶乱飘雨，芙渠发幽香。蝌蚪找妈妈，奔走询问忙。只缘执一体，再三认错娘。莫笑蝌蚪傻，人亦有如此。认识不全面，好心办坏事。莫笑故事诞，此中有哲理。画意与诗情，三美此全具。"

这部动画短片 1961 年获瑞士第 14 届洛迦诺国际电影节短片银帆奖；1962 年获第 1 届中国电影百花奖最佳美术片奖、法国第 4 届安纳西国际动画片电影节儿童片奖；1964 年获法国第 17 届戛纳国际电影节荣誉奖；1978 年获南斯拉夫第 3 届萨格勒布国际动画电影节一等奖；1981 年获法国巴黎蓬皮杜文化中心第 4 届国际儿童和青年电影节二等奖。

Tadpoles Looking for Mommy[1]

In 1960, *Tadpoles Looking for Mommy*[2], the first ink–and–wash animation film in the world, directed by Sheng Tewei and Qian Jiajun, was completed. The film is based on the fairy tale of the same name created by Fang Huizhen and Sheng Lude, telling the story: the mother frog left after laying eggs, and the little tadpoles slowly grow up with their tails, and then they decide to look for their mother. Along the way, they mistakenly regard goldfish, crabs, tortoises, and catfish as their mother. Finally, the little tadpoles have successully found their mother.

The ink–and–wash animation film is based on the image of fish and shrimp created by the artist Qi Baishi. At the beginning of the film, a simple and elegant Chinese painting album appeared on the screen. With the cover slowly unfolded, a quiet scene of a secluded lotus pond is presented before the audience. As the lens gradually move to the screen, the melodious ancient zithern and pipa music transports the audience into the animation world of beautiful and lyrical ink painting. In the spring pond, a school of little tadpoles slowly swim around. Seeing that the chicks on the shore are very affectionate with their mothers, the little tadpoles are very envious, so they decide to look for their own mother. They

---

1 The official website of Shanghai Art Film Studio, accessed on November 4, 2021, https://www.ani–sh.com/; referring to Sogou Encyclopedia, https://baike.sogou.com/v64820143. htm;jsessionid=1A87056C931700178D11E0A79876D03A, accessed on October 4, 2021.

2 There are several English translation of the title, such as *Baby Tadpoles Look for Their Mother, Little Tadpole Looks for Mommy, Tadpoles Looking for Their Mother.* Here I translate it into *Tadpoles Looking for Mommy,* because it is a title of animation film for children; referring to Baidu Encyclopedia, https://baike.baidu.com/item/%E5%B0%8F%E8%9D%8C%E8%9A%AA%E6%89%BE%E5%A6%88%E5%A6 %88/4820144?fr=aladdin, https://baike.sogou.com/v64820143.htm;jsessionid=1A87056C931700178D11E0A79876D03A, accessed on October 4, 2021.

don't know what their mother looks like, so they ask the senior shrimp, who describes the characteristics of their mother: "Your mommy has two big eyes." They begin to look for their mother. After going through twists and turns, they have mistakenly identified goldfish, crabs, tortoises, and catfish as their mother, but finally succeed in finding their own mother. The little tadpoles have met a goldfish with two big eyes have been are so happy they call "mommy". The goldfish says: "Your mommy has a white belly." Seeing that the crab has a white belly, the tadpoles have happily call "Mom". The crab says: "Your mommy has only four legs." Seeing that the turtle has four legs, the tadpoles go round calling "mommy". The little tortoise next to him shouts anxiously: "She is my mommy; mom and child look the same!" The little tadpoles have to swim forward and the catfish opens the mouth to scare them. At this time, mother frog has arrived, and the little tadpoles have finally found theirs. The little tadpoles in the film are lively and cute, just like innocent babies.

This animated short film, one of the representative works, is 14 minutes long, but it is famous all over the world. This cartoon uses the unique Chinese ink–and–wash painting effect for the first time. Cartoonist Fang Cheng said: "This film has a unique artistic style. It can be said that each shot is a moving picture, which makes the audience feel like they have entered the palace of art." French Le Monde commented on this film, praising it: "Chinese ink painting, with soft scenery, meticulous brushwork, and expressions of worry, hesitation, and happiness, make this film attractive and poetic." In 1962, Mao Dun watched the film and wrote a poem: "Baishi is treasured by the world, handsome and fresh. Rongbao is good at copying, and often chaotic. When it is on the stage of the film, the creation astonishes ghosts. The famous paintings are really movable, really being lifelike. Willow leaves are chaotic and rainy; lotuses send a fragrance. Tadpoles look for their mother, and are busy asking questions. They are only bound to one, and repeatedly recognize their wrong mothers. Don't laugh at tadpoles as stupid, and people are like this. They don't know well, and do bad things with kindness. Don't laugh at the story, and there is a philosophical reason. With painting and poetry, it has all the three beauties."

This animated short film won the Silver Sail Award for Short Film at the 14th Locarno International Film Festival in Switzerland in 1961; in 1962 it won the Best Art Film Award at the 1st Chinese Film Hundred Flowers Award and the 4th Annecy International Animation Film Festival in France for Children's Films Award; in 1964, it won the honorary award of the 17th Cannes International Film Festival in France; in 1978, it won the first prize of the 3rd Zagreb International Animation Film Festival in Yugoslavia; in 1981, it won the second in the 4th International Children of the Pompidou Cultural Center in Paris, France and the second prize of the Youth Film Festival.

水墨动画

中国画艺术有水墨画类别，中国影视有水墨动画艺术。随着上海美术电影制片厂第一部中国水墨动画片《小蝌蚪找妈妈》[1]的完成，水墨动画片可誉为中国动画界一大创举。它把典雅的中国水墨画与动画电影相结合，将传统的中国水墨画艺术引入到动画制作中，通过借鉴中国水墨画虚实相间的渲染意境和轻灵优雅的缥缈画面，形成了最具中国特色的动画电影艺术风格，使动画片的艺术格调有了重大突破。

水墨动画片借鉴中国水墨画，从中得到许多有益的启发，使中国水墨动画艺术具备了强烈的民族特色，蕴含了民族文化内涵。中国水墨动画蕴含水墨韵味的画面效果和意境，达到了一种独特的审美境界，将中国动画艺术推向了新的高潮，并在全世界得到了国际认同。

与一般的动画片技法不同，水墨动画片制作过程繁琐且耗时，水墨动画没有轮廓线，水墨在宣纸上自然渲染，浑然天成，一个个动画场景就是一幅幅出色的水墨画。角色的动作和表情优美灵动，泼墨山水的背景豪放壮丽，柔和的笔调充满诗意。然而，又并非人们所理解的动画创作都在宣纸上完成，水墨动画要分层渲染着色，制作工艺极其复杂，在每一张画面上分解、描线、分层着色，并且在摄影台上一而再、再而三地重复固定和拍摄。在影片的整个绘制过中，原画师和动画制作人员始终都用铅笔在动画纸上作业，一切工作如同画一般，原画师一样要设计动画片的主要动作，动画人员一样要精细地添加好中间画面，不能出现丝毫差错；一部短片耗费大量时间和人力。

水墨动画片的奥秘都集中在摄影部分。到了着色这一步，画在纸上的每一张人物或者动物，都必须分层上色，即同样一头水牛，必须分出四五种颜色，有大块面的浅灰、深灰或者只是牛角和眼睛边框线中的焦墨颜色，分别涂

1　上海美术电影制片厂官网，访问时间2021年11月4日，https://www.ani–sh.com/。

在数张透明赛璐璐片上。每一张赛璐璐片都由动画摄影师分开重复拍摄，最后再重合在一起，用摄影方法处理成水墨渲染的效果，也就是说，观众在银幕上所看到的那头水牛，最后必须靠动画摄影师“画”出来。动画制作工序十分繁复，仅是用在一部水墨动画片的摄制时间，就足够拍成四、五部同样长度的普通动画片。上海美术电影制片厂对水墨动画片投入巨大，除了盛特伟和钱家俊这样的老一辈动画大师，就连国画名家李可染、程十发也曾参与水墨动画片艺术指导。正是因为这样不惜工本的艺术追求，中国水墨动画在国际上才博得了人们的交口称赞。

在数字技术快速发展的今天，传统中国水墨动画也有了新载体和表现形式。水墨动画随着电脑技术的发展，动画也由二维向三维方向延伸，利用三维软件进行水墨动画的创作。制作者可以用 Photoshop 和 FLASH 两种软件结合来制作水墨动画。三维水墨动画，不再拘泥于传统的二维平面绘画，它可以创造出虚拟的三维空间，让人置身其中，创造出变幻莫测的视听感受。它与传统二维水墨动画的根本区别在于，它不是“画”出来的——而是“做”出来的，用三维动画制作软件来“搭建模型”和“渲染合成”出中国最传统的古老艺术形式。在这种影片中，制作人员一直着力于利用现代三维动画技术实现传统国画效果，但对于传统，又不能完全照搬，而是有所取舍。三维水墨不仅拓展了三维表现语言，而且可以突破表现出水墨所不能创建的运动空间。

三维水墨动画技术，始于 20 世纪 70 年代，随着超级图形工作站的出现，三维几何造型技术和真实感图形生成技术取得很大进展，促进了具有高度逼真效果的三维计算机动画技术迅速发展，并达到实用商品化地步。它可以创造出虚拟的影像，在观众看来可以达到水墨画的效果。数字的非线性编辑不但在技术上有一系列软件的支持，而且画面的组接有很大的自由性。运用数字技术调配各种各样的声音，制作十分便捷。

Ink–and–wash Animation

There is the category of ink–and–wash painting in Chinese painting art, and there is ink–and–wash animation art in Chinese film and television. With the completion of the first Chinese ink–and–wash animation *Tadpoles Looking for Mommy*[1] by Shanghai Fine Arts Film Studio, ink–and–wash animations can be regarded as a major innovation in the Chinese animation industry. It combines elegant Chinese ink–and–wash painting with animated films, and introduces traditional Chinese ink painting into animation production. By drawing on the rendering of the artistic conception of Chinese ink and wash paintings and the light and graceful ethereal images, the art style of animated films with the most Chinese characteristics has been formed, which has made a major breakthrough in the artistic style of cartoons.

Ink–and–wash animation draws on Chinese ink–and–wash painting, and has gained many useful inspirations from it, making Chinese ink–and–wash animation possess strong national characteristics, and containing national cultural connotations. Chinese ink–and–wash animation contains the artistic effect and artistic conception of watery ink charm, reaching a unique aesthetic state, promoting Chinese animation art to a new climax and gaining the international recognition in the world.

Different from ordinary animation techniques, the production process of ink–and–wash animation is tedious and time–consuming. Ink–and–wash animation has no outlines, with the ink and water rendered naturally on rice paper. Each animation scene is an excellent ink–and–wash painting. The characters'

1 The official website of Shanghai Art Film Studio, accessed on November 4, 2021, https://www.ani–sh.com/.

movements and expressions are beautiful and agile; the background of the splash–ink landscape is bold and magnificent, and the soft tone is full of poetry. But not all the animation tasks, as people understand, are done on rice paper. Ink–and–wash animation needs to be rendered and colored in layers, whose production process is very complicated. Each picture is broken down, lined, layered and colored, and it is done on the photography stage, fixing and shooting again and again. Throughout the entire course drawing of the film, the original artists and animators always used pencils to work on the animation paper, where everything is done like drawing. The original artist must design the main movements of the animation, and the animator must finely add the middle. There can be no mistakes in painting; a short film consumes a lot of time and manlabour.

The mysteries of ink–and–wash cartoons are concentrated in the photography part. When it comes to the coloring step, each figure or animal drawn on the paper must be colored in layers, that is, the same buffalo must be divided into four or five colors, with large areas of light gray, dark gray or just the dry scorched ink colors in the horns and eye border lines, that are painted on several transparent celluloid sheets. Each celluloid film is repeatedly shot separately by the animation photographer, and finally superimposed together, and processed into an ink–and–wash rendering effect in photographic methods. That is to say, the buffalo that the audience see on the screen must rely on the animation photographer "to paint" it out in the end. The production process is of great complexity, and only the time spent in the production of one ink–and–wash cartoon is enough to make four or five ordinary cartoons of the same length. Shanghai Fine Arts Film Studio has invested heavily in ink–and–wash animation. In addition to the older generation of animation masters such as Sheng Tewei and Qian Jiajun, even famous Chinese painters Li Keran and Cheng Shifa also participated in the art direction of ink–and–wash animation. It is precisely because of this kind of artistic pursuit that does not hesitate to work hard, Chinese ink–and–wash animation has won the international praise.

Nowadays, with the rapid development of digital technology, traditional Chinese ink–and–wash animation also has new media and forms of expression. With the development of computer technology, animation has also extended from two–dimensional to three–dimensional, which is used to create ink–and–wash animation. With the development of computer software, producers can use the combination of Photoshop and FLASH to make ink–and–wash animations. Three–dimensional ink–and–wash animation, no longer constrained to the traditional two–dimensional plane painting, can create a virtual three–dimensional space, let people be inside, and create an unpredictable audio–visual experience. The fundamental difference between it and the traditional two–dimensional ink–and–wash animation is that it is not "painted" —but "made", using three–dimensional animation production software to "build models" and "render and synthesize" the most traditional ancient Chinese forms of art. In this kind of film, the production staff have been focusing on the use of modern three–dimensional animation technology to achieve the traditional Chinese painting effect, but the tradition cannot be copied completely, and there are some trade–offs. Not only does three–dimensional ink–and–wash animation expand the language of three–dimensional expression, but also can break through the movement space beyond ink–and–wash's creation.

Three–dimensional ink–and–wask animation technology began in the 1970s. With the emergence of super graphics workstations, three–dimensional geometric modeling technology and realistic graphics generation technology have made great progress, which has promoted the rapid development of three–dimensional computer animation technology with highly realistic effects, reaching the point of practical commercialization. It can create virtual images that can achieve the effect of ink–and–wash painting in the eyes of the audience. Not only is digital non–linear editing technically supported by a series of software, but also has great freedom in the combination of pictures. The animation making is convinient and swiftly free, employing digital technology to adjust a variety of sounds into harmony.

Word bank

1.ink–and–wash painting n. 水墨画

2.ink–and–wash animation n. 水墨动画

3.*Tadpoles Looking for Mommy*《小蝌蚪找妈妈》

4.innovation n. 革新；变革

5.animate v. 使有生命；把……绘制成动画

6.breakthrough n. 突破

7.cartoon n. 动画

8.connotation n. 含义；含意

9.tedious adj. 冗长的；啰嗦的；单调乏味的

10.time–consuming adj. 耗时的

11.splash–ink landscape n. 泼墨山水

12.shoot v. 射死；投篮；拍摄

13.animator n. 赋予生气的人；动画师；动画片制作者

14.manpower n. 人力；劳动力

15.buffalo n. 水牛；野牛

16.scorched adj. 炙烤的；烧焦的

17.transparent adj. 透明的；受公众监督的；易察觉的

18.celluloid n. 赛璐珞

19.superimpose v. 把……放在另一物上；叠加

20.two–dimensional adj. 二维的

21.three–dimensional adj. 三维的

22.constrain v. 强迫；勉强；约束

23.unpredictable adj. 无法预测的；不定的；易变的

24.synthesize v. 使合成；综合

25.graphics n. 图形；图表算法

26.commercialization n. 商品化；商业化

27.non–linear adj. 非线型的；非直线的

饰 品

The Chinese Adornment

发饰[1]

饰品是用来装饰的物品，自古有之。因为爱美之心人皆有之，为了追求美，人们求助于饰品。沈从文在《中国古代服饰研究》中有言：

> 装饰品钻孔的小石珠，发现七件，白色，样式不甚规则，形体大小一致。砾石为黄绿色卵圆形，两面扁平。穿孔系两面对钻而成还有的海蜡、青鱼眼上骨和可以穿成串的鱼脊骨、刻纹的常等尤其是许多钻了孔的鹿、狐、獾的犬齿。其中有二十五件还用赤铁可粉涂染成了红色（是目前所知最早的矿物着色工艺染制品），分引人注目。据推测，这些五颜六色打孔小物件，是用皮于衣，或者系在颈项、手臂之上以为装饰的，是我国远古时代的原始工艺美术品。[2]

由此可知，人类爱美之心始自文明的开端，饰品历史悠久。古代饰品甚至成为身份的象征物，小小的首饰还承担着深厚的文化内涵，尤其是发饰。

古人特别看重头发，所以发明了很多发饰。发簪就是发饰之一，它又称

1 本文由编者编写。

2 沈从文：《中国古代服饰研究》，商务印书馆，2011年，第16页。

笄，古代汉族用来固定和装饰头发的一种首饰。古人多用发簪固定和装饰头发，因而发簪最初是无性别特征的饰品，古代男子也留长发。《辞海》解释为：簪，古人用来插定发髻或连冠于发的一种长针，后来专指妇女插髻的首饰。[1]据《仪礼》[2]等书记载，周代贵族女子在订婚以后、出嫁之前需举行成年嘉礼笄礼。行礼主要是在成年女子发上加笄即簪，故称笄礼。

其实古代男女发式都为发髻，著名唐代诗人白居易就赋诗多首描写自己梳头的情景。以挽髻为主，发髻挽成之后，就要设法将其固定，最常用的绾髻之具是发簪。在男子盛行带冠之时，发笄还有固冠作用，以免滑坠。《史记·滑稽列传》里说："前有堕珥，后有遗簪。"[3]杜甫《春望》[4]中也有"白头搔更短，浑欲不胜簪"之句。唐宋时期及以后各代，是发簪流行的盛世。唐代敦煌壁画中的众多妇女就是插满花簪的形象。唐代古画中也有众多满头插簪的妇女形象。《宋书·五行志》记载："宋代元嘉六年民间妇女结发者，……头上有花插簪梳等饰。"[5]宋代陆游《入蜀记》记载当时西南一带的女子头饰为"插银钗至六只，后插大象牙梳，如手大"[6]。

古代发笄形式繁多，仅以质料上看，就有骨、石、陶、蚌、荆、竹、木、玉、铜、金、象牙、牛角及玳瑁等多种。发簪式样十分丰富，主要变化多集中在簪首。它有各种各样的形状，还爱用花鸟鱼虫、飞禽走兽作簪首形状。常见的花类有梅花、莲花、菊花、桃花、牡丹花和芙蓉花等。《天水冰山录》中关于发簪名就有"金桃花顶簪""金梅花宝顶簪""金菊花宝顶簪""金宝石顶簪""金厢倒垂莲簪""金厢猫睛顶簪""金崐点翠梅花簪"等名称。以动物为簪首的发簪，常见的有龙凤、麒麟、燕雀及游鱼等，其中以凤簪最多，制作也

1 陈至立主编：《辞海》，上海辞书出版社，2020年。

2 《仪礼》，古诗文网，访问时间2022年1月23日，https://so.gushiwen.cn/guwen/bookv_46653F-D803893E4FC342454E3EB489A6.aspx。

3 （西汉）司马迁，《史记·滑稽列传》，访问时间2022年1月23日，https://www.thn21.com/wen/Famous/hdnj/shiji2116.html。

4 （唐）杜甫，《春望》，古诗文网，访问时间2022年1月23日，https://so.gushiwen.cn/shiwenv_89d3a63c6d7f.aspx。

5 《宋书·五行志》，访问时间2022年1月23日，http://www.guoxuemeng.com/guoxue/songshu/。

6 （宋）陆游，《入蜀记》，访问时间2022年1月23日，http://www.gushicimingju.com/gushi/wenyanwen/2282.html。

最为精致。[1]

发钗和发簪都用于插发，但两者的结构有异：发簪通常做成一股，而发钗则做成双股；另外在用途上也有一些区别。发钗用来绾住头发，也有用它把帽子别在头发上。五代马缟《中华古今注》[2]："钗子，盖古笄之遗象也，至秦穆公以象牙为之，敬王以玳瑁为之，始皇又金银作凤头，以玳瑁为脚，号曰凤钗。"发钗的普及大约在西汉晚期，自此以后，它一直是中国妇女的主要头饰之一，至今，发钗在女性梳妆品中演变为常用的发夹饰品。

发钗的特点还在于钗首上的不同装饰。如"蟠龙钗"，就是在钗首雕凿蟠龙形状。晋崔豹《古今注》[3]中就有"蟠龙钗，梁冀妇所制"的记载；历代妇女都崇尚饰有鸾鸟的发钗鸾钗，尤其在结婚首饰中，更为常见，因为鸾鸟在汉族民间一直被视为吉祥之禽。

发钗插法也多样，横插法、竖插法、斜插法、自下而上倒插法。所插发钗数量也各异，据需而定，可左右各一支安插两支；也可插数支，最多时两鬓各插六支，合为十二支。这让人联想到"金陵十二钗"[4]，钗喻指美丽的女子。

若在发钗上装缀活动的花枝，并在花枝上垂以珠玉等饰物，这就成了另一种首饰，名为"步摇"，因为插着这种首饰，走起路来，随着步履的颤动，钗上的珠玉会自然的摇曳。《释名》有首饰名称解释："步摇，上有垂珠，步则摇曳。"[5]"莲伐制度，皇后谒庙的服装，上衣天青色，下裳黑色。亲自祭祀蚕神时的服装，上衣青色，下裳淡青色。首饰是：假髻、步摇、八雀、九花，加上翡翠。"[6]现故宫博物院藏清代"银镀金点翠穿珠流苏"[7]，通长43厘米，宽4.5厘米。这件流苏由银钎和三串珍珠构成。银钎顶端为银镀金点翠云蝠纹饰，寓意"福在眼前"。云蝠有孔穿环，与三串珍珠相连，共计104粒珍珠。每串珍珠有珊瑚制成的"囍"字两枚以作点缀。珠下端有红宝石坠角3个。两块结牌将三

1 （清）吴允嘉（述）：《天水冰山录》，商务印书馆，1937年。

2 （五代）马缟：《中华古今注》，序晋崔豹《古今注》为《中华古今注》，《四部备要》。

3 （晋）崔豹：《古今注》，《四部备要》。

4 金陵十二钗是中国古典小说《红楼梦》中的十二位女性人物，也是经典艺术群像。

5 （汉）刘熙：《释名》，中华书局，2021年。《释名》别称《逸雅》，东汉末年刘熙著，是一部专门探求事物名源的经典著作。

6 《宋书·五行志》，访问时间2022年1月23日，http://www.guoxuemeng.com/guoxue/songshu/。

7 故宫博物院官网，访问时间2021年11月3日，https://www.dpm.org.cn/Home.html。

清　银镀金嵌珠双龙点翠长簪　故宫博物院藏
A long beaded double–dragon–pointed emerald silver–gilt hairpin, the Qing Dynasty, in the collection of the Palace Museum

串珍珠相连，结牌作银镀金点翠云蝠纹，两端各嵌红宝石一块。流苏俗称“挑子”，属于步摇一类，每逢宫中帝后大婚或吉庆节日，后妃皆喜欢佩戴此饰物。[1]

清代宫廷后妃们的首饰由广储司和造办处的撒花作、累丝作、玉作、牙作、镶嵌作、珐琅作等处承做。这些宫廷首饰造型高贵典雅，做工细致入微。同样，这些首饰也体现了严格的等级制度。

饰品自古多彩多样，品类繁多，可以按材料、工艺手段、用途、装饰部位和功能等来区分。现在随着社会的发展文明的进化，饰品更加多元化，而玉饰只是其中的一小部分。

1　赵桂玲，故宫博物院官网，访问时间2021年11月3日，https://www.dpm.org.cn/Home.html。

Hair Accessories[1]

Ornaments are articles used to decorate, and they have been there since ancient times. Because everyone has a love for beauty, in order to pursue beauty, people turn to jewelry and accessories. Shen Congwen said in *Research on Ancient Chinese Costumes*:

> Seven small stone beads drilled into the ornament were found, white, with irregular patterns and the same size. The gravel is yellow–green oval, flat on both sides. The perforation system consists of sea wax drilled on both sides, upper bones of herring eyes, fish spine bones that can be pierced into strings, and carved regulars, especially the canine teeth of many drilled deer, fox, and badger. Twenty–five of them were dyed red with hematite cocoa powder (the earliest known dyed products of mineral coloring process), and they are eye–catching. It is speculated that these colorful perforated small objects are made of leather on clothing, or tied to necks and arms for decoration. They are primitive arts and crafts of our country in ancient times. [2]

It can be seen from this that the love of beauty of mankind started from the beginning of civilization, and accessories enjoy a long history. Ancient accessories are even status symbols, and such small things also bear a deep cultural connotation, especially hair accessories.

The ancient people so especially greatly valued hair that many hair accessories were invented. Hairpin is one of these, also called 笄 , a kind of

---

1 This is compiled by the compiler of this book.

2 Shen Congwen, *Research on Ancient Chinese Costumes,* The Commercial Press, Beijing, 2011, p. 16.

accessory used to fix and decorate the hair of the ancient Han people. The ancient often used hairpins to fix and decorate their hair, so hairpins were originally non–gendered accessaries, for ancient men also had long hair. As interpreted in *Cihai*,[1] a hairpin is a long needle used by the ancient to fix the hair in a bun or to make a crown on the hair. Later, it specifically refers to the accessary for women to put in a bun. According to records in *Rituals*[2] and other books, the aristocratic women of the Zhou Dynasty were required to hold adult ceremonies between the period after getting engaged and before getting married. The salute is mainly to add Hairpin to the hair of an adult woman, called the Hairpin Ceremony.

In fact, to do up the hair styles of both men and women in ancient times, hairpins were in use. Bai Juyi, the famous poet of the Tang Dynasty, wrote several poems describing the scene of combing his hair. The main thing in doing up hair styles is to make a bun. After the bun is finished, it is necessary to try to fix it, with the hairpin as the most commonly used tool. When the men's crown is popular, the hair curler also has the function of fixing the crown to prevent slipping. In the *Historical Records·Funny Biographies,* it is said: "There is a fallen Er before, and a relic after it."[3] There is also a sentence in Du Fu's *Spring Hope* that "white–headed scratches are shorter, and lust is overwhelming."[4] The Tang and Song dynasties and subsequent generations were the flourishing age of hairpins. Many women images in the Dunhuang frescoes of the Tang Dynasty are the ones with flower hairpins. There are also many images of women with hairpins in the ancient paintings of the Tang Dynasty. According to records in *Songshu · WuXingzhi*: "The folk women who had haircuts in the sixth year of Yuanjia in the Song Dynasty…had ornaments such as hairpins and combs on

---

1 Chen Zhili (Editor–in–chief), *Cihai*, Shanghai Dictionary Publishing House, August 2020.

2 *Rituals*, Gushiwen.com, accessed on January 23, 2022, https://so.gushiwen.cn/guwen/bookv_46653F-D803893E4FC342454E3EB489A6.aspx.

3 (Western Han Dynasty) Sima Qian, *Historical Records·Funny Biography*, accessed on January 23, 2022, https://www.thn21.com/wen/Famous/hdnj/shiji2116.html.

4 (Tang Dynasty) Du Fu, *Spring Hope*, Gushiwen.com, accessed on January 23, 2022, https://so.gushiwen.cn/shiwenv_89d3a63c6d7f.aspx.

their heads."[1] Lu You of the Song Dynasty recorded in *Rushu Ji, The Story of Entering Shu,* that the women's headdresses in the southwest region at that time were "six silver hairpins inserted, and a large tooth comb inserted in the back, even as big as a hand"[2].

There were many forms of ancient hair wares. Just looking at the material, there were bone, stone, pottery, mussel, wattle, bamboo, wood, jade, copper, gold, ivory, horn and tortoiseshell. Hairpin styles are very rich, and the main changes are mostly concentrated on the hairpin head, which has a variety of shapes, using the images like flowers, birds, fish, insects, birds and beasts as hairpin shapes. Common flower species include plum, lotus, chrysanthemum, peach, peony and hibiscus. The names of hairpins in *Tianshui Bingshan Lu* in the Ming Dynasty include "Golden Peach Flower Hairpin", "Golden Plum Blossom Hairpin", "Golden Chrysanthemum Flower Hairpin", "Golden Jewelry Hairpin", "Golden Chamber Upside Down Lotus Hairpin", "Golden Box Cat Eye Top Hairpin", "Golden Kun Diancui Plum Blossom Hairpin" and other names. Among the hairpins with animals as their first hairpins, dragons and phoenixes, unicorns, chaffinch, and swimming fish are common ones, among which phoenix hairpins are the most popular and the most exquisitely crafted.

Faji and Fachai are both used for hair insertion, but the structure of the two is different: hairpins as Faji are usually made into one strand, while hairpins as Fachai are made into double strands; in addition, there are some differences in use. The latter is used to tie the hair, and also used to pin the hat to the hair. In the Five Dynasties it is recorded in "*Chinese Ancient and Modern Notes·Chaizi*"[3] that Chaizi, the image of the ancient 笄，is also covered, until the Qin Mugong

---

1 *Song Shu·Five Elements Chronicles*, accessed on January 23, 2022, http://www.guoxuemeng.com/guoxue/songshu/.

2 (Song Dynasty) Lu You, *Rushu Ji,The Story of Entering Shu*, accessed on January 23, 2022, http://www.gushicimingju.com/gushi/wenyanwen/2282.html.

3 (Five Dynasties) Ma Zheng, *Zhonghua Gujin Zhu, Annotation on Ancient and Modern China*, countinuing Cui Bao's *Gujin Zhu, Annotation on Ancient and Modern,* in the Jin Dynasty as *Annotation on Ancient and Modern China, Sibu Beiyao.*

used ivory as it, and King Jing used tortoiseshell as it, and the First Emperor had gold and silver as the crested head, with tortoiseshells as feet, its name is phoenix hairpin." The popularity of hairpin was in about the late Western Han Dynasty. Since then, it has been one of the main headwear for Chinese women. Until now, hairpin has evolved into a commonly used hairpin accessory in women's cosmetics.

The hairpin is also characterized by the different decorations on it. For example, the "Panlong Hairpin" is carved in the shape of a dragon on the head of the hairpin. Cui Bao's "*Annotation to Ancients and Moderns*" in the Jin Dynasty has a record of "Panlong Hairpin, made by the wife of Liang Ji"[1]; women throughout the ages have admired Luan hairpin decorated with phenix bird hairpin, especially in wedding jewelry; it is more common, because Luan birds have always been regarded as auspicious birds in the Han people. Hairpin insertion methods are also diverse, including horizontal insertion, vertical insertion, oblique insertion, and bottom–up inverted insertion.

The number of hairpins to be inserted is also different; depending on needs, you can install two on each of the left and right; you can also insert several, and at most, you can insert six on each sideburn, making twelve in total. This is reminiscent of the "Jinling Twelve Hairpins", which refers to beautiful women. [2]

If the hairpin is decorated with active flower branches, and hang beads and other ornaments on the flower branches, this becomes another kind, called "Bu Yao", because this kind of accessary is inserted and swaying along with walking. With the trembling of steps, the jade on the hairpin will sway naturally. *Shiming* has an explanation of the name, saying: "Walking every step, there is a bead

1 (Jin Dynasty) Cui Bao, *Gujin Zhu, Annotation on Ancient and Modern, Sibu Beiyao.*

2 The Twelve Hairpins of Jinling are twelve female characters in the Chinese classical novel *Honglou Meng, A Dream of Red Mansions,* and they are also a group of classic art portraits.

on it, swaying every step."[1] According to the Lotus Cutting System, when the Queen pays a visit to the temple, her clothes should be that the top is in sky blue, and the bottom in black; when the Queen worships the Silkworm God in person, her clothes should be in blue on the top and in light blue on the bottom, with jewelry and accessories of fake bun, Bu Yao (stepping shake), eight sparrows, nine flowers, as well as jade Feicei.[2] "Silver–plated Dotted Emerald Fringed Tassel" of the Qing Dynasty, collected now in the Palace Museum, is 43 cm long and 4.5 cm wide. This tassel consists of silver brazing and three strings of pearls. The top of the silver brazing rod is decorated with silver gilded dotted green cloud bats, which means "fortune is in sight". The cloud bat has holes pierced and connected to three strings of pearls, a total of 104 pearls; each string of pearls is decorated with double Xi 囍 made of coral; there are 3 ruby pendants at the bottom of the bead; two knots connect the three strings of pearls, which are made of silver gilded dots and bat patterns, with a ruby embedded at each end. Tassels, commonly known as "Tiaozi (choose sons)", belong to the stepping shake category, which are worn by concubines during the wedding or auspicious festivals of the emperors and queens in the palace. [3]

The jewellery of the imperial concubines in the Qing Dynasty was made by the bureau of the Cantonese Reserve and the manufacturing offices of the flowers, silk, jade, tooth, inlay, and enamel. These palace jewels are noble and elegant, with meticulous craftsmanship. Similarly, these jewellery also embodies a strict hierarchy.

Jewelry and accessories have been colorful and diverse since ancient times, and there are many categories, which can be distinguished by materials,

---

1 (Han) Liu Xi, *Shiming, Explanation of Names*, Zhonghua Book Company, 2021. *Shiming*, also known as *Yi Ya*, was written by Liu Xi in the late Eastern Han Dynasty. It is a classic work devoted to exploring the origin of names.

2 *Song Shu• Five Elements Chronicles*, accessed on January 23, 2022, http://www.guoxuemeng.com/guoxue/songshu/.

3 Zhao Guiling, official website of the Palace Museum, accessed on November 3, 2021, https://www.dpm.org.cn/Home.html.

techniques, uses, decorative parts and functions. Now with the development of society and the evolution of civilization, accessories is more diversified, and jade ornaments are just a small part of it.

玉雕[1]

玉文化在中国文化中占有独特位置。良渚文化属于中国古代玉文化的典型代表。《礼记》中载有弟子问孔子："君子何以重玉？"孔子曰："夫昔者君子比德于玉焉。"中国人皆爱玉器。中国著名的特种工艺之一玉雕又称玉器，是中国最古老的雕刻品种之一。精雕玉器被清代皇帝乾隆称为"玉图画"[2]。早在新石器时代晚期，中华民族就有了玉制工具。商周时期，制玉成为一种专业，玉器成了礼仪用具和装饰佩件。用玉石雕刻成各种形状的器物，多为工艺美术品，主要产地是北京，北京玉雕的技艺源远流长，深厚精湛，在制作上量料取材，因材施艺，尤以俏色见长。玉雕讲究量料取材、因材施艺，最终雕成精美的玉器。

古老的经典《山海经》里提到许多山都产玉，玉门关为古"丝绸之路"北路的重要关隘，在甘肃省敦煌西北。传说古代西域的玉器必经此关输入中国，故得名。现仅存方形关口一座，全为黏黄土版筑。[3]

玉在中国的文明史上有着特殊的地位，《五经通义》说玉："温润而泽，有似于智；锐而不害，有似于仁；抑而不挠，有似于义；有瑕于内必见于外，有似于信；垂之如坠，有似于礼。"[4]孔子曰："玉之美，有如君子之德。"他认为玉具有仁、智、义、礼、乐、忠、信、天、地、德、道等君子的品节。《诗经》里有"言念君子，温其如玉"之句。古人给美玉赋予了那么多人性的品格，以至于人们仍将谦谦君子喻为"温润如玉"。

据儒家经典《礼记·玉藻》记载，古代君子必须佩玉：

1　本文由编者编写。

2　［德］劳悟达著，殷凌云、毕夏译：《中国艺术中芭蕉的图像学·叶展叶舒》，中国美术学院出版社，2022年，第194页。

3　沈善洪：《中国语言文化背景汉英双解词典》，商务印书馆，2010年，第488—489页。

4　（汉）刘向撰，（清）马国翰辑：《五经通义》。

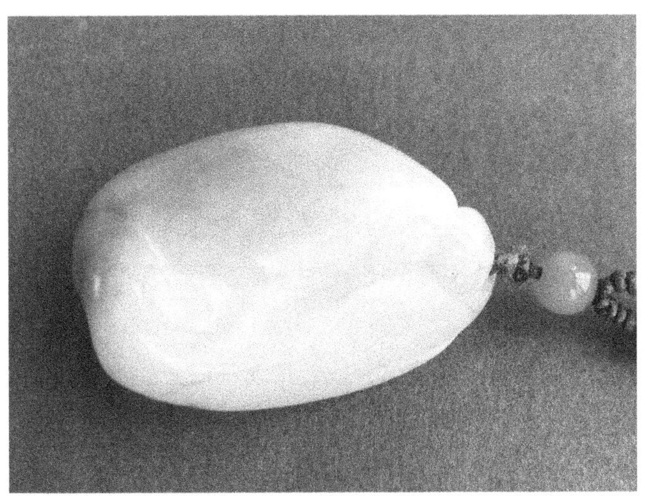

和田玉瑞兽玉佩　私人收藏
A Hetian jade auspicious animal, a private collection

玉佩　战国　故宫博物院藏
A Jade pendant, Warring States Period, Collected in the Palace Museum

古之君子必佩玉……然后玉锵鸣也。故君子在车，则闻鸾和之声，行则鸣佩玉，是以非辟之心，无自入也。君在不佩玉，……凡带必有佩玉，唯丧否。……君子无故，玉不去身，君子于玉比德焉。天子佩白玉……公侯佩山玄玉，……大夫佩水苍玉……世子佩瑜玉……士佩瓀玟……孔子佩象环五寸……[1]

1　杨天宇：《礼记译注》，上海古籍出版社，2016年，第458页。

由此可知，不同品质的玉标志不同的社会身份等级。故此，在汉语中含“玉”字的词语象征着美好的事物，“玉帛”：古时国与国之间交际时，用作礼物的玉器和丝织品。“玉成”意为请求别人成全。“玉洁冰清”，像玉石、冰块那样纯洁、清透。人的气质、风度高纯洁。“玉宇”传说中神仙住的用美玉建成的宫殿；“玉石俱焚”美玉和石块一齐烧毁。比喻好的和坏的、善良的和丑恶的一同毁掉。玉碎与“瓦全”相对，比喻为保持气节而牺牲，如：“宁为玉碎，不可瓦全。”玉人为雕琢玉器的工人，或者用玉雕成的人像，或者容貌美丽的人，多指美女。敬辞玉体称别人的身体，或者指女子润泽的身体。文学作品中也常常以玉作为创作要素。《红楼梦》写宝玉自出生就自带通灵宝玉，成为整部作品的灵魂。

中国古人爱玉，很早就在身上佩戴精美玉器饰物即玉佩。《诗经·秦风·渭阳》：“何以赠之？琼瑰玉佩。”《论语》中也有孔子“执圭”的描写，“圭”即玉。故宫博物院藏还藏有古老的宋代“白玉镂雕凤凰坠佩”，长5厘米，宽3.5厘米，厚0.5厘米。此坠佩呈片状，正面略鼓，背面稍平。双面雕工，镂雕凤凰衔草纹，刀法简洁。宋代玉制佩饰品种极多，有带饰、佩饰等多种形式。从目前发现的宋代佩玉看，属璜、环、珩、冲牙体系的古代佩玉已不再流行，而代之以鱼、花、鸟、兽、人物等坠佩。其中鸟形玉佩极多。整体采用镂雕技法，透空的比例几乎等同于留料处，显示出独特的风格和玉质的莹润与坚实。[1]由此可见，宋代人极其喜欢玉佩。清人王士禛在《香祖笔记》中载有一件轶事：

尝有咏宋高宗一绝云：“千金空买玉孩儿”。不得其解。读《西湖志余》，高宗尝宴大臣，见张循王俊持扇，有玉孩儿扇坠，上识是旧物，昔往四明，误坠于水者。问俊所从得，对曰：“臣从清河坊铺家买得之。”询铺家，云得之提篮人；复询之，乃从候潮门外陈宅厨娘处得之；询之厨娘，云破黄花鱼腹中所得也。上大悦，铺家、提篮入补校尉，厨娘封孺人。[2]

玉佩雕刻中的中国传统图案内容丰富，形式多样，大体有吉祥如意、长

1 梁科，故宫博物院官网，访问时间2021年11月3日，https://www.dpm.org.cn/Home.html。
2 （清）王士禛：《香祖笔记》卷三，上海古籍出版社，1982年，第47页。

寿多福类、家和兴旺类、安宁平和类、事业腾达类和辟邪消灾类等，其中以吉祥如意类图案为多。随着朝代更迭，社会变迁，特别是商业的发展，佩挂的严肃性越来越少，装饰意味越来越重，成为佩挂于身、寄意标高的玩赏之物。这种风气，晚清尤盛。

Jade Sculpture[1]

Jade culture occupies a unique position in Chinese culture. Liangzhu culture is a typical representative of ancient Chinese jade culture. Recorded in the *Book of Rites*, a disciple asked Confucius why superior men set such a high value on jade. Confucius answered that superior men found the likeness of all virtues in jade. The Chinese all love jades. Jade carving is one of the oldest carving varieties in China, as a special Chinese handicraft. Finely carved jade articles were called "jade painting" by Emperor Qianlong of the Qing Dynasty. [2] As early as the late Neolithic Age, the Chinese nation had jade tools. During the Shang and Zhou Dynasties, jade making became a profession, and jade wares became ceremonial utensils and decorative pieces. Jade carvings are done in various forms of human figures and objects and are regarded as valuable art works. Most of the jade carvings are produced in Beijing in China. The skills of Beijing jade carving enjoy a long history and are profound and exquisite. In jade carving, the carver finally sculpts the material into exquisite jade sculptures, paying great attention to employing the material measuring it and applying the craftsman–ship based on the manterial.

The ancient classics *Shanhai Jing, The Classic of Mountains and Seas,* mentions that jade comes from many mountains. The Yumen Pass, an important pass at the north end of the "Silk Road", is located in the northwest of Dunhuang County, Gansu Province. It is said that just through this pass could the jade of the

1 This is compiled by the compiler of this book.

2 (Germany) Uta Lauer, *Leaves Unfurl: The Iconography of the Banana Plant in Chinese Art*, translated into Chinese by Yin Lingyun and Bi Xia, China Academy of Art Press, 2022, p.194.

Western Regions be imported into China in the ancient times. As a relic site, only a square tower mainly made of loess is left there now.[1]

Jade enjoys a special place in the history of Chinese civilization. The *Five Classics* says that jade is "Warm and moist, it is like wisdom; sharp but not harmful, it resembles benevolence; if it is inflexible, it resembles righteousness; That flaws in the inside must be seen outside resembles faith; if it hangs like a pendant, it resembles ritual."[2] As Confucius said, "The beauty of jade is like the virtue of a gentleman." He believes that jade has the qualities of gentlemen such as benevolence, wisdom, righteousness, courtesy, joy, loyalty, faith, heaven, earth, virtue, and Tao. There is a sentence in The Book of Poetry that speaking to a gentleman warms like a jade. The ancients endowed beautiful jade with so many human qualities that people still refer to the modest gentleman as warm and moist as jade.

It is recorded in the Confucian classic *Liji·Yuzao* that the gentleman in the ancient times must wear a jade:

A gentleman in ancient times must wear a jade... and then the jade chimes. Therefore, when a gentleman is in the carriage, he hears the sound of harmony, and when he walks, he rings the sound of chiming jade on him, and therefore all evil thoughts will never enter the gentleman's mind. The servants do not wear jade in front of the monarch...Everyone must wear jade, except when he is mourning. ...If there is no special reason for a gentleman, jade will not leave his body, because a gentleman uses jade to symbolize his virtue. The emperor wears white jade...the princes wear the jade with color like the mysterious mountain and mixed with texture...the ministers wear the jade with color like water and mixed with texture...the prince wears the beautiful jade... the scholars wear the Ruwen jade which is the beautiful stone next to jade...When Confucius

---

1 Shen Shanhong, *A Chinese–English Dictionary with Cultural Background Information*, the Commercial Press, 2010, pp. 488–489.

2 (Han Dynasty) Liu Xiang, (Qing Dynasty) Ma Guohan ed., *Wujing Tongyi*.

lived alone, he wore the jade as an elephant ring with a diameter of five inches...[1]

It can be concluded form the above that jade of different quality stands for different social status in the hierarchical society. Therefore, Chinese idioms and phrases containing the character "Jade 玉" in Chinese symbolize beautiful things. "Yubo" stands for jade objects and silk fabrics, presented as gifts between ancient states; "Yucheng" is a polite formula to ask somebody to help accomplish a task; "Yujing bingqing" is as pure as jade and as clean as ice, meaning pure and noble; "Yuyu" represents in legend the grand palace of the immortals, made of jade; "Yushi jufen" is both jade and rock burning together, meaning all things, good and bad, beautiful or ugly, are destroyed together in a fire; "Yusui" is to die with honour, as against "Waquan—as complete as a tile"; "Yuren" is a jade carver, or a jade statue, or a beauty ; "Yuti" is polite formula of the body of a person, the nude body of a woman. Jade is often used as an element in literary works. *Dream of Red Mansions* writes that Baoyu has been born with psychic treasures Precious Jade， as the soul of the book.

The ancient Chinese loved jade, and they liked to wear exquisite jade ornaments or jade pendants on their bodies for a long time. As is the poem in Weiyang of Qin Wind in *The Book of Poetry*: "Why donate it? Qiong and jade pendant." In the *Analeats of confucius* can be found the description of "holding the jade scepter", a jade. The jade object, "White jade carved phoenix pendant" of the ancient Song Dynasty in the collection of the Palace Museum, is 5 cm long, 3.5 cm wide and 0.5 cm thick. This pendant has a flake shape with a slightly bulging front and a slightly flat back, with double–sided engraving, carved phoenix–like pattern, with simple carving technique. There are many kinds of jade ornaments in the Song Dynasty, including belt ornaments and other objects. Judging from the jade wares of the Song Dynasty currently discovered, the ancient jade belonging to

1 Yang Tianyu, *Annotation of the Book of Rites*, Shanghai Ancient Books Publishing House, Shanghai, 2016, p.458.

the semicircular jade ornament, ring, plover, teeth–punching systems is no longer popular, and instead is replaced by fish, flowers, birds, beasts, and figures. Among them, there are many bird–shaped jade pendants. The carving technique is adopted as a whole, and the proportion of the open space is almost equal to that of the reserved material, showing the unique style as well as the luster and firmness of the jade quality. [1] Therefore, it can be seen that the people of the Song Dynasty liked jade very much. Wang Shizhen of the Qing Dynasty contained an anecdote in his *Xiangzu Biji*:

There is a unique saying about Gaozong of the Song Dynasty: "Pay a thousand gold entirely for a jade boy". I couldn't understand it until I read *West Lake Zhiyu*, reading that Emperor Gaozong invited his ministers to a banquet, and recognized it was his old thing, on seeing Zhang Jun Xun King holding a fan with a jade boy as the fan pendant. When the Emperor asked Jun where he got it, he replied: "I bought it from the shop on the Street Qinghefang." When the Emperor asked the shopper about it, the answer was it was from the basket carrier; When the Emperor asked the basket carrier again, the reply was it was got from the chef of Chen's house outside the Chaochao Gate; the chef, when breaking a yellow croaker, she found it in the fish belly. After that, the Emperor was greatly pleased, and the shopper and the basket carrier were awarded as the captain, and the chef lady as the Ruren.[2]

The traditional Chinese patterns in engraving of jade pendants are rich in content and diverse in forms, generally including types of auspiciousness and wishfulness, longevity and happiness, home prosperity, peace and quietness, career thriving, and evil and disaster elimination, among which there are many auspicious and wishful patterns. With the change of dynasties, social changes,

1 Liang Ke, official website of the Palace Museum, accessed on November 3, 2021, https://www.dpm.org.cn/Home.html

2 (Qing Dynasty) Wang Shizhen, *Xiangzu Biji*, Vol. 3, Shanghai Ancient Books Publishing House, 1982, p. 47.

especially the development of commerce, the seriousness of the decoration is becoming less and less, and the decoration is more and more important. This kind of atmosphere was especially prosperous in the late Qing Dynasty.

Word bank

1.handicraft n. 手艺；手工艺

2.Neolithic Age n. 新石器时代

3.utensil n. 器皿；用具

4.the Yumen Pass n. 玉门关

5.moist adj. 微湿的；潮湿的

6.benevolence n. 善行；仁慈

7.inflexible adj. 坚定不移的；不屈不挠的

8.righteousness n. 正直；正义

9.pendant n. 垂饰；坠子

10.courtesy n. 有礼貌；谦恭

11.loyalty n. 忠诚；忠心

12.endow v. 向（人、机构）捐赠；资助；赋予

13.fabric n. 布；织物

14.immortal adj. 不死的；永生的

15.psychic adj. 通灵的；超自然的

16.phoenix n. 凤凰；长生鸟

17.flake n. 薄片；一小片

18.bulging n. 膨胀；打气

19.luster n. 光泽；有光泽的物质

20.auspicious adj. 有助于成功的；有利的

21.longevity n. 长寿

22.prosperity n. 繁荣；昌盛；成功

23. elimination n. 淘汰；消除

24. prosperous adj. 成功的；富足的

25. semicircular jade ornament n. 璜

26. plover n. 珩

参考文献

[1] Basil Gray, “Sloan and the Kämpfer Collection,” in The British Museum Quarterly, 18. London, 1953; Joseph Vedlich, The prints of the Ten Bamboo Studio followed by Plates from the Kämpfer Series and Perfect Harmony. Fribourg/Geneve, 1979; Wolfmar Zacken, Die Kämpfer Drucke, Wien, 1995.

[2] Cf. Christopher de Hamel, The Book: A History of the Bible, London, 2001.

[3] Cf. L. Febvre and H. Martin, The Coming of the Book, London, 1993.

[4] Charles O. Hucker, A Dictionary of Official Titles in Imperial China, Peking University Press, 2008.

[5] E. H. 贡布里希著，杨思梁、范景中、严善淳译:《艺术与科学：贡布里希谈话录和回忆录》，浙江摄影出版社，1998 年。

[6] Fritz Saxl，A Volume of Memoria Essays from his Friends in England, ed., D. J. Gordon, London, 1957.

[7] J.Turnered. The Dictionary of Art，Volume 6, Grove, 1998.

[8] James Cahill Chinese Painting, Rizzoli International, Inc., New York, 1977.

[9] Reid, D. A Handbook of Chinese Healing Herbs, Singapore: Periplus.

[10] 北京大学古文献研究所编:《全宋诗》，北京大学出版社，1998 年。

[11] 徐惟诚总编:《不列颠百科全书》，中国大百科全书出版社，1999 年。

[12] 参照百度百科，https://baike.baidu.com/item/%E5%B0%8F%E8%9D%8C%E8%9A%AA%E6%89%BE%E5%A6%88%E5%A6%88/4820144?fr=aladdin

[13] 参照搜狗百科，https://baike.sogou.com/v64820143.htm;jsessionid=1A87056C931700178D11E0A79876D03A，登录时间为 2021 年 10 月 4 日。https://baike.sogou.com/v64820143.htm;jsessionid=1A87056C931700178D11E0A79

876D03A

[14] 陈至立主编:《辞海》,上海辞书出版社,2020 年。

[15] [德]劳悟达著,殷凌云、毕夏译:《中国艺术中芭蕉的图像学·叶展叶舒》,中国美术学院出版社,2022 年。

[16] 范景中:《套印本和刻本及其〈会真图〉》,《新美术》,2005 年第 4 期。

[17] 范景中:《序言:套印本和闵刻本及其〈会真图〉》,载董捷:《明清刊〈西厢记〉版画考析》,河北美术出版社,2006 年 .

[18] 傅申著:《书史与书迹》,台湾历史博物馆,1996 年。

[19] (汉)刘熙:《释名疏证补》,中华书局,2008 年。

[20] (汉)刘向著,(清)马国翰辑:《五经通义》。

[21] (汉)史游:《急就篇》,岳麓书社,1989 年。

[22] 故宫博物院官网,https://www.dpm.org.cn/Home.html

[23] (明)陈继儒:《读书十六观》,道光刊本。

[24] (明)丰坊:《真赏斋赋》,光绪二十四年缪荃孙刻《藕香零拾》本。

[25] (明)李日华:《味水轩日记》,《嘉业堂丛书》本。

[26] (明)刘侗、于奕正著:《帝京景物略》,北京出版社,1963 年。

[27] (明)刘若愚著:《酌中志》,北京古籍出版社,1994 年。

[28] (明)田汝成:《西湖游览志余》,上海古籍出版社,1980 年。

[29] (明)汪砢玉:《汪氏珊瑚网法书》,卷十六,《适园丛书》本。

[30] (明)徐一夔:《始丰稿》,卷十三光绪间钱塘丁氏嘉惠堂刻《武林往哲遗著》本。

[31] (明)臧懋循:《负苞堂文选》,卷《续修四库全书》影印天启元年尔炳刊本,上海古籍出版社,1994–2002 年。

[32] [美]贺凯:《中国古代官名辞典》,北京大学出版社,2008 年。

[33] 黄涛、王心愿:《中秋月饼考》,《温州大学学报(社会科学版)》,2014 年第 2 期。

[34] 蒋玄佁:《中国绘画材料史》,上海书画出版社,1986 年。

[35] 《江令君集》，卷一，光绪五年信述堂重刊《汉魏六朝百三家集》本。

[36] （清）卞永誉著:《式古堂书汇考》,《中书画全书》本，上海书画出版社，1994 年。

[37] 《仪礼》，古诗文网，https://so.gushiwen.cn/guwen/bookv_46653FD803893E4FC342454E3EB489A6.aspx.

[38] （清）顾文彬:《过云楼书画记》，卷五，《续修四库全书》影印光绪刊本，上海古籍出版社，1994—2002 年。

[39] （清）嵇曾筠等修:《浙江通志》，上海古籍出版社，1991 年。

[40] （清）沈虹屏著:《春雨楼集》，卷十，乾隆刻本。

[41] （清）王士禛:《香祖笔记》，上海古籍出版社，1982 年。

[42] （清）吴允嘉述:《天水冰山录》，商务印书馆，1937 年。

[43] （清）杨宾:《大瓢偶笔》,《中国书画全书》本，上海书画出版社，1994 年。

[44] （清）袁枚:《随园食单》，三秦出版社，2005 年。

[45] 《钦定天禄琳琅书目》卷二《清人书目题跋丛刊》本，中华书局，1995 年。

[46] 《全宋笔记》，大象出版社。

[47] 曲阜市官网网上资料，http://www.qufu.gov.cn/，访问时间 2021 年 10 月 10 日；以及 https://baike.sogou.com/v110419.htm，访问时间 2021 年 10 月 10 日。

[48] （宋）洪迈:《容斋随笔》，北京燕山出版社，2008 年。

[49] （宋）陆游:《入蜀记》，http://www.gushicimingju.com/gushi/wenyanwen/2282.html.

[50] （宋）孟元老等著:《东京梦华录》，文化艺术出版社，1998 年。

[51] （宋）沈括:《梦溪笔谈》，中华书局，2016 年。

[52] （宋）苏轼:《苏轼诗集》，中华书局，1982 年。

[53] （宋）陶谷，《清异录》，中国商业出版社，1985 年。

[54] （宋）吴自牧:《梦粱录》，浙江人民出版社，1984 年。

[55] （宋）周密:《武林旧事》，浙江古籍出版社，2011 年。

[56] 《石渠宝笈》，卷三，上海古出版社影印文渊阁《四库全书》本，1987 年。

[57] 《书法丛刊》，总第 28 期，文物出版社，1991 年。

[58] 《四部丛刊》初编本，卷四十六。

[59] 《宋书·五行志》，http://www.guoxuemeng.com/guoxue/songshu/.

[60] 上海美术电影制片厂官网，https://www.ani–sh.com/.

[61] 沈从文:《中国古代服饰研究》，商务印书馆，2011 年。

[62] 沈善洪:《中国语言文化背景汉英双解词典》，商务印书馆，1998 年。

[63] 滕军:《日本茶道文化概论》，东方出版社，1992 年。

[64] （唐）陈陶《陇西行四首（其二）》，《全唐诗》，http://qts.zww.cn/#

[65] （唐）杜甫，《春望》，古诗文网，https://so.gushiwen.cn/shiwenv_89d3a63c6d7f.aspx.

[66] （唐）陆羽:《茶经》，北京时代华文书局，2020 年。

[67] 汪榕培、潘智丹译:《英译诗经·国风》，上海外语教育出版社，2008 年。

[68] 王仲荦:《金泥玉屑丛考》，中华书局，1998 年。

[69] （五代）马缟:《中华古今注》，崔豹《古今注》。

[70] 《吾国与吾民》，https://www.haoshuya.com/11/8288/565700.html#headid.

[71] 徐海荣主编:《中国饮食史》，华夏出版社，1999 年。

[72] 《新疆维吾尔自治区博物馆画册》，香港金版文化出版社，2006 年。

[73] （西汉）司马迁:《史记》，中华书局，2011 年。

[74] 杨琳:《中国传统节日文化》，宗教文化出版社，2000 年。

[75] 杨天宇:《礼记译注》，上海古籍出版社，2016 年。

[76] （元）陶宗仪:《说郛》，卷十三，民国十六年上海商务印书馆铅印本。

[77] 尤汪洋主编:《中国画技法全书》，河南美术出版社，2002 年。

[78] 张伯英著:《张伯英碑帖论稿》，河北教育出版社，2006 年。

[79] 《中国书法全集》（赵孟頫卷），荣宝斋出版社，2002 年。

[80] 《中华文苑》，《文物天地》，www.china–culture.com。